The Contest of Faculties

The
Contest of Faculties

Philosophy and theory
after deconstruction

Christopher Norris

METHUEN
London and New York

First published in 1985 by
Methuen & Co. Ltd
11 New Fetter Lane, London EC4P 4EE

Published in the USA by
Methuen & Co.
in association with Methuen, Inc.
733 Third Avenue, New York, NY 10017

© *1985 Christopher Norris*

Photoset by Rowland Phototypesetting Ltd
Bury St Edmunds, Suffolk
Printed in Great Britain
at the University Press, Cambridge

British Library Cataloguing in Publication Data

Norris, Christopher
The contest of faculties:
philosophy and theory after deconstruction.
1. Deconstruction
I. Title
801'.95   PN98.D43

ISBN 0-416-39930-4
ISBN 0-416-39940-1 Pbk

Library of Congress Cataloging in Publication Data

Norris, Christopher
The Contest of Faculties.
Bibliography: p.
Includes Index.
1. Deconstruction.   2. Narration (Rhetoric).
3. Literature – Philosophy.   I. Title.   II. Title:
Philosophy and Theory after Deconstruction.
PN98.D43N58 1985   801'.95 85-15426

ISBN 0-416-39930-4
ISBN 0-416-39940-1 (Pbk.)

Contents

For my mother

Acknowledgements

These essays were written over a two-year period, often starting out as lectures or seminar papers and then being much revised in the light of subsequent discussion. Certainly the book would never have taken shape without the help and encouragement offered on those occasions. It is conventional practice to save oneself the labour of detailed acknowledge-ment by saying that one's debts are too many to record. If I exploit this convention having first denounced it (a good deconstructionist move), at least I can hope that the many who listened and criticized will again pick up the threads of a continuing dialogue. But to name just a few: my thanks to Terence Hawkes and Kate Belsey of the Cardiff Critical Theory Seminar, for much time spent in discussion of these and related topics; to Andrew Belsey and Robin Attfield for casting a cool philosophical eye over the typescript; and to Stephen Bygrave, Richard Machin, Dan Latimer and Jamal Samir for reading early drafts and supplying much-needed stimulus and interest.

If the book had any single starting-point, then it must have been the six weeks I spent at the School of Criticism and Theory, Northwestern University, in the summer of 1983. My thanks to Geoffrey Hartman for inviting me to participate and for showing such a generous interest in my subsequent work. Richard Rorty, as Visiting Fellow at Northwestern, did more than anyone to clarify my thinking on the issues raised by a certain 'neo-pragmatist' reading of deconstruction. I trust that he will take it as no backhanded compliment when I say that nearly all the ideas in this book have been arrived at through disagreement with Rorty. At least he can relish the irony of a situation where literary critics are more and more talking 'philosophy' while he is mainly anxious to have done with it and talk on a level with the critics. I am also very grateful to Joseph Margolis for pointing out some questionable passages of argument in my dealing with modern analytical philosophy. Any muddles that remain are, of course, my own responsibility.

Philip Sturgess arranged for me to visit Poland during 1984 and take part in some memorably live and stimulating seminars. To Jerzy Jarniewicz and Maria Jedrzejkiewicz, in particular, I extend warm greetings and thanks for making me so welcome. Gary Wihl invited me to give an early version of the chapter on Empson and de Man for a session he chaired at the 1984 MLA Convention in Washington. Derek Roper, Tom Docherty and Paul Hamilton provided similar opportunities in Sheffield and Oxford. I am grateful to Linden Stafford for reading the typescript with exemplary editorial care and for offering a number of valuable suggestions, particularly on the topics of photography and film.

My thanks are also due to the editors and publishers of the following journals for permission to reprint portions of this book that first appeared in their pages: *Comparative Criticism*, *Enclitic*, *Genre*, *Meridian*, *Southern Humanities Review*, and *Southern Review*. 'Narrative theory or theory-as-narrative' has also been published in the volume *Marxism and the Interpretation of Culture*, edited by Cary Nelson and Larry Grossberg (University of Illinois Press, 1986).

Introduction: philosophy, theory and the 'contest of faculties'

I

Literary critics interpret texts. By and large they get on without worrying too much about the inexplicit theories or principles that underwrite their practice. Some of them very actively resist the idea that such theories can be found, or that bringing them to light could serve any useful purpose. At its most obscurantist this attitude takes the Leavisite form of a down-right refusal to engage in such discussion. Elsewhere, distinctions are drawn between 'theory' and 'principle', the latter being conceived as a realm of tacit values and assumptions beyond reach of further analysis. At a more philosophical level, the issue is joined by those in the 'hermeneutic' camp (like Hans-Georg Gadamer), who argue that each and every act of understanding is embedded in a context of cultural meanings and presuppositions which can never be exhausted by rational explanation.[1] From this point of view there is simply no appeal to a higher 'theoretical' order of knowledge independent of cultural conditioning. To interpret a text is to enter, willingly or not, into the 'hermeneutic circle' which constitutes the basis of all understanding. Theory is deluded if it thinks to get a hold upon texts from some ideal vantage-point of pure, disinterested knowledge.

On the other hand there are those who reject such arguments as merely a species of conservative pleading for the 'commonsense' status quo. They would argue that theory can indeed be justified in its claim to transcend the various kinds of naturalized or pre-reflective knowledge that make up a given cultural consensus. To deny such a power vested in rational reflection is to give up the very idea of enlightened critique. If acted upon consistently, it would amount to a vote of no confidence in reason itself, or the capacity of reason to criticize its own unexamined presuppositions. The 'hermeneutic circle', thus, becomes a pretext for conservative philosophies of language and culture which refuse to question the values implicit in the discourse of society at large.

These objections have been argued most forcefully in recent years by the philosopher Jürgen Habermas.[2] Thought can indeed transcend its rootedness in cultural tradition and attain a standpoint of rational self-understanding from which to criticize 'commonsense' ideas. To deny this possibility, Habermas argues, is to yield up reflection to the forces of prejudice and mere cultural inertia. Rather we should see that the knowledge-constitutive interests which motivate our thinking are capable of a positive, emancipating thrust as well as the negative drive toward conformist dogma. Knowledge has an interest in removing those blocks to enlightened understanding which come of its attachment to a narrow, unreflective or positivist paradigm. Reason requires that its own claims to truth be constantly questioned through the kind of open, dialogical exchange which can only take place under conditions of free and reciprocal human understanding. Hence the appeal to what Habermas calls the 'ideal speech situation', intended as a yardstick by which to measure the past and present distortions of genuine rationality.[3] Though it remains – of necessity – a purely hypothetical construct, this notion enables Habermas to mobilize the powers of reflective critique against the various forms of entrenched unreason that resist such dialogue. He can thus maintain a pragmatics of communicative discourse which engages with present social realities but also insists on the need for a higher ('metalinguistic') dimension of critical enquiry.

This debate between Habermas and Gadamer has large implications for philosophy, criticism and every branch of the human sciences. What the issue comes down to at root is the choice between rival paradigms of reason, meaning and interpretation. On the one side are those advocates of 'hermeneutic' thinking who argue that *all* forms of knowledge – even the most abstract or theoretical – have their origin within a context of tacit assumptions and values which can never be reduced to any 'rational' explanation. On the other are thinkers like Habermas who reject such inherently conservative attitudes and argue thàt reason is empowered to comprehend – and hence potentially to criticize and change – its background of motivating interests. Those who take this second (broadly rationalist) line are likely to play down the idea that the humanistic disciplines have their own distinct mode of intuitive or possibly pre-logical understanding. They will tend to regard such distinctions, in whatever sophisticated form, as a species of merely subjectivist retreat before the truth-claims of a science itself given over to unreflecting positivist method. Such thinkers (Habermas among them) want to re-establish the human sciences on the basis of a critical self-understanding which could also serve as a corrective model for other disciplines, the 'hard' sciences included. Hermeneutics would likewise challenge this distinction, but with wholly different ends in view. Here it would be a matter of denying that any one discipline (say, philosophy) could set up as a privileged discourse that was somehow more 'rigorous', or closer to the truth, than any other (say, literary criticism). In fact that relationship tends to be reversed, since the paradigm case of hermeneutic understanding is often sought in the encounter between literary text and responsive reader. From this standpoint it looks as though philosophy took a wrong turn when it moved towards logic and scientific method, rather than acknowledging its kinship with the humanistic disciplines at large.

Richard Rorty, for one, argues that philosophy had better give up its delusions of intellectual grandeur and learn to regard itself as just another voice in the medley of present-day cultural exchange.[4] He is frankly impatient with literary critics who think to make their discipline more 'rigorous' by hitching their wagon to some theory (of language, intentions, or whatever) supposedly possessed of 'philosophic' dignity and truth. They have not caught up with the simple fact that philosophy is no more a master discipline – and no less subject to interpretative vagaries – than the practice of literary criticism. What these 'weak textualists' all have in common, according to

Rorty, is 'a tendency to think that literature can take the place of philosophy by *mimicking* philosophy – by being, of all things, *epistemological*'.[5] What they fail to see (unlike their 'strong textualist' counterparts) is the non-privileged status of philosophy as one kind of writing among others, and the pointlessness of setting up 'philosophic' theories as if they possessed some kind of ultimate, metalinguistic truth. In the current state of play this gives a clear advantage to the undeceived critic who is content with offering 'strong' new readings of literary texts. To claim anything more – like a philosophic *theory* to back up those readings – is to miss the whole point, as Rorty sees it.

It is hardly surprising that these arguments have proved highly attractive to literary critics and not so convincing to academic philosophers, tenured or otherwise. Rorty thinks that philosophy still has a future, but only if it comes to see the error of its ways and takes up a decently moderating stance *vis-à-vis* the other 'human sciences'. This means accepting that literary critics may well have the best of it at present. Quite simply, philosophy gives up its age-old legislative claims and settles down to the much less exalted business of *interpreting texts*. This shift is not dictated by any new 'theory' that would somehow *prove* that literary critics have the truth of the matter. It is merely to recognize that what is going on among literary intellectuals is currently more interesting, useful or productive than what is going on among philosophers. As Rorty puts it:

> The claims of a usurping discipline to preside over the rest of culture can only be defended by an exhibition of its ability to put the other disciplines in their places. This is what the literary culture has been doing recently, with great success. . . . Science did not *demonstrate* that religion was wrong, nor philosophy that science was merely phenomenal, nor can modernist literature or textualist criticism *demonstrate* that the 'metaphysics of presence' is an outdated genre. But each in turn has managed, without argument, to make its point.[6]

'Without argument' because, in Rorty's view, no *argument* could possibly serve to adjudicate the claims of such rival discourses. Their relative standing can only be assessed from time to time by deciding which has most to offer in the way of useful or relevant new ideas. Until recently it seemed (to philosophers at least) that the different kinds of knowledge could be slotted into a firm hierarchical structure, with philosophy either securely on top or in place among the rational foundations. Just what those foundations rested on at bottom was the main topic of debate. Rorty lists some of the candidates: 'clear and distinct ideas, sense-data, categories of the pure understanding, structures of prelinguistic consciousness and the like'.[7] But this debate begins to look rather pointless, he thinks, with the growing recognition that paradigm changes amount to nothing more than a shift of governing metaphors or 'final vocabulary'. Philosophers had better make peace with this new situation and strike up dialogues wherever they can at the present stage of intellectual conversation.

II

'In Defence of Reason' might have been the (somewhat grandiose) title for the essays in this book. 'Rescuing Philosophy' would fit just as well, though it might seem more than a little presumptuous, coming from one who lacks any clear institutional warrant to argue such a case. There is, of course, a handy line of defence in Rorty's suggestion that we scrap this old-fashioned way of carving up the disciplines and make 'philosophy' an open house to whatever is going on in the liveliest adjacent fields. The literary critic should be quick to see the benefits of a radical pragmatism like Rorty's, one that has the effect of levelling out truth-claims to a point where they all appear as options thrown up by different kinds of cultural self-interest. From a pragmatist viewpoint, Rorty writes, 'there is no interesting difference between tables and texts, protons and poems'.[8] These objects are defined, for all practical purposes, by the role they play in this or that context of ongoing present debate. They are all just 'permanent possibilities for use', their cognitive status always open to 'redescription, reinterpretation, manipulation'. There is more comfort here for literary critics than philosophers, since critics are mostly in the business of interpreting texts. They stand to gain something in cultural self-esteem if it comes to be accepted that other disciplines are similarly placed, though without the same well-practised means of turning this position to advantage. 'Strong textualists' of whatever colour would apparently have reason to rejoice in Rorty's new dispensation.

These essays argue, on the contrary, that critics – let alone philosophers – will be throwing too much away if they accept such pragmatist reasoning at anything like face value. Rorty would have it that literary theory is a pointless attempt to emulate philosophers on ground which they are anyway about to vacate for wider horizons and pastures new. Epistemology, as Rorty puts it,

> still looks classy to weak textualists. They think that by viewing a poet as having an epistemology they are paying him a compliment. They even think that in criticizing his theory of knowledge they are being something more than a mere critic – being, in fact, a philosopher.[9]

No doubt there is a good deal of cumbersome and misconceived pseudo-philosophy currently passed off upon credulous readers in the name of literary theory. But this hardly justifies Rorty's claim that the enterprise was wrong from the start and should now be viewed as just another chapter in the history of failed ideas. 'Hostility to theory', Terry Eagleton remarks, 'usually means an opposition to other people's theories and an oblivion to one's own.'[10] Eagleton backs his position with a comment of John Maynard Keynes, whom he quotes as observing how 'those economists who disliked theory, or claimed to get along better without it, were simply in the grip of an older theory'.

This should remind us that issues of politics are rarely far from the surface in any such debate between 'theory' and commonsense pragmatics. Free-market doctrine (the 'older theory' that Keynes alluded to) was based on the assumption that one didn't need a worked-out strategy of state intervention, since the economy would function best if left to establish its own equilibrium of prices, profits and wages. Rorty's pragmatist arguments look very much like extending this idea to the realm of philosophy and intellectual culture at large. 'Theory' is mistaken if it thinks to intervene and criticize notions which have got themselves decently established as part of an ongoing cultural dialogue. If there is no last appeal to ultimate truths ('clear and distinct ideas', etc.), then equally there is no firm vantage-point of theory from which to conduct such criticism. Rorty brings out this suggestive parallel with free-market economics in one of the metaphors he chooses to describe the pragmatist position. It is a matter of accepting, as he writes,

> that there are no constraints on inquiry save conversational ones – no wholesale constraints derived from the nature of the objects, or of the mind, or of language, but only those retail constraints provided by the remarks of our fellow-inquirers.[11]

Interventionist 'theory' would put this conversation out of joint by substituting abstract precepts for the working system of checks and balances that makes up a cultural tradition. Rorty is quite explicit in equating this desirable context of debate with present-day North American consensus politics. It would hardly make sense, his argument implies, to mount the kind of 'wholesale' ideological critique which sought to break with that tradition and show up its prejudiced or distorting character. Thus Rorty clearly sides with Gadamer as against Habermas on the question of how far reason can go in backing up its own foundational truth-claims. If pressed to the point of saying what would *count* as 'undistorted communication', Habermas (according to Rorty) inevitably 'goes transcendental and offers principles'.

These essays argue the opposite case: that 'going transcendental' (or, as Habermas would have it, keeping faith with enlightened reason) cannot be simply dismissed as a species of outworn metaphysical delusion. They often run up against the kinds of problem that Rorty would like to see removed from the agenda of worthwhile topics for discussion. These include the relationship of 'sense' and 'reference' (construed in Fregean terms), the cognitive status of narrative explanations and – in the chapter on Rorty – the reasons for *not* adopting a thorough-going pragmatist position. In each case they are open to the Rortyan charge of being hooked on age-old problems which philosophy should now put away, having arrived at a more realistic sense of its own powers and limitations. In so far as these essays manage to rebut that charge, it is by showing that the problems in question are not so easily pushed out of view, or only by means of a pragmatist counter-philosophy which carries its own specific charge of ideological assumptions. The move to foreclose on certain 'technical' aspects of epistemological critique is seen as falling in all too readily with the interests of a present-day cultural status quo.

An important part of this argument has to do with deconstructionist literary theory, a development which Rorty views with some interest, though for largely tactical reasons. What he likes about Derrida is his refusal to *play the game* of philosophy on rules made up by all those 'serious' thinkers, from Kant onwards, who have thought to find 'constructive' answers to genuine problems. What he doesn't like so much is the other, more rigorous form of deconstructionist argument which looks like rejoining that same superannuated line. On his good side it is a game of wits between 'bad brother Derrida' and 'honest old uncle Kant'. On his retrograde side, as Rorty sees it, Derrida 'succumbs to nostalgia, to the lure of philosophical system-building, and specifically that of constructing yet another transcendental idealism'.[12] Deconstruction, in short, is a kind of abortive or half-hearted pragmatist venture. It is willing to dispense with most of the truth-claims and illusions of method which have so far served to prop up an ailing philosophical enterprise. But it still has this unfortunate (Kantian) tendency to take its own arguments seriously and – like Habermas – to 'go transcendental' at the drop of a hat.

It is rare enough to find philosophers admitting that they've read Derrida, let alone writing about him (as Rorty does) with a measure of sympathetic insight. For a literary critic to reject Rorty's reading might seem like a case of not merely looking a gift-horse in the mouth but kicking it squarely in the teeth. All the same, I want to urge that deconstruction is *not*, as Rorty would have it, an offshoot of pragmatism that is merely too precocious to recognize its own true lineage. In the case of Paul de Man especially, the drive to demystify traditional concepts of philosophic truth goes along with a rigorous thinking-through of their textual *and* their epistemological consequences. In his late essay 'The Resistance to Theory' de Man has some pertinent reflections on the motives that work to assimilate deconstruction to other, more conventional kinds of activity.[13] He picks out its most subversive aspect as the power to problematize relations between logic, grammar and rhetoric, the latter (through its surplus of 'deviant' figuration) undermining the assurance of a 'proper' relationship between language and thought. This certainly looks like an attack on traditional epistemology from the standpoint of a thorough-going deconstructive rhetoric of tropes. But it also holds out against the kind of accommodating pragmatist 'solution' which Rorty sees beckoning at the end of every road. De Man remains the most rigorous of anti-philosophers, undermining the truth-claims of epistemology only by way of an exhaustively thought-out rhetorical critique.

This leads on directly to the question – much canvassed by Marxist critics – of the *politics* of deconstruction. The aspects which Rorty picks out for approval are those that give rise to the Marxist claim that deconstruction is really nothing more than a species of Nietzschean reactionary creed indifferent to history, politics and reason alike. Such polemics might seem justified in the light of what Rorty has to say about Derrida's textual strategies. Thus he writes, for example, that Derrida wants to hang on to Hegel's historical way of doing philosophy, though 'without its teleology, its sense of direction, its seriousness'.[14] This would ultimately point to a pragmatist conclusion, a 'naturalized Hegelianism' (as Rorty puts it) minus all the needless machinery of theory, dialectics and mediating concepts. What always drops out in the pragmatist argument is any form of ideological critique which would challenge that 'naturalized' relation between history, reason and present-day consensus values. From Rorty's reading of Derrida (at least on its 'positive' side) the Marxist might well feel confirmed in a blanket diagnosis of 'American deconstruction' as yet another form of disguised apologetics for the intellectual status quo.

But this is to ignore the demystifying thrust of those deconstructive arguments which *do* precisely bear on the workings of common sense or naturalized perception. De Man puts the claim most strongly in a passage from 'The Resistance to Theory':

What we call ideology is precisely the confusion of linguistic with natural reality, of reference with phenomenalism. It follows that, more than any other mode of inquiry, including economics, the linguistics of literariness is a powerful and indispensable tool in the unmasking of ideological aberrations, as well as a determining factor in accounting for their occurrence.[15]

These sentences would stand a good deal of conceptual unpacking. What they help to explain at this stage is the fact that the politics of any given theory are not to be read off directly in terms of its commitment (or otherwise) to a realist ontology of language and reference. The Marxist hostility towards deconstruction is most often expressed in precisely those terms: by attacking the so-called 'idealist' leanings of a theory which operates in the problematic space between conflicting codes of textual representation. Thus Rorty and the Marxists are oddly united in condemning what they see as deconstruction's tendency to 'go transcendental'. I argue, on the contrary, that it is *only* by preserving this moment of epistemological critique that philosophy (or literary theory) can keep its effective radical edge. The passage from de Man goes on to make this point with more than a touch of self-vindicating passion.

> Those who reproach literary theory for being oblivious to social and historical (that is to say, ideological) reality are merely stating their fear at having their own mystifications exposed by the tool they are trying to discredit. They are, in short, very poor readers of Marx's *German Ideology*.[16]

This is to argue that textual theory has a power to demystify commonsense assumptions, a power that is all the more effective for its calling into question such doctrinaire (phenomenalist) notions of meaning and reference. It is also to insist, *contra* Rorty, that the business of epistemological critique remains firmly on the agenda, for politics as well as philosophy.

This is why these essays refuse the Rortyan option of collapsing philosophy into literary criticism, or a version of literary criticism which excludes 'theory' as just one more effort to smuggle philosophy in by the back door. De Man once again tries to pinpoint what is at issue in this present-day 'contest of the faculties'. Literary theory, he writes, is a 'relatively autonomous version of questions that also surface . . . in philosophy, though not necessarily in a clearer and more rigorous form'.[17] Philosophy has tended to bypass the problems of coming to terms with its own textual or rhetorical constitution. Literary theory (at least since the advent of deconstruction) has made these problems its peculiar concern, and in this sense has moved into regions of enquiry closed off to 'philosophy' as such. This is *not* to say, with Rorty, that philosophy should henceforth be treated as just one 'kind of writing', along with all the others that make up a flourishing culture. Rather, it is to argue that deconstructive theory has uncovered certain problematic aspects of philosophy which can now be thought through in more rigorous fashion *without* losing sight of philosophy's distinctive concerns.

Aesthetics is one of those contested sectors in the philosophic enterprise where de Man finds these unsettling tensions at work. It is here that reflection has tended to pass, as if unproblematically, from the level of idealized speculative *concepts* to the level of first-order concrete *perception*. In so doing, according to de Man, it has contrived to short-circuit the rhetorical problems which a deconstructive reading brings to light. It is in Kant's *Critique of Judgement* that these blind-spots of argument are most clearly revealed. Aesthetics, for Kant (as for Hegel after him), occupies a far from marginal place in the systematic project of philosophy.[18] It is the ground on which 'pure' and 'practical' reason are notionally reconciled, where *a priori* concepts are thought to find their validating content of sensuous perception. Aesthetic judgement thus tends towards a moment of phenomenalist reduction which seeks a grounding in sensory experience but fails to give an adequately argued account of that grounding. Literary theory (as opposed to 'philosophy', in this respect at least) shows up these questionable passages of argument in the form of unlooked-for textual aberrations.

This may help to explain the common misreading of de Man which takes him to deny all practical commerce between language and reality. 'In a genuine semiology', he writes, 'the referential function of language is not being denied – far from it; what is in question is its authority as a model for natural or phenomenal cognition.'[19] Aesthetics is the critical ground on which this authority has often been claimed by philosophers. In deconstructing such claims, de Man is simultaneously opening a space for reflection on the *ideological* motives that work to naturalize a certain model of 'commonsense' thought and perception. My own chapter here on Roger Scruton's aesthetics comes at these questions from a similar angle. It asks, that is to say, what interests are involved in the mode of argument which grants the 'aesthetic understanding' a privi- leged place above matters of theory and ideological reflection. It is not, Scruton argues, *'subtlety* that is required in order to make the theory of history relevant to aesthetics'. More speci- fically: the question of the relevance of theory 'can only be decided from the standpoint of aesthetics, and is not a ques- tion for the theory itself to answer'.[20] It is the function of such argumentative moves to cut out theoretical reflection at pre- cisely the point where it might undermine the supposedly self-evident truths of aesthetic understanding.

Scruton stands in a line of conservative critic-philosophers, from Burke to T. S. Eliot, who valorize the aesthetic by placing it beyond reach of ideological critique. Eliot discovered a whole range of techniques for achieving this desired separation of realms. For Donne, he wrote, 'a thought . . . was an experi- ence; it modified his sensibility'.[21] Thought and feeling existed in a state of harmonious adjustment which required no elab- orate provision of *theory* by which to adjudicate their claims. This happy condition Eliot equated with the kind of 'organic' culture which supposedly flourished in English society prior to the turmoils of the Civil War period. What then came to pass – according to this influential myth – was a wholesale 'dissocia- tion of sensibility', such that the qualities of thought and emotion tended to separate out and develop in a state of unhealthy isolation. The Romantics inherited this deep-laid cultural malaise, the effects of which – in their poetry and criticism alike – Eliot was quick to diagnose. What he chiefly deplored was the strain of 'undisciplined' emotional licence, along with the increased self-consciousness trained upon the workings of poetic creativity and feeding on its own deep conflicts of motive. Hence the need, as Eliot saw it, for a strict demarcation of bounds between philosophy and literary criticism. Otherwise critics would be all too easily seduced from their proper vocation by 'the sad ghost of Coleridge, beckoning from the shades'. Coleridge comes to figure for Eliot as a type-case of the literary intellectual in whom abstract reflection gets the upper hand over unforced, spontaneous creativity.[22] This cautionary tale goes to reinforce the message: that 'theory' and criticism don't mix, or only at the cost of dissociating thought from its natural element of lived experience.

Thus Eliot, like Rorty, sees nothing but multiplied error and delusion in criticism's desire to 'go transcendental' and look for legitimating theories beyond its first-order practical concerns. It is the critic's proper business, as Eliot defines it, to pass as directly as possible from detailed local perception to generalized statements of method and principle. This is what he found most perfectly embodied in Aristotle's practice: 'intelligence itself, operating the analysis of sensation to the point of principle and definition'.[23] One can see how an essay like 'Tradition and the Individual Talent' sets out to emulate this classicist ideal. On the one hand, there are those passages of exemplary 'close reading' which exerted such an influence on later critics. On the other, there is the constant readiness to let drop statements of an offhand nature on such large questions as the limits of ethical individualism, the metaphysics of identity and (of course) the concept of 'tradition' itself. What is excluded in the process is any kind of reasoned *theoretical* account of how language achieves (or fails to achieve) that harmonious inwardness of thought and emotion which Eliot so prizes in a poet like Donne. There is something distinctly disingenuous about Eliot's statement that 'this essay proposes to halt at the frontiers of metaphysics'.[24] In fact it contains a good deal of 'metaphysical' argument, though presented in such a way as to sidestep the awkward middle-ground of theory. Practical criticism can thus get on with the business of sharpening its local perceptions, while the essay advances its larger (ideological) claims without risking any kind of detailed *textual* engagement.

The 'perfect critic' is therefore one who lives up to that ideal of co-operative thought and sensibility which marks out the finest of seventeenth-century verse. This paradigm seemingly holds for all time, no matter what changes might since have been wrought by the fall from metaphysical grace. Indeed, this collapse of history itself into a timeless, idealized 'tradition' – an imaginary museum of cultural exhibits – goes along with Eliot's resistance to all forms of mediating theory. Tradition is conceived as the co-ordinating medium of ideas, perceptions and values which rise clean above the crass contingencies of historical event. The poet, in Eliot's well-known phrase, must write with a sense of the entire European tradition immemorially 'in his bones'. Such deep-laid sympathies will hardly permit themselves to suffer disturbance by reflecting too nicely on the complex mediations of history, language and 'tradition'. They exist in a sealed-off aesthetic domain where perception is raised directly into abstract principle, leaving no room for theory on the one hand or historical reflection on the other. Scruton is yet more doctrinaire in his claims for the primacy of aesthetic understanding. His strategies of argument fully bear out what de Man has to say about the mystification of philosophic discourse through its constantly resorting to aesthetics as a means of short-circuiting rational critique. They also lend colour to de Man's strongest claim: that deconstruction has radical effects precisely in so far as it suspends the commonsense equation between language and the order of phenomenal experience.

III

Deconstruction thus engages with philosophy at those points of more or less visible strain where philosophy fails to follow out its own more rigorous *textual* implications. In this sense it substitutes a 'literary' reading – a reading trained up on techniques of rhetorical analysis – for other, more conventionally 'philosophical' forms of argument. Yet it also refuses the pragmatist option of declaring philosophy henceforth redundant except in so far as it renounces all claim to epistemological rigour. Deconstruction goes counter to received ideas of what 'philosophy' is about, but only by consistently pressing those ideas beyond their presumed self-evident basis in the

nature of phenomenal perception. De Man's reading of Kantian aesthetics exemplifies this double movement of thought. It
may be the case (stage one of his argument) that Kant is
passing off tropes as concepts, presenting not so much a strict
transcendental deduction as 'a story, a dramatized scene of the
mind in action'.[25] But this is not to license a last-ditch retreat
from the claims of philosophical critique. Ideology and criticism may be 'interdependent' to the point of creating all
manner of confusion in texts which strive to keep them apart.
But simply to *collapse* that distinction – as the pragmatist
argument implies – is to give up all hopes of rational understanding. In de Man's words:

> philosophies that succumb to ideology lose their epistemo-
> logical sense, whereas philosophies that try to bypass or
> repress ideology lose all critical thrust and risk being repos-
> sessed by what they foreclose.[26]

This is the aspect of deconstruction – the moment of ideological critique – which tends to be ignored by its Marxist detractors, as well as by 'post-modern' pragmatists like Rorty. De
Man's deconstructive 'allegories of reading' have nothing in
common with the pragmatist insistence that theory should at
last give way before the levelling regime of first-order narrative
conventions.

Critical theory has its work cut out for the present in maintaining a sense of this crucial distinction. Without it, thought
seems destined to collapse into a state of passive acquiescence
in the myths, ideologies and naturalized half-beliefs which
make up commonsense wisdom. Already there are those, like
Jean-François Lyotard,[27] who welcome this emergent 'revolution' of attitudes as a sign of long-delayed cultural maturity.
Lyotard's case can be summarized roughly as follows. Philosophers (political theorists especially) have always cast their
ideas in some kind of *narrative* form. Mostly they have wanted
to disguise that fact, as by shifting from a first-order 'natural'
narrative to a higher plane of understanding where the story
would yield up its true (e.g. 'dialectical') significance. What
the post-modern era signifies, according to Lyotard, is an end
to all such consoling myths of intellectual mastery and
truth. Straightforward narratives are all we have, and their

significance is strictly a matter of what *makes sense*, in the way of explanations, at any given stage of cultural history.

This diagnosis bears a striking resemblance to Rorty's account of post-Kantian philosophy. In each case the upshot is a summons to put away the false meta-narrative security of system and method, and to come out fully on the side of 'post-modern' pragmatism. Politically, the message is equally clear: that all those totalizing schemes of explanation (Marxist meta-narratives especially) are henceforth redundant, since nothing could intelligibly *count* as supporting their truth-claims. The position is the same (so this argument would have it) in philosophy and the human sciences at large. The time is long past when it was rational to place any faith in theories which sought to criticize their native culture from a standpoint of masterly detachment. Such perspectives are deemed irrelevant from the standpoint of a generalized social con-sensus which sets its own terms for debate. The only kind of argument which then makes sense is the kind that sticks to naturalized narrative pragmatics and surrenders all claim to a higher (dialectical) order of knowledge.

The utopian aspect of Lyotard's argument comes from his belief that modern technology is evolving away from its re-pressive uses as an instrument of centralized power and control. He predicts that the spread of information networks will break down monopolistic structures of authority and work to promote the free circulation of ideas. As the networks become more densely interactive, so society will learn to make do without absolute legitimating truths, and to live with its own kinds of 'narrative' understanding. What counts as viable 'knowledge' will be wholly determined by the complex sys-tems of power and interest which make up the totality of social relations. The destinies of post-modern culture are seen as interlocking at every point with those of post-industrial socie-ty. The arts and sciences are alike subject to a process of 'delegitimation' which removes their transcendent ('meta-narrative') authority and opens them up to all the winds of cultural change. 'Linguistic practice' and 'performative power' thus become the only effective measures of a statement's truth, since truth is what holds for a given society at a given stage in its cultural evolution. As Lyotard writes:

The performativity of an utterance, be it denotative or prescriptive, increases proportionally to the amount of information about its referent one has at one's disposal. Thus the growth of power, and its self-legitimation, are now taking the route of data-storage and accessibility, and the operativity of information.[28]

Lyotard sees clearly enough that there is another possible upshot to this story, one which would turn the new technology into a 'dream machine' for the purposes of ever more sophisticated social control. But these doubts count for less than his hopeful belief that truth and power are already well on the way to being 'delegitimized', and that socio-political structures must inevitably soon follow suit. Thus: 'the ideology of communicational "transparency", which goes hand in hand with the commercialization of knowledge, will begin to perceive the State as a factor of opacity and "noise".'[29] Such reflections enable Lyotard to sustain a broadly optimistic viewpoint alongside (or despite) his technological-determinist creed.

It will be seen how this puts him squarely at odds with a thinker like Habermas, committed to the quest for legitimating principles of reason while acknowledging the forms of 'repressive rationality' that work to distort those principles. The only point of contact between Habermas and Lyotard is that both diagnose a deep-lying crisis in the present state of cultural and scientific knowledge. From here on their reasonings are sharply divergent. Habermas rejects the consensus view of truth entailed by Lyotard's pragmatist outlook. He seeks a way beyond the present 'legitimation crisis' by recalling thought to the Enlightenment tradition of rational critique. Lyotard denies that such ideas can be of any use in the post-modern context of debate. And where Habermas would criticize our present 'distorted' rationality from the standpoint of enlightened reason, Lyotard sees no possible *grounds* for any such argument. There is no last appeal beyond the 'rational' norms which decide what shall count as genuine contributions to knowledge at any given time. For Lyotard, reason is a product of consensus and can only be judged in light of its 'performative' status, its role in furthering the present aims of knowledge. For Habermas, conversely, it is incumbent upon reason to transcend all forms of unreflective cultural consensus in the quest for a better, more enlightened rationality. And among the social forces which resist such understanding is precisely that pragmatist equation of *truth* and *power* – or knowledge and instrumental reason – which Lyotard so readily accepts.

I have tried to give the reader some idea of how these essays hang together on a range of connected topics. Central to them all is the issue between Habermas and Lyotard: the question, that is, of how theory can justify its claims when faced with various forms of sceptical or relativist argument. The chapters on deconstruction are likewise concerned to challenge the idea that 'textualist' readings always come down to a species of Nietzschean irrationalism. On the contrary: the point of de-construction is to argue with the utmost *logical* rigour to conclusions which may yet be counter-intuitive or at odds with commonsense (consensual) wisdom. And it is here, I maintain, that critical theory is most effectively deployed in questioning the stereotypes and cultural self-images of the age. The resistance it has met with in various quarters – not least from professional philosophers – is perhaps the best measure of this salutary power to disturb.

1

Narrative theory or theory-as-narrative: the politics of 'post-modern' reason

I

Some large claims have recently been put forward in the name of narrative theory. Might it not be that *all* forms of knowledge partake of a certain narrative or storytelling interest? Such ideas have taken hold not only (as might be expected) among literary theorists, but also among philosophers and historians. Of the latter, Hayden White goes furthest in asserting that history is always a species of narrative construct, a discourse whose meaning is actively produced by the tropes and devices employed to make sense of an otherwise inchoate material.[1] The positivist assumption – that 'truth' must surely emerge if 'the facts' are just set down in their proper, self-evident order – is the merest of delusions, according to White. What it serves to disguise is the way in which competing ideologies work to reorganize the discursive field in pursuit of their own particular ends. The various kinds of narrative emplotment are closely bound up with these varieties of ideological world-view. One would have to go back to the earliest, most primitive forms of history – the bare-bones chronicle of events – to find a plausible counter-example to White's sophisticated arguments. And even there, as he shows, the supposedly 'factual' record is by no means innocent of certain narrative designs.

A similar idea is gaining ground among current 'post-analytic' philosophers like Richard Rorty.[2] In their case the story goes roughly as follows. Philosophy has traditionally pinned its hopes on various kinds of logical or *a priori* truth which would offer a solution to its problems. That no such

solutions were yet forthcoming – that the same old problems
remained on the agenda – was cause for regret but not despair.
It meant that new methods had better be tried, new ways of
posing the great central issues so as to render them amenable,
at last, to strictly *philosophical* treatment. There was always a
fresh terminology at hand for describing these successive
'revolutions' of thought. We have already seen some of Rorty's
nominees for the list of failed candidates: 'clear and distinct
ideas, sense-data, categories of the pure understanding, structures of prelinguistic consciousness, and the like'.[3] Each of
them (and others more recent) seemed to mark a decisive
advance towards philosophic clarity and truth. There was a
choice at every stage – or so it appeared – between merely
rehearsing the history of past errors or actually *doing* philosophy, pushing back the limits of thought. One was either a
'genuine' philosopher or the kind of hanger-on who might
claim the title 'historian of ideas'. The latter had their uses, if
only to legitimize the latest revolution by making it the upshot
of a new, revisionist history. The plot could always be rewrit-
ten, or angled from a different omniscient viewpoint, so as to
bring it into line with enlightened modern opinion.

   Rorty's argument, in brief, is that philosophy ('real', first-
order philosophy) has failed to deliver the goods. Too many
revolutions have come and gone without providing the
looked-for enlightenment. In fact, Rorty argues, they were
never much more than local variations on a theme laid down
by the deep metaphorics of traditional discourse. The narrative
might take a different turn from time to time, but the moves
were pretty well mapped out in advance, episodes in a story
which offered no last-minute ultimate truths. To the question
'Whither philosophy now?' Rorty replies that it can keep up
the narrative interest *without* still subscribing to its old, deluded claims of authorial omniscience. The philosopher, that is
to say, steps down from an imaginary privileged position
vis-à-vis the cultural community at large, and learns to make
peace with the fact that there are no valid methods, truths or
techniques which would set philosophy firmly apart from
other, less elevated forms of intellectual life. There is still a
whole range of interesting narrative *connections* to make –
different ways of interpreting the same basic story – without

the illusion of a God's-eye view. The one constraint on this activity, as Rorty sees it, is the need to make sense within the larger, continuing story of western (= present-day North American) cultural life. The good news is that this tradition has come round to a healthy pragmatist sense of the non-availability of ultimate truths, the uselessness of large-scale explanatory 'systems', and the fact that ideas are interpretable only in terms of their (past and present) cultural relevance. Thus Rorty's narrative can claim to get things right (from a pragmatist standpoint) while consistently denying that truths are to be had in any other, more ultimate or 'philosophic' form.

One could multiply examples of this 'narrative turn' in recent intellectual debate. It mostly goes along with a marked reaction against the kinds of wholesale explanatory theory which would seek to transcend their own special context or localized conditions of cultural production. Foucault is the most obvious example, with his rejection of Marxist theory (especially in its Althusserian or 'scientistic' guise), and his espousal of a 'micro-politics' of local intervention, carried on by 'specific intellectuals' with no grand claims to universal truth.[4] This interventionist strategy is also a kind of first-order narrative pragmatics. It denies what the Marxists (some of them, at least) would most emphatically claim: that history unfolds according to laws which reason – dialectical reason – can ultimately grasp and promote. Foucault rejects the possibility of any such grand meta-narrative. The point is best made by a text like *I, Pierre Rivière . . .* , where the central 'event' – the multiple murder – is recounted from various partial viewpoints including that of the eponymous protagonist.[5] The other viewpoints represented – doctors, psychiatrists and lawyers with various professional interests involved – are neither more nor less 'authoritative' than Pierre's first-person narration. And the same applies (we must surely conclude) to the diagnostic commentaries appended by Foucault and his colleagues. There is no meta-narrative stance which might permit these diverse reports to be channelled into some kind of masterly general 'truth'. First-order narratives are all we have, and the truth is what is given only from a limited perspective which other such narratives can always claim to demystify. This would leave no room for the Marxist assumption that knowledge is in some sense defined in *opposition* to the workings of ideological false consciousness. For all its Althusserian refinements, this notion remains indispensably a part of the Marxist theoretical standpoint.

So there is a sense in which the emphasis on *narrative* (narrative, that is, as a limit-point of rational explanation) comes into conflict with the truth-claims of critical theory. Hayden White would see the various 'logics' of historical explanation as merely the legitimating cover adopted by different ideologies in search of narrative hegemony. For Rorty, the presumptive 'truths' of traditional philosophy are really nothing more than a species of metaphorical delusion, best treated as so many first-order narrative episodes. What they both reject (along with Foucault) is the kind of totalizing theory which would claim to demystify such narrative understanding in the name of a higher, dialectical truth. And this creates problems – very sizeable problems – when it comes to describing the present state of what is loosely referred to as 'narrative theory'. On the one hand there is the fact that narrative explanations are currently in the process of dislodging some of the most basic concepts and methods of traditional thought. That process has generated a great deal of useful and productive discussion. Yet 'theory' (in a certain sense of the term) is precisely what seems to be excluded – or drastically curtailed – if one accepts these current claims for the priority of first-order narrative explanations.

There is a curious paradox (or maybe just a law of diminishing returns) at work in this present situation. Critical theory tends to *textualize* all forms of knowledge, alerting (for instance) historians and philosophers to the elements of narrative or figural sense that typically shape their discourse. Yet this very unmasking of rhetorical strategies often lays claim to the status of theoretical knowledge. It seeks to comprehend them at a higher stage of dialectical awareness, a vantage-point of theory that would somehow transcend the first-order rhetorics of narrative telling. Theory is scarcely conceivable without this implicit claim that thought is in possession of cognitive powers more adequate – less mystified or ideologically distorted – than the texts it presumes to interpret. Some such conviction must always be at work in those varieties of 'enlightened' critique that think to articulate the difference between naturalized myths and the forms of rational under-standing. Otherwise reflection is entirely in the power of those pre-reflective fantasies and 'commonsense' assumptions which thrive on the absence of critical thought. Such would be the upshot of a thoroughgoing pragmatism that went all the way in equating its own present interests with the cultural self-image of society at large.

Yet this is very much the message given out by those 'post-modern' thinkers (like Jean-François Lyotard[6]) who de-clare wholeheartedly in favour of first-order narratives. There is no going back, they insist, to an age of 'totalizing' theories when thought could take shelter in abstract systems of its own devising. Such systems – whether Kantian, Marxist, or what-ever – have now been shown up as so many failed and delusive master-plots, wholly out of touch with the cultures they claimed to transcend. 'An end to meta-narratives' is Lyotard's way of expressing this hard-earned pragmatist wisdom. The mistake is to imagine – like certain old-fashioned novelists – that there exists some kind of ultimate, self-validating view-point from which all the other limited perspectives would suddenly fall into place. The only cure for this chronic delusion is to recognize (like Rorty or Lyotard) that knowledge is always inescapably complicit with the first-order myths and enabling fictions that underwrite its claims to truth.

In view of this, the term 'narrative theory' assumes a prob-lematical, even disjunctive character. As the idea gains ground that *all* theory is a species of sublimated narrative, so doubts emerge about the very possibility of *knowledge* as distinct from the various forms of narrative gratification. Theory presup-poses a critical distance between its own categories and those of a naturalized mythology or commonsense system of assumptions. Simply to collapse that distance – as Lyotard suggests – is to argue away the very grounds of rational critique. It amounts to a vote of no confidence in the idea that theory can obtain a critical hold on the limiting assumptions of its own time and place. There is just no *room* for such 'enlight-ened' rationalist notions, if thought has no more active role to play than that of willing participant–narrator in present-day cultural myths. The 'post-modern condition' – as Lyotard interprets it – thus seems to share the essential characteristics of all conservative ideology, from Burke to the current New Right. It rests, that is to say, on the idea that *prejudice* is so deeply built into our traditions of thought that no amount of rational criticism can hope to dislodge it. Any serious thinking about culture and society will have to acknowledge the fact that such enquiries have meaning only within the context of a certain informing tradition. It is a delusion – so this argument implies – to elevate critique above the everyday, practical knowledge that simply *makes sense* of things as they are. Such mistaken ideas are characteristic of the left-wing intellectual, who is convinced that reason – mere reason – can overcome the deep continuities of custom and prejudice.

This conservative ideology has clear affiliations with Lyotard's idea of naturalized narrative pragmatics. It also brings out the very marked political implications of any such wholesale, deliberate retreat from the claims of rational critique. These issues are stated most forcefully by Jürgen Habermas in his long-running public debate with Hans-Georg Gadamer.[7] On the one side is Gadamer's contention (derived from a post-Heideggerian hermeneutic standpoint) that rational explanations must always be grounded in a sense of meaningful *dialogue* with past tradition.[8] Otherwise, he argues, we would simply lack the means to grasp their present validity, since there is no power of abstract argument which carries an ultimately authenticating context along with it. Hermeneutic understanding, as Gadamer conceives it, thus claims a naturally privileged status *vis-à-vis* the rival presumptions of rational critique. There is no breaking out of the hermeneutic circle, the paradox which Gadamer (like Heidegger before him) locates at the heart of all understanding. How can understanding get a hold on any text without in some sense *knowing beforehand* what would count as a valid interpretation? And again: where does interpretation start, given the reciprocal interdependence between 'part' and 'whole' in the process of textual understanding? On the basis of these and other such paradoxes, Gadamer concludes that hermeneutic 'method' can never be reduced to any form of theoretical critique. Rather, it involves a process of open-ended dialogue whereby the interpreter both questions the text and comes to comprehend his or her own inevitably partial viewpoint.

What Habermas chiefly objects to in Gadamer's argument is the assumption that *all* understanding is embedded in a context of pre-reflective meanings and motives which reason is effectively powerless to criticize. To accept this position, he argues, is to throw away the whole tradition of enlightened 'liberal' thinking and regress to an almost dark-age state of passive acquiescence in received ideas. For Habermas, there *must* be certain positive norms – structures of rational understanding – which allow thought to criticize the current self-images of the age. In his early writings this critique took the form of a genealogical enquiry into the growing divorce between instrumental reason (or scientific positivism) and the powers of reflective self-understanding.[9] More recently, Habermas has developed a theory of 'communicative competence' whereby to assess the distortions of rational consensus present in all existing societies. From this critical perspective (that of an ideal 'speech situation' generalized to the public sphere) he can claim to theorize the workings of repressive social institutions.[10] His quarrel with Gadamer follows from the need to establish this basis for a critical theory independent of prevailing consensual norms. To Gadamer's way of thinking, such a theory would be out of the question – or merely unintelligible – since nothing makes sense in isolation from its own informing cultural context.

Habermas rejects what he sees as the inbuilt conservatism of Gadamer's hermeneutic stance. This results from its appeal to established consensual values, assumed to lie so deep – or so close to the sources of articulate thought – as to preclude any radical critique. Such consensus, according to Habermas, merely embodies the prevailing lack of rational reflection which Gadamer misguidedly seeks to perpetuate. Hermeneutics in this guise would thus become the guilty philosophical accomplice of a social order bent upon naturalizing its own irrational truth-claims. For Gadamer, as Habermas interprets him,

Any attempt to suggest that this (certainly contingent) consensus is false consciousness is meaningless since we cannot transcend the discussion in which we are engaged. From this Gadamer deduces the ontological priority of linguistic tradition before all possible critique.[11]

Any talk of 'ideology' would have to be renounced as implying that thought can gain a vantage-point decisively beyond the past or present stages of cultural consensus. As with Lyotard, so with Gadamer: the limits of reflection are those implicit in the culture or tradition under scrutiny.

For Habermas, on the contrary, consensual values are always open to rational critique. They are not to be treated as an unsurpassable horizon of meaning beyond which thought cannot go without surrendering its claims to intelligible sense. From this point of view,

> every consensus, in which the understanding of meaning terminates, stands fundamentally under suspicion of being pseudo-communicatively induced . . . the prejudgmental structure of the understanding of meaning does not guarantee identification of an achieved consensus with a true one.[12]

This plainly controverts the pragmatist or hermeneutic thinking which would deny all access to higher (meta-narrative) modes of understanding. Repressive rationality has its counterpart, for Habermas, in the forms of potentially enlightened or emancipating reason implicit in human language. The ideal of undistorted communication is something like a latter-day linguistic equivalent of Kant's *a priori* structures of transcendental reason. It thus differs crucially from Gadamer's appeal to language as a pre-reflective source of understanding anterior to all the rational constructions which enlightened critique would place upon it. For Habermas, this kind of 'ontological' grounding ignores both the negative (repressive) and the positive (emancipating) aspects of social rationality. It fails to see that consensus may embody forms of unreflective self-interest which work to legitimate large-scale patterns of socio-economic domination. At the same time it is blind to that other, enlightened form of cognitive interest which enables reason to grasp and transcend its present, self-alienated condition. Such are the grounds for Habermas's long-running quarrel with Gadamer.

II

This debate has a crucial bearing on current issues in narrative theory. On the one hand there is a clear affiliation between Gadamer's broadly conservative hermeneutic stance and the idea that all understanding is shaped by pre-existent patterns of narrative organization. For Gadamer, there is finally no escape from the circle of tacit or intuitive foreknowledge that makes interpretation possible. The same line of argument underlies Lyotard's claim that first-order narrative 'explanations' are all that we can reasonably hope for, given the failure (as he sees it) of other, more ambitious systems of thought. In both cases, theory is brought up against its limits by reflecting on a supposedly prior 'hermeneutic' level of understanding which its own concepts and categories cannot fully grasp. Central to Gadamer's argument is the Diltheyan distinction between *Verstehen* and *Erklären*. The former kind of knowledge (characteristic of the 'human sciences') involves a rich but largely tacit dimension of enabling motives and assumptions. The latter sets out, on the other hand, to explain where those assumptions come from, to expose them to rational critique and demonstrate their structural genealogy. It is *this* kind of knowledge that Habermas invokes by way of preserving the critical impulse in the discourse of hermeneutic reason. And it is here also that narrative theory has to choose between two divergent paths of development.

The choice can be stated roughly as follows. Theory can claim to have a knowledge of narrative structures and devices beyond the kind of first-order storytelling interest that most narratives provide. It may likewise claim to unmask (or deconstruct) elements of textual *ideology* which the narrative is unable to acknowledge in itself, since to do so would be to destroy its own (illusory) coherence. Theory, in short, presumes a knowledge of the text which the text makes possible only in so far as it lends itself to a different, more rigorously argued form of discourse. Such is the premiss of most Marxist criticism, especially in the wake of Althusser's distinction between 'ideology' (as the mode of lived but illusory experience) and 'science' (as the work of *theoretical* production which aims to explain such illusions). Thus, in Macherey's words,

'the themes immediately extracted from *literary* works can
have no value as concepts'.[13] And again, for Terry Eagleton
(writing in 1976, very much under Althusser's influence),
criticism must 'break with its ideological prehistory, situating
itself outside the space of the text on the alternative terrain of
scientific knowledge'.[14] Such arguments stand squarely
opposed to Lyotard's assumption that first-order narratives
exhaust all the powers of conceptual explanation. They require, that is to say, a sharp distinction between the kind of
self-knowledge that a narrative obscurely possesses but cannot *articulate*, and the means by which criticism works to draw
out that knowledge. To Lyotard, such theories would amount
to nothing more than pointless variations on a grand but
superannuated theme.

This difference of views clearly has large implications for the
politics of critical theory. Lyotard's version of narrative
pragmatics leads him to formulate what is, in effect, an 'end of
ideology' thesis. It takes for granted the existence of a broad-
based consensus on what *makes sense* at the present stage of an
ongoing, open-ended cultural tradition. Any claim to unmask
the ideology inscribed in that consensus – to deconstruct it, in
Eagleton's words, from the 'alternative terrain' of theory – is
overruled on straightforward pragmatist grounds. As narrative becomes, in effect, the basis of all explanations, so narrative *theory* begins to lose its powers of cognitive and critical
grasp. The theorist is implicitly caught up in a narrative
situation which permits no escape to the high ground of
'science' or totalizing meta-critique. It would then seem impossible to argue, like Eagleton, that criticism can break
altogether with its own ideological prehistory. Such arguments are merely a product (according to Lyotard) of the bad
old rationalist thinking which sets up an abstract, hierarchical
relation between different orders of discourse.

So there is a sense in which 'narrative theory' tends to
undermine its own cognitive status as its claims become more
sweepingly ambitious. A similar pattern of development
emerges if one looks at the passage from 'structuralist' to
'post-structuralist' theories of the narrative text. Structuralist
narratology in its 'classical' phase took over the systematic
aims and aspirations of the earlier Russian Formalists. Eschew-

ing mere 'interpretation', it sought to place criticism on a scientific footing by the study of supposedly *invariant* structures and devices present in all literary texts. This quest for a universal narrative 'grammar' underwent successive refinements of method, from Propp's *Morphology of the Folk-Tale* (1928) to Barthes's middle-period essays. There then occurred a marked shift of interest, with Barthes (in *S/Z*, 1970) declaring an end to the structuralist dream of reducing all narratives to a single, prototypical pattern. Henceforth, he suggested, criticism should renounce this reductive ideal and seek instead to liberate those plural energies of meaning which even the 'classic realist' text cannot wholly repress.[15] Of course there were still critics of a structuralist persuasion (Todorov and Genette chief among them) who continued to work at the taxonomic ordering of narrative forms and devices. But the effect of *S/Z* was to inaugurate a new, more adventurous hermeneutics of reading, one which valued 'theory' not so much for its explanatory power as for its speculative uses in exploding traditional concepts of method. Theory no longer laid claim to a knowledge of the text which the text could only yield under pressure of articulate theory. It was now more a case of the theorist being drawn into labyrinths of textual 'undecidability' where any kind of systematic truth-claim could only tell the story of its own undoing.

Deconstructionist critics (among them Barbara Johnson and Shoshana Felman) have traced in elaborate detail some of the unconscious ruses to which criticism is forced in its efforts to 'master' the literary text. Interpreters become the dupes (the 'straight-men', Johnson calls them[16]) of a narrative undecidability which draws them to identify (sometimes obsessively) with one partial viewpoint and actively *suppress* all others. Felman puts the case with extraordinary subtlety and vigour in her reading of various critics on James's *The Turn of the Screw*. The interpreters, she argues, cannot help but confirm the narrative's contagious power to distort and disfigure their perceptions. In Felman's words,

> The actors, or *agents* of this textual action, are indeed the readers and the critics no less than the characters. . . . Reading here becomes not the cognitive observation of the

text's pluralistic meaning, but its 'acting-out'. Indeed it is not so much the critic who comprehends the text, as the text which comprehends the critic.[17]

This brings out the curious reversal of roles between 'theory' and 'narrative' produced by reading critical texts with an eye to their duplicitous rhetoric. As it turns out, the various reductive 'theories' of James's interpreters all have their own strange story to tell of fixations, repressions and more or less blatant misreadings. Criticism is most in error when it thinks to attain a knowledge of the text which the text can harbour only obliquely or unconsciously. In fact – as Felman shows in the case of self-styled 'Freudian' readings – it is the critics who display the most striking symptoms of unconscious motivation. They habitually misread both James's tale *and* the very texts of Freud whose authority they think to invoke.

Felman makes the point that this whole debate (between 'Freudian' and 'anti-Freudian' readings) is based on a reciprocal misunderstanding of what it *means* to read one text in the light of another. Critics on both sides tend to assume that the 'truth' of Freud's writings is unambiguously there to be consulted, taken over and applied at will. As a matter of 'theory', its truth-claims in any given case can be tested against the literary 'evidence' and judged on their explanatory merits. This is to assume that theory has access to a knowledge independent of the doubts and perplexities which beset literary interpretation. But it is precisely *that* assumption, Felman argues, which has to be jettisoned by a reading that is alert to the textual complications of Freudian discourse. That there is no metalanguage immune to 'unconscious' lapses and displacements is indeed the chief lesson to be read in Freud's (as well as in James's) exemplary texts.

> A 'Freudian reading' is thus not a reading guaranteed by, grounded in, Freud's knowledge, but first and foremost a *reading of Freud's 'knowledge'*, which as such can never *a priori* be assured of knowing anything, but must take its chances *as* a reading, necessarily and constitutively threatened by error.[18]

Reading thus becomes a veritable allegory of errors, most

'rigorous' (or least deluded) precisely where it knows and makes allowance for its own, irreducibly *textual* predicament.

What is evident here is perhaps not so much a retreat from theory as a way of redefining it in textualist or narrative terms. Felman's treatment of Freud is typical of many such post-structuralist (or Lacanian) readings, which insist that there is no last ground of appeal, no 'truth' beyond the writings which make up Freudian discourse. For Lacan, the unconscious is 'structured like a language', but not in such a form as to yield up its logic to a 'structuralist' theory securely possessed of its own legitimating method. It may appear sometimes that Lacan is proposing a systematic *scheme* of tropological equivalents for Freud's less sophisticated language of unconscious functions. Thus he argues that Freudian 'displacement' and 'condensation' can be rendered precisely in terms of the distinction which Jakobson draws between 'metonymy' and 'metaphor' as the ultimate structuring principles of language.[19] But this is not to claim that any *theory* of language could hope to master the field of unconscious desire or its rhetorical effects. The notorious 'difficulty' of Lacan's style – its elliptical constructions and density of metaphor – is clearly meant as a reminder that language is not to be reduced to some pristine, intelligible structure of sense. The style goes along with a rooted resistance to theory, if by 'theory' we understand the rationalist (Cartesian) commitment to 'clear and distinct ideas'. It is expressly the purpose of Lacan's writing to show (like Felman on *The Turn of the Screw*) how ubiquitous are the effects of desire in language, and how easily they work to subvert any confident distinction between 'rational' and 'irrational' processes of thought. Theory could hardly go further in deconstructing the truth-claims of traditional epistemology.

What bearing might this have on the attempt by thinkers like Habermas to revive rationalist philosophy in the form of a reflective social critique? Clearly the Lacanian account of language puts problems in the way of that 'ideal speech situation' which Habermas assumes to lie within the powers of human cognitive grasp. This would then seem, not merely 'utopian' (as Habermas of course admits), but hopelessly misguided in its ignoring of the *unconscious* factors that work to complicate all possible speech situations. Thus Rainer Nägele criticizes

Habermas for basing his theory on a simplified version of ego-psychology which elides (or represses) the disruptive effects of unconscious meaning.[20] How can one assume that reason aspires to an ideal of pure, undistorted communication if this means neglecting the very *real* possibility of other, less amenable effects within language? Dominick LaCapra pursues this line of argument, concluding that 'from the perspective of ordinary and literary language, the ideal speech situation might in one sense appear to be a technocratic fantasy'.[21] Such criticisms chime with Lyotard's mistrust of all those grand meta-narratives or totalizing theories which claim to *ground* knowledge once and for all.

So what remains of 'theory' if its best, most articulate efforts might always be subject to narrative drives (or textual distortions) beyond its power to control? Habermas returns a confident reply. Theory is indeed an impossible ideal if one takes it in the root etymological sense of a pure, disinterested contemplation of timeless truths. But there remains a vital role for the kind of reflective critique which would work to situate existing forms of discourse by examining the knowledge-constitutive *interests* that sustain them. These interests are presumed to have a critical dimension – an inbuilt drive towards self-understanding – which redeems them from the status of 'mere' ideology. Hence the resemblance, as Habermas sees it, between Critical Theory and Freudian psychoanalysis.[22] Both involve a *dialogue* which seeks to illuminate the symptomatic blind-spots of a language distorted by forms of repressive unreason. Both have to fix their sights (so the argument runs) on an ideal speech situation where the language of 'private' desire would no longer be invaded and disfigured by the pressures of 'public' ideological conformity. Critical Theory sets out to unmask the irrational (because counter-communicative) structures of dominance involved in this pitiless divorce between private and public spheres. It thus carries over into social critique the Freudian project of enlightened dialogical exchange. 'Where Id was, there shall Ego be' is the programmatic sub-text of Habermas's enterprise.

But it is here precisely that his critics locate the fundamental weakness of the theory. It assumes too easily that unconscious interests can always be brought to light by the activity of a rational self-knowledge capable of grasping its own (hitherto occluded) motives and desires. And this assumption, it is argued, goes along with the 'Enlightenment' values which Habermas adopts without sufficiently questioning their sources. His ideal of free and open communication between private and public spheres is a variant of that eighteenth-century rationalism which drew sharp limits to what counted as 'reason'. By seeking to push back the frontiers of unconscious discourse, Habermas effectively empowers a regime of lucid, accountable, 'public' reason which operates its own form of ideological repression. His idea of rational consensus entails a drastic restriction on those elements of fantasy and wish-fulfilment which may find genuine if limited expression in the 'private' sphere. To regard such expression as merely symptomatic of distorted rationality is to write off the hope that unconscious desire might actively *resist* the structures of instituted reason. What Habermas has to ignore, in short, is that *other* 'dialectic of Enlightenment' which his Frankfurt mentors, Horkheimer and Adorno, equated with the growth of repressive rationality.

Nägele provides the most forceful critique of this component in Habermas's theory.[23] He traces it back to the final section of *Knowledge and Human Interests* (1971), where Habermas develops his reading of Freud in terms of the knowledge-constitutive interests built into the dialogue of patient and analyst. What Nägele objects to here is the assumption that psychoanalytic discourse can *succeed* (i.e. 'cure' the patient) only by attaining an ideal of perfect, undistorted rationality. Habermas compares the Freudian enterprise with the model of interpretative clarity and method established by philologists in the high tradition of humanistic scholarship.[24] The object would then be to work progressively through layers of accumulated error and distortion to the point of restoring a pristine 'original' sense. But this is to assume a utopian dimension of discourse in which meaning, intention, truth and rationality should always ideally coincide. And this premiss needs questioning, Nägele argues, for two main reasons. First, it assumes the kind of 'rational' consensus (or perspicuous relationship of knowledge and interests) that Freudian analysis calls into doubt. Secondly, it works to legitimate this ideal rationality in terms that would effectively deny or repress any deviant symptoms of unconscious desire. A Lacanian reading, such as Nägele proposes, would insist on the signifying surplus in language that escapes the exactions of a theory grounded in rational consensus.

III

It is Marxism that most often figures, expressly or obliquely, as the target of these current attempts to demote 'theory' from its classical high standing. For Lyotard, Marxism is clearly to be counted among those delusive 'meta-narratives' that think themselves capable of delivering up the truth of history from a standpoint of omniscient detachment. In place of such delusions Lyotard advocates a 'post-modern' readiness to accept that no narrative (or narrative *theory*) could possess the kind of ultimate, truth-telling power that would lift it decisively above all the others. The upshot in political terms would be a 'liberal' consensus forswearing the idea of social improvement through rational critique and relying instead on the free circulation of communal myths and values. Such thinking translates readily enough into the present condition of western 'liberal' democracy, where the appearance of open, pluralist debate (sustained by the mass media) disguises the monopolistic interests of power. The turn against theory in the name of first-order narrative explanations is a part of the process by which such interests are shielded from rational critique.

This political alignment is obvious enough in the case of Lyotard and his updated version of the 'end of ideology' thesis. But it is not so clear where the lines are to be drawn when it comes to the debate between Habermas and his post-structuralist critics. On both sides the argument is advanced on behalf of a radical critique of existing social structures and conventions. Habermas sees his opponents as betraying the very idea of enlightened critique by their denial that thought can ever reach the stage of adequately grasping its own ideological prehistory. In Gadamer he finds a mystified version of the hermeneutic process which refuses to analyse the knowledge-constitutive interests implicit in its own activity. With regard to post-structuralism – and Foucault in particular – Habermas rejects the relativist outlook according to which all varieties of 'discourse' are products of the power–knowledge relation, indifferently ranked in point of truth or rationality. In short, he holds out for a power of reflective understanding (or rational critique) equal to the prospects for enlightened reform of social institutions at large.

His critics, as we have seen, regard this way of thinking as a species of 'technocratic fantasy', tending to repress the marginal (or subliminal) in the name of a sovereign rationality. Their arguments can equally be mounted on behalf of a 'radical' critique which works to *deconstruct* such established oppositions as 'conscious'/'unconscious', 'centre'/'margin' and others of the same hierarchical form. Michael Ryan has argued persuasively that this should be the means by which deconstruction is harnessed to the purposes of Marxist social critique. There is, Ryan asserts, a necessary relationship between the structures of thought and the structures of political power. Privileged concepts exert the kind of force that makes them unavoidably complicit with forms of social domination. And this gives deconstruction a *political* leverage far beyond the narrowly 'textual' domain to which (as the Marxist opponents would claim) its activities are limited. As Ryan argues,

> the deconstructive critique of absolutist concepts in the theory of meaning can be said to have a political-institutional corollary, which is the continuous revolutionary displacement of power toward radical egalitarianism and the plural diffusion of all forms of macro- and microdomination.[25]

This means that deconstruction effectively lines up with the 'margins' as against the 'centre'. It works to unseat any concept of legitimating reason which promotes the interests of a vanguard party (or centralized bureaucracy) against those in whose name strategic decisions are taken. Deconstruction is not an antagonist discourse which Marxism must work to discredit by exposing its ideological motives. Neither is it merely a handy appendage that Marxists can adapt – with a little ingenuity – to their own more practical purposes. Rather, it is the currently most advanced form of that critical reflection upon knowledge and interests which remains indispensable to Marxist thought.

What is perhaps most valuable about Ryan's approach is that it works to revise the operative concepts of Marxist rationality without, in the process, falling prey to irrationalist arguments. This gives it a significant bearing on the issue between Habermas and his post-structuralist opponents. Ryan takes the point of Nägele's contention that theory may become a species of repressive rationality if its powers are unchecked by 'marginal' resistances and counter-examples. But this is not to say that theory (or reason) have finally come up against their own constitutive limits. What it shows is the need to reflect *rationally* upon the forms of distorted instrumental reason thrown up by unreflective self-interest. And this suggests a way beyond those deadlocked antinomies which characterize the present state of critical theory. Deconstruction provides the most effective strategy for pressing the critique of wholesale explanatory systems *without* giving way to a 'post-modern' outlook of passive liberal consensus.

Ryan offers two main examples of what a 'deconstructed' socialist politics might amount to once freed from the dead hand of centralized power. One is the radical feminist movement which challenges a patriarchal Marxist tradition by refusing to accept its own 'marginal' status as defined by the prevalent (male-dominated) concept of historical necessity. Feminism, according to Ryan, 'sees consciousness as multiple and contradictory, not as a locus of absolute truth and power'.[26] His other main practical inspiration is the Italian socialist 'autonomy' movement, one of whose slogans – as Ryan reports – is taken from Derrida: 'the margins are at the centre'. These instances are both seen as exerting a powerful deconstructive leverage on the forms of centralized socialist 'planning' embodied in Leninist precept and practice. Ryan repeatedly makes the point that in deconstructing texts one is also and inseparably deconstructing the practical *effects* which may follow from a partial or distorted reading. Thus Lenin in his own writings 'consistently overlooks (literally) Marx's text and goes straight for the undistorted truth'. Yet this very belief (in 'truth' as something absolute and homogeneous) prevents him from perceiving that Marx's text 'is crosshatched with strands of reference linked to a specific history (itself highly complex) which do not resolve into an ideal meaning or essence'.[27] Thus Lenin falls victim to the kind of repressive or instrumental reason that elevates theory above the interests of enlightened rationality.

Ryan pursues this argument into the texts of Marx himself, especially those passages of *Kapital* which seem to give rise to contradictions by alternately proposing the 'economic' and the 'political' as ultimate or primary causes of social change. In fact, Ryan argues, this apparent 'confusion' is a sign that Marx has decisively rejected the kind of binary categorical distinction that would draw a clear line between the one and the other. 'A paradigm would decide which of the two is primary, which logically or ethically prior. A deconstructive argument would point out the undecidability of the two in history.'[28] Subsequent appropriations of Marx's text have failed to maintain a due sense of this 'rigorous' undecidability. They have thus been misled into setting up rigid *concepts* on the basis of exclusive *oppositions*, as between 'theory' and 'practice', 'mental' and 'manual' labour, economic 'base' and sociocultural 'superstructure'. In each case the effect is to reduce a complex and heterogeneous reality to the terms of a one-track dialectical reason, a concept of history working to exclude all threats to its centralized authority and power.

Ryan's argument therefore has important implications for the current stand-off between Marxism and deconstruction. It shows convincingly that 'theory' can allow for the narrative or tropological movement in its own explanations *without* falling prey to a wholesale scepticism *vis-à-vis* history and reason. Deconstruction is often reviled – by Marxist critics especially – for its supposed irrationalist leanings and lack of political engagement. Certainly Ryan has to measure his distance from those proponents of 'American' deconstruction – like Paul de Man – whose extreme attentiveness to language in its figural aspect might seem to justify such charges. But this is to ignore the possibility that specialized reflection on the powers and limits of textual understanding may have consequences beyond its avowed or immediate ends. Deconstruction differs in at least one crucial respect from the philosophy of first-order narrative pragmatics advanced by Lyotard. It preserves that dimension of enlightened critique wherein the myths and pseudo-satisfactions of naturalized meaning are subject to reflection at a higher theoretical level. This formulation would undoubtedly be suspect from an *echt*-deconstructionist stand-point. Theory, after all, is nothing if not a product of *textual* understanding, and therefore it would seem inconsistent to think of one text as having cognitive priority (or 'higher' theoretical standing) as against another. But to grasp this argument is also *de facto* to claim a degree of emancipated knowledge unattainable on the level of naturalized common-sense wisdom. Deconstruction may deny that any 'theory' can advance to the stage of comprehending the textual operations which everywhere exceed and prevent its full conceptual grasp. Yet the process of thinking through to this conclusion by way of the rigorous close reading of texts is itself a powerful form of reflective meta-critique. Deconstruction has at least the very positive political virtue of opposing itself squarely to the naturalized consensus of 'post-modern' liberal reason.

Of course there is a long prehistory to this issue between 'theory' and 'narrative' as modes of explanation. It was Hegel's main argument against Kant that he elevated certain ideas to *a priori* status which really had only a transitory place in the narrative of world-historical reason. Kant was claiming an ultimate, God's-eye view of the plot in which he actually figured as just one (albeit a leading) protagonist. But Hegel's philosophy equivocates here, since it claims to deconstruct the protocols of Kantian reason from a standpoint of higher dialectical knowledge. Hilary Putnam makes the point most succinctly:

> Hegel, who introduced the idea that reason itself changes in history, operated with two notions of rationality: there is a sense in which what is rational is measured by the level to which Spirit has developed in the historical process at a given time. . . . And there is a limit notion of rationality in Hegel's system; the notion of that which is destined to be stable, the final self-awareness of Spirit which will not itself be transcended.[29]

Putnam is not so much criticizing Hegel for having it both ways as pointing to a root dilemma in the nature of historical reflection. To reduce all philosophy to a series of episodes in a narrative devoid of any rational truth-claims is to give up the very idea of enlightened critique. It can only amount to a form of out-and-out cultural relativism which would thus undermine its own critical premises at every turn. Thus Putnam objects on logical grounds to the assumption (in Foucault among others) that truth-claims compete in an open field of ideological differences, so that no given 'discourse' is inherently more rational than any other. This position is simply untenable, he argues, since it wants to demystify various forms of ideological investment while effectively denying itself the rational grounds to comprehend their working.

Putnam raises the same objection to those latter-day versions of Hegel that avoid inconsistency by cutting out the rational machinery and sticking to first-order narrative pragmatics. 'When present-day relativists "naturalize" Hegel by throwing away the limit-concept of true rationality, they turn the doctrine into a self-defeating cultural relativism.'[30] Putnam is not arguing from a Marxist standpoint. In fact he goes on to criticize Althusser for thinking to avoid such a relativist upshot by identifying 'science' with the knowledge-constitutive interests of working-class awareness. Yet it is clear that Marxism cannot do without some means of articulating 'reason' and 'history' in other than purely narrative terms. What Putnam calls the 'limit-concept of true rationality' is implicit in any claim to demystify the forms of ideological misrecognition. And this claim is built into the self-understanding of historical-materialist critique, no matter what refinements Marxism may bring to its current working concept of ideology. The real issue between Marxism and deconstruction has to do with the powers and limits of rational explanation. It is not centrally a question (as current polemicists would have it) of 'realist' versus 'idealist' accounts of how language relates to the outside world of tangible objects and events. Ontologically speaking, both sides to this dispute are in broad agreement about the mediating character of language and representation, and hence the need for a critical theory which *interrogates* the knowledge thus produced. What they are both opposed to is the kind of inertly consensual or naturalized thinking which denies that theory can possibly transcend the cultural conditions of its own production.

IV

This calls for some revision of prevalent ideas about the politics of theory and the way that political 'positions' can be read off from various kinds of detailed textual activity. I want to conclude by looking briefly at two major thinkers – Fredric Jameson and Paul de Man – who are widely regarded as out-and-out antagonists in the context of 'advanced' current thinking on critical method. For Jameson, Marxism is the source and horizon of a massively ambitious totalizing drive to harness every available theory to the purposes of Marxist historical understanding.[31] This project he conceives as a positive, even 'utopian' counterpart to the work of ideological demystification which mostly preoccupies critical theory. The object is to open up the texts of tradition to a powerfully appropriative reading which would seek to draw out the radical potential – the latent figurations of hope and desire – concealed within the structures of dominant ideology. And this totalizing movement also applies to the various hermeneutic or critical perspectives that Jameson brings into play. Their specific limitations (like the static, ahistorical character of the structuralist model) are turned to account through a diagnostic reading which looks beyond such reductive effects to the larger possibilities they ignore or repress. Thus Jameson proposes yet another way of reading Hegel, one which adopts neither a God's-eye rationalist perspective nor a naturalized commonsense-pragmatist view. Hegel's idea of Absolute Spirit is seen as a 'strategy of containment', a move which allows Hegel's thinking 'to seem internally coherent in its own terms, while repressing the unthinkable (in this case, the very possibility of collective praxis) which lies beyond its boundaries'.[32] Marxism is thus implied as the next and decisive stage in a process of 'totalizing' auto-critique which nowhere comes to rest in placid self-acceptance.

Jameson's argument displays a constant movement back and forth between narrative and meta-narrative stances. On the one hand it requires that Marxist rationality be capable of grasping the logic implicit in those episodes of thought which make up its own prehistory. On the other, it has to deny that such knowledge could ever be fully or consciously achieved, since the 'untranscendable horizon' of Marxist thought is a state of perpetually open possibility. At times this issues in the kind of formulation that might seem compatible with Lyotard's 'post-modern' liberalism. Thus Jameson argues that the problem of conceptualizing history – the central question of Marxist theory – is 'essentially a narrative problem, a question of the adequacy of any storytelling framework in which History might be represented'.[33] But the pragmatist overtones are qualified here by the notion of an 'adequate framework' which would serve to *articulate* the first-order sense of narrated events at a higher, meta-narrative level. This catches precisely the shuttling movement of thought by which Jameson avoids the liabilities of premature abstraction while holding on to the 'totalizing' drive which effectively under-writes his whole argument. Debates around this issue have become, as Jameson notes, 'the most dramatic battle-ground of the confrontation between Hegelian and structural Marxisms'.[34] His own response is to situate criticism in a space of theoretical reflection midway between narrative and meta-narrative status.

De Man's deconstructive 'allegories of reading' are implac-ably opposed to any totalizing habit of thought.[35] They are typically deployed with the intention of undoing that assur-ance of intelligible sense and logic which governs most inter-pretative styles. For de Man, criticism is most deluded when it thinks to have mastered the play of textual figuration and arrived at a stable, self-authenticating sense. Such mastery is achieved only at the cost of systematically ignoring whatever resists its drive towards unified meaning. Interpretation be-comes an allegory of errors, an endless reflection on its own inability to set firm limits to the textual aberrations of sense. Naïvely referential or 'totalizing' readings are treated by de Man as a species of self-willed mystification tantamount to mere bad faith. Certain tropes (like metaphor and symbol) are especially apt to solicit such reading through their inbuilt appeal to organicist notions of an ultimate, transcendent rapport between mind, language and reality. To deconstruct these delusive truth-claims involves showing, first, how the privileged figures themselves decompose into *other* kinds of trope (like metonymy) which exert no such mystified power over thought. Thus metaphor is deprived of its sovereign status by a reading which demonstrates the extent of its dependence on merely *contingent* or associative transfers from detail to detail of a metonymic chain. Deconstruction then pursues this undoing of sense to the point where it appears a constitutive or *necessary* moment in the reading of texts. There is no escaping a process whose effects, according to de Man, are coextensive with the uses of language. But this doesn't mean that deconstruction can, so to speak, pull itself up by the bootstraps and theorize from a standpoint of masterly detachment. Its readings will always leave 'a margin of error, a residue of logical tension that prevents the closure of the deconstructive discourse and accounts for its narrative or allegorical mode'.[36]

Clearly, de Man has none of Jameson's faith in the virtues of a 'totalizing' meta-critique which would open up dimensions of meaning undreamt of in the current, depressed condition of cultural awareness. De Man's is indeed a hard teaching, perhaps the most rigorous form of that modern 'hermeneutics of suspicion' that Jameson so strenuously seeks to overcome. But Jameson is also careful to insist (like Marx before him) that utopian thinking is merely delusive except where it passes through that stage of critical reflection (or 'labour of the negative') required to chasten its more extravagant claims. And it is here that Marxism might find a use for the extreme demystifying rigour of de Man's hermeneutics. Above all, deconstruction holds out to the last against those forms of pre-emptive consensus thinking which substitute a naturalized 'narrative' ethos for the work of critical reflection. Jameson himself, as I have argued, comes close to entertaining such ideas when he seems to collapse the categories 'reason' and 'history' into a generalized space of 'narrative representation'. What de Man brings out with exemplary rigour is the *consequence* of reading texts (including 'political' texts) in the light of their rhetorical organization. On the face of it such criticism is no doubt open to the charge of inventing ever more ingenious textual complications to keep itself in business *and* avoid reflecting on its own political situation.[37] But this is to ignore the very real and pointed implications of de Man's writing for a politics of theory inextricably tied to the problems of textual and narrative representation.

These problems are posed most insistently in the chapter on Rousseau's *Social Contract* in de Man's *Allegories of Reading*. Certainly this essay contains its share of those offhand 'textual-ist' pronouncements that Marxist critics seize upon as evidence of a will to foreclose all discussion of history and politics. Thus:

> We are not here concerned with the technically political significance of this text, still less with an evaluation of the political and ethical praxis that can be derived from it. Our reading merely tries to define the rhetorical patterns that organize the distribution and the movement of the key terms – while contending that questions of valorization can be relevantly considered only after the rhetorical status of the text has been clarified.[38]

That 'rhetorical status' is furthermore shown to consist in a perpetual oscillation between modes of language (metaphor and metonymy, constative and performative) which problematize the *Contract* beyond all hope of extracting a coherent political 'message'. Worst of all, from the Marxist standpoint, is de Man's repeated assertion that history is intelligible *only* as a product of these conflicting rhetorical codes. It is the non-coincidence of method and meaning that opens up a gap of deferred understanding where 'history' can then take hold. De Man sees this process strikingly at work in the *Social Contract*. If Rousseau's text could be read as political *theory* pure and simple, then it would serve as an unproblematical blueprint, a kind of 'constitutional machine' to which one could resort 'for the elaboration of specific constitutions'. The 'text of the law' and the 'law of the text' would thus coincide perfectly and lay down all the necessary rules for their own interpretation. The *Social Contract* could then be lifted out of history – the history of its various disputable readings – and rendered an object of purely scientific knowledge.

That this is not the case is explained, for de Man, by the

Contract's literal 'unreadability' at the level of straightforward constative utterance. Thus it turns out

> that the 'law of the text' is too devious to allow for such a simple relationship between model and example, and the theory of politics inevitably turns into the history, the allegory of its inability to achieve the status of a science.[39]

It is the field of tension set up between 'model' and 'example' (or constative and performative modes) which thus creates the need for endless reinterpretations. Hence de Man's claim, in the provocative closing sentence of this chapter, that 'textual allegories on this level of rhetorical complexity generate history'.[40] The question is whether such pronouncements have to be written off by Marxists as a species of last-ditch 'textualist' retreat from history and reason alike. I have argued that this is not the case, and that deconstruction – even when pushed to the limits of rational accountability, as by de Man – remains on the side of enlightened critique. We should not take too lightly de Man's statement (in his chapter on Rousseau's *Discourse on Inequality*) that 'far from being a repression of the political, as Althusser would have it, literature is condemned to being the truly political mode of discourse'.[41] There are two ways of reading such passages. One is to regard them as an obvious extension of de Man's strategy for reducing politics to a mere epiphenomenon of textual signification. The other is to follow out the logic of his argument and see what specific kinds of dislocating *force* it might exert upon received categories like 'literature' and 'politics'. This second way of reading would take into account – among other things – the deconstruction of totalizing metaphors which assimilate language, politics and reason to a Rousseauist mythology of natural origins.

De Man's texts quite explicitly *ask* to be read in this 'political' mode. They insist that the field of rhetorical tensions is always ('contrary to what one might think') a space where the politics of reading is inevitably brought into play. One further lengthy quotation from de Man on Rousseau may help to substantiate this claim. The argument at this point is directed against those forms of 'traditional' Rousseau criticism that go straight for the literal meaning of the text and refuse to acknowledge the existence of complicating tensions. Such readings precisely *exclude* politics by collapsing all distinctions between nature, truth and linguistic figuration. On the other hand, de Man writes:

> if society and government derive from a tension between man and his language, then they are not natural (depending on a relationship between man and things), nor ethical (depending on a relationship among men), nor theological, since language is not conceived as a transcendental principle but as the possibility of contingent error. The political thus becomes a burden for man rather than an opportunity, and this realization . . . may well account for the recurrent reluctance to accept, or even to notice, the link between language and society in the works of Rousseau.[42]

It may also account for a similar reluctance, among Marxist critics, to notice these passages of explicitly political reflection in de Man. To some extent that response is well founded, since the 'burden' of politics, as de Man conceives it, is a negative labour (like that of deconstruction) relentlessly trained upon its own liability to error and delusion. Yet the *room* for such error (which de Man locates in the gap between referential and figural meaning) is precisely what enables texts to be read against the literalizing tendency of critical tradition. This is the message that, according to de Man, 'the classical interpretation of Rousseau has stubbornly refused to hear'. If the political unconscious is structured like a language, then the politics of reading is both more error-prone *and* more radically unsettling than criticism (Marxist or otherwise) can easily allow.

Jameson's ideal of interpretative method is one that transcends every restricted definition of 'narrative' and 'theory' in an open-ended, totalizing movement of thought. It occupies its own tropological domain between the organicist metaphors of Hegelian dialectic and those other, deconstructive or demystifying tropes which (as Jameson argues) 'reconfirm the status of the concept of totality by their very reaction against it'.[43] De Man's is the opposite but in a sense *complementary* movement. It likewise aims to undo the distinction between 'theory' and 'narrative', but in this case by means of those

cautionary 'allegories of reading' which posit the stark impossibility of reconciling method and meaning, logic and sense.
Undoubtedly there are passages in de Man that might be
singled out as deeply resistant to the kind of historical understanding that Jameson seeks. Thus, on Rousseau again:

> the distinction between metonymic aggregates and
> metaphorical totalities, based on the presence, within the
> latter, of a 'necessary link' that is lacking in the former, is
> characteristic of all metaphorical systems, as is the equation
> of this principle of totalization with *natural* process.[44]

But it would still be mistaken to conclude from this that
deconstruction must be either hostile or indifferent to the
politics of Marxist criticism. On the contrary, as I have tried to
show, it is often at those points of sharpest theoretical divergence that de Man's texts bear insistently on questions that
Marxism cannot ignore. One of these is the question of how
theory relates to the claims advanced by various proponents
of first-order narrative explanation. In light of this debate
I would argue that deconstruction belongs firmly on
Habermas's side of the argument, rather than Gadamer's. And
it is this alignment, I would further suggest, that most accurately situates current contributions to the politics of theory.

2

Sense, reference and logic: a critique of post-structuralist theory

I

Post-structuralism has often been attacked for its seeming commitment to a 'textualist' position which fixes an insuperable gulf between language and reality. This charge has come from various quarters. It is pressed most frequently by Marxist critics, irate at what they see as an attempt to claim 'radical' status for a theory quite devoid of political force or effectivity.[1] Post-structuralism can then be written off as a last desperate ploy of that irrational strain in bourgeois ideology which had always sought to drive an idealist wedge between subject and object, knowledge and the real. On the other side similar accusations are heard from defenders of a robust commonsense empiricism, anxious not so much to change the world as to keep it solidly there for all practical purposes.[2] If the Marxist and the bourgeois empiricist agree on nothing else, at least they are united in condemning post-structuralism as a species of self-serving mystification, a theory marooned in metaphysical problems of its own wilful creation.

It has been suggested in several recent essays that an answer to these problems might be found in the writings of Frege and other philosophers in the modern 'analytic' tradition.[3] More specifically, it is claimed that Frege's philosophy of language provides the conceptual tools for arguing a different, more properly *materialist* relation between language and reality. What is in question here is a theory of reference that would offer an alternative to Saussure's purportedly 'idealist' theory

of meaning. That distinction – between 'reference' and 'meaning' – is a cardinal point in Frege's philosophy and also for
those, like Michael Dummett,[4] who regard Frege as having
radically transformed modern thinking about language and
logic. The claim, roughly speaking, runs as follows. Frege was
the first to see clearly that genuine philosophic problems could
only come down to problems about our use of language. These
in turn needed treating on the logical basis of a theory which
would properly determine how language performed its legitimate (i.e. meaningful or logically accountable) role. Not for
Frege the late-Wittgensteinian idea that meaning can only be
grasped within one or other of the manifold 'language games'
which make up a given cultural repertoire. This view went
along with a sharp reaction against the kind of one-track logical
thinking that had characterized Wittgenstein's earlier philosophy. Certainly, Frege treats meaning as determined by context to the extent that words have no specific role apart from
the *sentences* within which their function is defined. But he
doesn't take the further Wittgensteinian step of expanding the
idea of 'context' to include the whole of a given linguistic
culture. For Frege, the task is to specify how words possess a
definite, assignable meaning as components of the sentences
which effectively specify their truth conditions. And this entails a clear demarcation between cases where this logic can be
seen to operate and others where it gives no hold for understanding. Sentences of the latter type are 'incomplete' in terms
of their logical-semantic specification, and thus fall outside the
purview of a strict philosophical account.

It remains to enquire what use might be found for Frege's
terms and distinctions within the discourse of current post-
structuralist theory. In addressing this question I shall draw
very largely on Michael Dummett's book *Frege: Philosophy
of Language*. Dummett's interpretation is by no means
unchallenged,[5] but it represents a powerful and consistent
reading of Frege's arguments. (It is also an obvious source-text
for most of those literary theorists who have lately made
reference to Frege's philosophy.) Dummett makes no bones
about the fact that his reading is strongly predisposed towards
a certain interpretation of Frege, one that tends to concentrate
on his earlier writings and pass over (or deplore) some later

irregularities. That these tensions are of interest – especially in a post-structuralist context – is a point I shall return to in the course of this chapter. For the moment, let us say that 'Frege' is more specifically *Dummett's* Frege, an authority appealed to only in so far as his thinking has lately given rise to certain crucial debates in the discourse of philosophy and critical theory at large.

Dummett has his own points to make about this question of proper names and the role they play in legitimizing statements of fact. What are the operative truth conditions, he asks, for a sentence like 'Frege was a great philosopher' (Dummett, p. 235)? Clearly it is not a matter of singling out a real-life referent, such that only those who had met or known Frege could be in a position to judge of the statement's truth. Having the man pointed out to them – Frege *ipse* – would be of no use to somebody who had not actually read Frege's *writings*, or at least picked up a competent secondhand knowledge of their significance. What Dummett is rather neatly illustrating here is the crucial Fregean distinction between *sense* and *reference* as components of meaning. What if Frege had defied all the laws of common mortality and lived on to the present day? There might be some neighbour, Dummett imagines, who heard the name 'Frege' as applied to 'that antique individual whom he saw being wheeled in his Bath chair'. But his being thus pointed to the *referent* of the name would help the neighbour not a whit in deciding on the truth of the given proposition, 'Frege was a great philosopher'. What the neighbour would need to do is 'not only to read Frege's writings, but also to establish that the old man he knew as "Frege" was the man who formerly wrote those works' (Dummett, p. 235). Establishing the reference of a proper name is not just a matter of ostensive definition, of matching up the name with an undifferentiated real-life referent.

Dummett offers this as a whimsical but not untypical instance of the way language works to specify reference only by way of a prior *sense* (or set of defining attributes) attached to the word in question. Thus 'Frege' is given a meaningful reference only if one takes it 'as standing for the man who wrote *Die Grundlagen der Arithmetik*, "Über Sinn und Bedeutung" and all the rest'. Nor is this argument restricted to the somewhat specialized instance of personal names. Frege's point can be extracted as the maxim that *sense precedes reference*, or – differently put – that our use of language to designate objects always depends on our possessing a set of definitional criteria by which to pick those objects out. Language, that is to say, is established as a referential medium only in so far as we can specify *what counts* as an achieved or felicitous act of reference. To think of words as somehow matching up one-to-one with their real-life objects is to beg the question of how we can *know* when the requisite grasp has been achieved. The notion of reference, as Dummett says, 'is of interest only if it can be made to do some work in the model we give for the senses of the expressions of our language' (Dummett, p. 236). For Frege (at least as Dummett reads him) this model necessarily involves an account of how the logical-semantic structure of language operates to pick out whatever referent the sentence seeks to specify.

It may be asked how Frege's ideas, thus construed, could possibly serve as an antidote or corrective to current post-structuralist thinking. Certainly Frege finds room for reference as a proper – indeed indispensable – component of any theory of meaning. Saussure takes account of the referent only as a kind of Kantian *Ding-an-sich*, presumed to exist but strictly inaccessible to knowledge, since everything we know must always be structured *a priori* by the terms and categories of our language.[6] The fundamental relationship for Saussure is that between signifier and signified, the *word* as (spoken or written) sign and the *concept* which it serves to communicate. This creates an effective closed circuit of exchange where 'reality' is admitted only in so far as it conforms to the pre-existent grid of relationships laid down by language. This is not to say (as certain current polemicists would have it) that post-structuralism is a species of solipsist delusion serenely convinced that there is no real world outside the play of textual signification. The argument is more like a latter-day version of Kantian rationalism, with language assuming the place once occupied by Kant's *a priori* concept of reason. Kant declared firmly against the kinds of paradox engendered when reason ran wild in theoretical problems of its own abstract creating.[7] It had to be assumed that the real world existed, if only as a check to the puzzles thrown up by pure, unaccommodated reason. The idea of the real plays a similar, limiting role in post-structuralist thinking. It is not so much excluded as granted a strictly anterior and even (as it were) preconscious status. The question is whether Frege's philosophy of language can provide a referential grounding which manages to bypass or simply invalidate this model of semantic accountability.

It is certainly true that reference plays an essential role in Frege's theory of meaning. If the truth conditions of a sentence are the ultimate criteria for its meaning, then there must be some relation between the sentence and the world it purports to describe. 'The notion of reference', as Dummett writes, 'ought not to be idle within the theory of meaning' (Dummett, p. 147). Knowing what a sentence *means* is synonymous with knowing how its truth value might be recognized if the knower was ideally placed to grasp it. And this entails the further assumption, as Dummett sees it: that such knowledge must always presuppose a *referent* or real-world state of affairs to which the judgement 'true' or 'false' would bear a strictly decidable relation. If this is not the case, Dummett thinks, then 'the only conclusion can be that most of the time we do not succeed in referring to anything at all' (Dummett, p. 147). Our predications must then be neither true nor false, since they would be devoid of any strict or ascertainable reference. And any such conclusion, he declares, is simply 'too absurd to be entertained'.

This lends a certain *prima facie* plausibility to the claim that Frege points a way beyond the inbred puzzles and problems of post-structuralist thinking. Certainly Frege is steadfastly opposed to any mentalist theory which treats of meaning as wholly comprised within the order of conceptual representations. Like Kant, he insisted that his was a realist philosophy, making the detour through problematic regions only to provide a firmer grounding for our claims to legitimate knowledge. It is this side of Frege's thinking – his apparent provision of a theory of *reference* as part of his theory of meaning – that might be considered a realist antidote to the post-structuralist malaise. For Frege, in Dummett's words, 'we really do succeed in talking about the real world, a world which exists independently of us, and it is in virtue of how things are in that world that the things we say are true or false' (Dummett, p. 198). It looks as if philosophy has powerful arguments for restoring reference to the central role in any theory of language, a role that Saussure effectively denied it. Frege's rejection of 'idealist' notions – his denial that sense can be a matter of mental representation – would then seem to offer an alternative to Saussure's argument that meaning is a relation between word and concept (signifier and signified), rather than a link between word and referent. More precisely, it would offer grounds for supposing that the two relationships are inseparably bound up together, and that no philosophy of language can get along without a proper and integral theory of reference. Post-structuralism would then stand revealed as a species of abstract-idealist theory condemned by its Saussurean logic to a false set of assumptions about language, truth and reason.

Such, in broad outline, is the case for Fregean philosophy of language as a needful corrective to the post-Saussurean paradigm. It seems to promise a decisive shift of theoretical terrain, such that language might again be shown to hook up with reality, but now on the basis of a philosophic theory purged of empiricist residues. Hence the current interest in Frege among Marxists and others who resist what they see as the idealizing, counter-materialist tendencies of recent critical theory. However, the argument runs into problems as soon as one examines more closely how the notion of reference figures in Frege's logical economy of meaning. For it is basic to Fregean philosophy – at least on Dummett's influential reading – that *sense precedes reference* as a matter of logical-semantic necessity. That is to say, our use of a word to pick out some object must always be dependent on our knowing the *criteria* by which to judge the word's proper meaning in context. As Dummett explains it:

> The sense of any expression less than a complete sentence must consist only in the contribution it makes to determining the content of a sentence in which it may occur. For this reason, assigning a bearer to a name would be merely an empty ceremony if it did not serve as a preliminary to introducing a means of using that name in sentences whereby something was said about the object assigned as the bearer. (Dummett, p. 183)

The best-known illustration of Frege's argument is the case of expressions (like 'the Morning Star' and 'the Evening Star') which have identical *referents* but different *senses*. Or, again, there is the instance of two explorers who approach the same mountain from different directions and then carry the news back to their native country where the story gets about that there are *two* mountains, each baptized with a different name. If the sense of a word was exhausted by its reference, then any statement of identity in either case would be simply redundant or uninformative. In fact, Frege argues, there is a crucial difference between grasping the sense of a given expression and knowing what object it refers to. 'The Morning Star' and 'the Evening Star' may both have as object the planet Venus, but they go (so to speak) different ways around in specifying that object. To state their identity (i.e. their possession of a single, indivisible *referent*) could be informative only so long as their *senses* remained distinct. Otherwise such statements would be simply undecidable as to their truth or falsehood.

This principle (that 'sense determines reference') is the heart of Frege's linguistic philosophy as Dummett persuasively reads it. What consequences follow for the attempt to derive a realist theory of reference from Frege's writings? Clearly they afford no grounds for dispensing with Saussure's cardinal insight: that language is always already at work in our notion of what constitutes 'the real'. Far from rejecting this position, Frege makes it a major plank in his case against naïvely referential theories of meaning. Such theories assume that the world offers itself up to description as so many discrete chunks of reality to which we need simply attach the appropriate labels. Frege agrees with Saussure in decisively rejecting this view. Reference can only be established on the basis of certain 'criteria of identity' which determine what is to count as the 'same' object from one context to another. Again, it is the *sense* of any given word – that is to say, the relevant truth conditions which determine its role within a sentence of the language – that ultimately fixes its reference.

Dummett sees this as one of Frege's most powerful contributions to modern philosophy of language, helping to resolve certain longstanding problems bequeathed by classical logic. Thinkers like Mill, according to Dummett, 'wrote as though the world already came to us sliced up into objects, and all we have to learn is which label to tie onto which object' (Dummett, p. 179). But this ignores the way in which the words that we use 'determine principles whereby the slicing up is to be effected, principles which are acquired with the acquisition of the uses of those words' (ibid.). It now begins to seem that Fregean philosophy may not, after all, represent an alternative to post-structuralist theory. Rather, it provides a useful sharpening of some logical arguments that might be mustered on behalf of Saussure's basic paradigm. Frege may object to any theory, like Saussure's, that locates meaning in the tie between word and 'mental' representation. But he strongly endorses the Saussurean claim that there is no intelligible access to reality except by way of the mediating structures of language. The appeal to Frege as a 'realist' philosopher must first take account of his argument that the notion of reference is of use only in so far as it is given real work to do within a first-order theory of sense. And this creates problems scarcely less taxing than Saussure's 'idealist' conception of language.

II

That the term 'realism' is capable of such diverse and often contradictory meanings is a further source of theoretical confusion. At one extreme it may designate a hard-line materialist creed which insists that we conceive of reality as always pre-given to cognition and existing in a mode of objective truth absolutely prior to our knowledge of it. This attitude still finds a place in certain forms of 'vulgar' Marxist polemic. It runs up against the obvious (Kantian or post-structuralist) objection that reality is inescapably structured by the concepts and categories of human understanding. Any claim to have direct, unmediated access to the real must always founder on the Kantian logic of this case against 'transcendental realism'. Quite simply, there is no possible grounding for a materialist theory of knowledge that would bypass the question of what must *count* as self-evident, rational truth. This is the argument that Frege restates in logical-linguistic terms. Any theory of reference must always presuppose an adequate account of the sense-making structures (the logical semantics) which make up an intelligible language.

So Frege is clearly not a 'realist' in anything like that hard-line sense of the term. In fact, as Dummett argues, there is nothing in Frege's philosophy of language that would always demand some real-life object or state of affairs corresponding to 'truthful' propositions. Abstract entities (like numbers) were equally 'real' to Frege's way of thinking, so that questions of whether an object 'actually existed' – out there, so to speak, in the world of material things and events – was often philosophically beside the point. As Dummett puts it:

> The truth of the relevant existential statement is to be determined by the methods proper to that realm of discourse, i.e. in accordance with the truth-conditions that we are supposing have been stipulated for sentences of that kind. There is no further, philosophical, question about whether there *really* exists an object to be the referent of the name. (Dummett, p. 497)

Reference can therefore be established in the absence of any actual, empirical *object* by which to affirm its validity. What counts for Frege is the set of internally consistent criteria which constitute the relevant truth conditions of a given 'discourse' or instance of language. If these can be properly determined, then 'there exists something satisfying the condition given in the statement, and that is an end of the matter' (Dummett, p. 497).

Dummett concedes that there are problems in reconciling Frege's 'realism' with his adherence to what is, in effect, a wholly context-bound theory of meaning. It would seem that there is no distinction to be drawn between 'concrete' and 'abstract' varieties of reference, those that designate some real-world object and those that signify concepts (e.g. numbers or logical functions). This follows from Frege's philosophic programme, in particular his efforts to place mathematics on a firm logical basis. Above all, there has to be a sharp distinction between mere subjective 'ideas' and the elements of logical *sense* which constitute a valid argument. Concepts must be shown to possess an order of demonstrable truth-claim wholly independent of psychological vagaries. 'The idea is subjective: one man's idea is not that of another.'[8] Ideas are a species of 'mental image' that arise from the memory of sense impressions and are thus confined, for each individual, to his or her private sphere of experience. 'Such an idea is often saturated with feeling; the clarity of its separate parts varies and oscillates.'[9] The *sense* of a sign, on the other hand, is something held in common by various possessors of the language within which it plays a meaningful role.

Idea, sense and reference must therefore be firmly distinguished if language is to be treated from a logical point of view. Frege expresses the distinction most clearly in his cardinal essay 'On Sense and Reference'. The reference of a sign, he writes,

> is the object itself which we designate by its means; the idea, which we have in that case, is wholly subjective; in between lies the sense, which is indeed no longer subjective like the idea, but is not yet the object itself.[10]

It should now be evident in what precise sense Frege may be counted a 'realist' philosopher. His intention is to set up logical safeguards against any variety of relativist thinking which reduces concepts to a merely intuitive or subjective status. Hence Frege's reiterated stress on the distinction between 'sense' and 'idea'. To grasp the operative *sense* of a word is to understand it in accordance with rules that are logically self-evident to competent users of the language in question. It involves, that is to say, an appeal to the relevant truth conditions which determine how the word should be understood to function in a given context. Such grasp is 'objective' in the sense that it is available to anyone who has mastered the appropriate truth-conditional semantics. 'Ideas', on the other hand, are subject to no such determinate validating logic. Comparisons are possible, up to a point, between different spheres of individual experience and memory; but no precise account can be given because, as Frege says, 'we cannot have both ideas together in the same consciousness'.[11] It is in these terms that Frege wants to distinguish the elements of objective *sense* from the more or less private, associative realm of 'ideas'.

It will be seen that this leaves little room for any realist interpretation based on the idea of language as a referential medium. Frege is a 'realist' in two specific senses of the word. First, he insists on the objective character of those concepts that we need in order to make sense of language, mathematics and other forms of organized discourse. Secondly, he argues that reference is indeed a necessary component of any such theory, but only in so far as the sense-giving context (along with the relevant truth conditions) makes reference possible in any given case. This amounts to a kind of objective idealism, with reference playing only a very qualified and second-stage explanatory role. To make reference *prior* to sense – as the hard-line materialist might have it – would create logical problems which Frege thinks insoluble. For one thing, it would entail the claim that reference always already contained all the relevant criteria (or complex definitional attributes) required for the object in question to be picked out. 'Comprehensive knowledge of the reference would require us to be able to say immediately whether any given sense belongs to it. To such knowledge we never attain.'[12] Dummett has a chapter specifically contesting the arguments of those (like Saul Kripke in *Naming and Necessity*[13]) who want to reverse the Fregean dictum and establish reference as prior to sense in the semantics of natural language. The upshot of Dummett's argument is that no such model can possibly satisfy the requirements of logical consistency. And this for the reason, as Frege argues, that reference must always *presuppose* the logical and semantic criteria needed for us to pick out the object referred to.

This is *not* to suggest that the notion of reference is largely idle or redundant within Frege's theory of meaning. Rather it is the case that Fregean semantics *always and necessarily* includes some appeal to a referential grounding, though not in any sense readily adaptable to the purposes of hard-line materialism. For Frege, reference is presupposed in the fact that no *sense* can finally attach to sentences lacking the determinate truth conditions by which to establish or reject their validity. 'Why is the thought not enough for us? Because, and to the extent that, we are concerned with its truth value.' And again: 'it is the striving for truth that drives us always to advance from the sense to the reference.'[14] But the presupposition of reference might always be mistaken, as, for instance, in the case of imaginary elements like phlogiston, or of those who once believed that 'the Morning Star' and 'the Evening Star' referred to different planetary bodies. What is in question always is the presupposition that words *normally and properly* possess some determinate reference, and that users of language standardly *intend* to fall in with this enabling condition. That the putative reference may turn out to be mistaken – that such mistakes have indeed quite often occurred – Frege does not seek to deny. Rather, he rules it strictly irrelevant for the purposes of logical argument. Thus: 'in order to justify mention of the reference of a sign it is enough, at first, to point out our intention in speaking or thinking. (We must then add the reservation: provided such reference exists.)'[15] This brings out the sharp divergence between Frege's idea of referential presupposition and any attempt to ground language as a 'material' signifying practice. Certainly there seems small warrant here for the belief that Fregean semantics may have its uses as a 'realist' counter-argument to current post-structuralist theory.

Yet there is clearly more to this suggestion than my case has so far allowed. The idea of reference does, after all, figure importantly in Frege's philosophy, and bears – as we have seen – a more than notional weight of argument. One further extended quotation from Dummett may help to clarify the position.

> When someone knows the sense of a sentence, what he knows is how the truth-value of the sentence is to be recognized, whenever we are in a position to do so; and if a reference is to be significantly attributed to a word, then, for at least some sentences containing the word, the account of the process of recognizing that such sentences have one or other truth-value must involve the recognition of something as the referent of that word. (Dummett, p. 147)

This indicates a stronger sense of 'presupposition' than might be apparent from the argument so far. Reference – or at least the *possibility* of successful reference – becomes a precondition of intelligible language. It is still the case that language may sometimes (self-evidently) be dealing with fictions or imaginary entities which lack any determinate reference. But we manage to identify such instances as fictions precisely by virtue of their *not* inviting the usual question as to truth or falsehood. Thus – to borrow Frege's example – we may choose to set aside the requirement of reference when we read the sentence: 'Odysseus was set ashore at Ithaca while sound asleep.' Its fictional status creates a kind of willing suspension whereby we rest content with the *sense* of the words and refrain from following up the matter of their reference. 'The thought', says Frege, 'remains the same whether "Odysseus" has reference or not.' But, at the same time, 'the fact that we concern ourselves at all about the reference of a part of the sentence (i.e. the name "Odysseus") indicates that we generally recognize and expect a reference for the sentence itself.'[16] Thus fictions are marked as a distinctive or peculiar class of utterance precisely in so far as they work to inhibit the usual inferential advance from 'sense' to 'reference'.

III

Some provisional summing-up may be in order here. I have argued that Fregean logical semantics offers no possible hold for a theory of reference which would seek to bypass the Saussurean detour via language as a system of mediating signs and concepts. The *arbitrary* nature of the sign – the absence, that is to say, of any 'natural' or one-to-one relation between signifier and signified – is as much a point of principle for Frege as for Saussure. It is integral to Frege's argument that statements of identity hold between the *senses* and not the *referents* of words. (Otherwise, as he points out, there could be nothing informative about holding that 'the Morning Star' and 'the Evening Star' referred after all to the same object.) Semantic relations, of whatever logical status, necessarily take hold within the signifying structure of language, and not as a matter of straightforward designative naming. The assertion '$a = b$' can only be mediated, Frege argues, by 'the connection of each of the two signs with the same designated thing'. But this relation is strictly arbitrary, since 'nobody can be forbidden to use any arbitrarily producible event or object as a sign for something'.[17] Thus for Frege, as for Saussure, language constitutes a structure of signifying relationships which always interpose between word and object, semantic sense and empirical reference.

But this is not to say that Fregean semantics has no useful bearing on the problems thrown up by current post-structuralist theory. Frege's form of 'abstract' realism might have more to offer, by way of corrective emphasis, than any return to a pre-critical materialist ontology. That Marxists might at least entertain such a claim is evident from a study published in 1962 by the Soviet logician B. V. Birjukov.[18] The object of this essay is to evaluate Fregean semantics from the standpoint of dialectical materialism, the latter defined by constant reference to Marxist-Leninist norms. Very briefly, Birjukov's argument seeks to interpret Frege as affirming the 'objective' character of thought against all varieties of 'Platonist' abstraction. He acknowledges the problems in the way of such a reading, not least Frege's insistence that abstract entities (like numbers) are fully on a par with material objects so far as their semantic and logical status is concerned. But he points to the crucial distinction between 'idea' and 'sense' as evidence of a clear understanding, on Frege's part, that meaning is *objective* and cannot be reduced to mere private intuition. Birjukov's translator calls this 'a kind of intra-linguistic anti-idealism', much weaker in its claims than the Leninist variety but still within the broad parameters of Marxist philosophic discourse. It thus becomes plausible to argue that Frege's programme, for all its abstract-idealist tendencies, had nevertheless an 'historically progressive character'.[19]

The major contention of Birjukov's essay has to do with the relationship in Frege between thoughts and things, concepts and their material extension. Fregean concepts, he writes,

> do not belong to the world of spirit, of thinking, and are something objective, existing in reality itself. Frege understood by 'concept' the common property of things. He did not doubt either the objectivity of things or the objectivity of their common properties.[20]

Thus the Fregean assertion that 'sense precedes reference' (i.e. that 'concepts' logically predetermine our grasp of the real) can be given at least a debatably materialist gloss. Such is Birjukov's case against the Platonist reading of Frege, a reading he associates (predictably enough) with western 'bourgeois' logicians. Since concepts refer necessarily to *classes* of objects – sets, that is to say, which possess some common distinguishing property – it follows that thought must always presuppose the material existence of things. The *extension* of a concept (the range of objects it refers to) must always presuppose a realist ontology. 'Precisely in the concept (common property of things) is included the foundation of its being as a *class*.'[21] And from this point Birjukov can go on to argue that Frege's stress on the priority of concepts was a justified rebuke to those ('nominalists' and 'empiricists') who denied their very existence. He even suggests that this accords, up to a point, with the Marxist dialectic of universal and particular. Where Fregean logic comes up against its limit is in failing to recognize the historical character of this mediating process. Hence the lingering 'metaphysical' strain in Frege's logical programme, its confinement to what Birjukov finally classifies as a form of 'moderate realism'.

I have no wish to claim any special authority for Birjukov's frequently tortuous and procrustean argument. Too many questions are begged by his attempt to fit Frege's ideas into the standard framework of Marxist-Leninist philosophical polemics. Birjukov's account is plainly at odds with Dummett's more overtly Platonist reading, which is argued with much greater thoroughness and analytic power. What I want to suggest is that the problems confronting post-structuralism have more to do with its *logical* status than with its failure to envisage a proper referential matching-up between language and reality. That 'sense determines reference' – that we can only pick out significant features of the world as provided for by the semantic structure of language – is a doctrine common to Frege and Saussure. Indeed, it is shared by almost every variety of modern thinking about language (hard-line neo-realists like Kripke excepted). However, this is not to say that the notion of reference is everywhere treated with the same degree of theoretical indifference or marginalization. For Saussure, it is a third term only in the triangle signifier–signified–referent, a term about which linguists have little to say, since their interest is properly in language as a signifying system, a structured economy of words and concepts. Of course it is no part of Saussure's programme to deny that language *does* have referential uses which serve perfectly well for most practical ends. It is in the interest of linguistics as a systematic study that Saussure brackets (as it were) the referential dimension and concentrates on the 'arbitrary' relation between signifier and signified. The problem with much post-structuralist thinking is that it takes this methodological convenience for a high point of philosophic principle. And it is here that a Fregean logical semantics might serve to reintroduce a working concept of reference without falling prey to a naïve ontology of language.

The argument can perhaps be clarified by taking up Saussure's best-known illustrative instance: that of the 8.25 p.m. Geneva-to-Paris Express.[22] There is a sense in which this is the same train every day, despite the fact that engine, coaches and driver may be subject to endless daily substitutions. Its designation, that is to say, is a matter of distinguishing *that* particular train from all the other services, departure times, and so forth which make up the railway network. The 8.25 is not so much a referent – an object picked out by straightforward designative naming – as a term within that larger, differential context. And this, according to Saussure, is how language ought to be conceived: as a network of distinctive signifying features, 'differences' rather than 'identities'. The train as a physically embodied referent is less important, from this point of view, than the train as it figures in a railway timetable, one distinctive entry among others. Analogously, language is a system of relations, 'differences without positive terms'. Any local act of reference is always already mediated by the network of signifying contrasts and relationships that makes up language as a whole. It is this priority that has to be respected if linguistics is to achieve a scientific status. For linguists to make reference their primary datum – as distinct from the signifier–signified relationship – would be rather like insisting upon travelling in one particular *carriage*, no matter when and where it was scheduled to arrive.

In Frege, by contrast, the notion of reference can only be suspended in cases (like fictional sentences) which are marked out precisely by their *deviation* from the logical norm. Even then, it is the normative assumption – the 'striving for truth', as Frege puts it, which 'drives us always to advance from the sense to the reference' – that effectively enables us to recognize the fictional instance and make the appropriate adjustment. This is the crucial difference between Frege's logical semantics and Saussure's semiological theory. Saussure has nothing to say about the relations between meaning, logic and reference. In his terms, the basic distinction to be drawn is that between the paradigmatic (axis of selection) and the syntagmatic (axis of combination). These dimensions are both conceptualized from the standpoint of the signifier–signified relationship. They involve no recourse to either reference or logic, the former placed outside this model in its 'vertical' aspect, the latter having no role to play in its 'horizontal' (syntagmatic) unfolding. It is by means of this precisely regulated framework of description that Saussure seeks to bring new rigour to the science of linguistics.

This is not to go along with the perverse misreading which imputes to Saussure (and post-structuralism generally) a denial that there exists any 'real' world beyond the signifying codes of language. Saussure is clear enough that 'the entities are not abstract', since 'we cannot conceive of a street or train outside its material realization'.[24] What he doesn't allow for is the *logical* role that such assumptions play in the fabric of intelligible meaning which constitutes our grasp of language. Thus Saussure can also claim – as if unproblematically – that 'what makes the express is its hour of departure, its route, and in general every circumstance that sets it apart from other trains'. The identity of signs within the system of language is *not*, Saussure argues, the same kind of identity which attaches to objects in the world. An example of the latter would be the case of a suit which was stolen and then recognized in the window of a secondhand store. In terms of this comparison, Saussure insists, 'linguistic identity is not that of the garment; it is that of the train and the street'.[25] Meaning, that is to say, is entirely an affair of arbitrary signs or appellations whose reference depends on the role they play within a set-up of purely relational significance. And this results in turn from Saussure's view of language as a system of related but non-contextualized *signs*, rather than a network of intelligible *sentences* or truth-functional propositions.

What is left out of account in Saussure's methodology is precisely what Frege seeks to provide in his logico-semantic theory of language. Dummett again offers a useful point of comparison in his Fregean critique of the logician W. V. Quine. For Quine, language can only be construed holistically, as the network of interrelated meanings and propositions which make up a given cultural context. Language, he argues, is like a man-made fabric that impinges upon experience only at the periphery.[26] The centre is composed of that class of judgements which philosophy has often regarded as strictly analytic or *a priori* in character. Such judgements are thought to be immune to revision, true by virtue of their logical form and hence not open to empirical testing or falsification. This would distinguish them sharply from those other, 'synthetic' propositions whose bearing on matters of empirical fact renders them always liable to revision in the face of recalcitrant experience. For Quine, however, there is no such clear-cut distinction to be drawn between hard-core analytic truths and the corrigible statements of factual observation. *All* propositions are capable of being revised in the light of changed assumptions about the way that language, truth and reality hang together. The most basic logical axioms (i.e. those near the 'centre' of the fabric) are in principle as open to conceptual revision as statements of a straightforward empirical nature. The analytic/synthetic distinction – so deeply entrenched within philosophy at least since the time of Kant – is demoted by Quine to the status of a mere heuristic fiction. There is no central core of logical statements so basic to the rules of thought that their truth holds fast against every possible assault.

This leads to Quine's well-known thesis of the indeterminacy of radical translation.[27] It is impossible, he argues, to provide any firm or sufficient criteria for translating statements out of one language context into another. This follows from Quine's holistic conception of language, his refusal to countenance distinctions of kind between logical (analytic) and empirical propositions. Any theory one might offer would always derive its notions of 'logical' sense and force from the context of a given (culture-bound) natural language. There could be no getting outside the pragmatics of first-order natural language by way of achieving an adequate theory of translation. Any such claim would always run up against the difficulty of knowing for sure what conventions of sense and reference governed the other language in question. One might hope for certainty at least in the case of straightforward acts of naming by ostensive definition. Yet doubt must prevail even here, Quine argues, since it could always be the case that one's native informant was using a word, not to single out some object in its entirety, but to focus attention on some aspect, attribute or specialized property of the object. There are simply no criteria of reference or sense by which to save language from its structural condition of inherent undecidability. Such is Quine's argument for the species of rigorous agnosticism that characterizes his dealing with questions of meaning and truth.

There are clear enough parallels between Quine's position and the discourse of post-structuralist thinkers like Foucault. In both cases, language is conceived as a network of discursive codes and conventions, their claims to truth always subject to a principled qualifying doubt. Foucault treats knowledge, in Nietzschean terms, as a product of the will-to-power within language, a product whose structured genealogy allows of no final, authoritative truth.[28] Theory is deluded if it hopes to rise above this arena of competing rhetorics and establish itself as a discourse exempt from such contaminating influence. For Foucault, as for Quine, there is no juridical line to be drawn between the fabric of more or less coherent assumptions that make up a given state of knowledge, and the discourse that seeks to uncover those assumptions in terms of their rhetorical organization. Critique is always already caught up in the toils of its own demystifying will-to-truth. Hence the present tensions between Marxist critical theory and the claims of Foucauldian discourse analysis. Marxism may have abandoned (after Althusser) the presumption that theory can break with ideology to the extent of constituting itself as a rigorous, self-sufficient 'science'. But it remains crucial to Marxist thinking that there must exist some means of establishing critique on a higher dialectical level than the forms of ideological misprision which it seeks to explain or demystify. Otherwise there are simply no grounds for supposing that Marxism offers any kind of privileged critical standpoint.

It is for this reason that Quine's argument, like Foucault's, tends to undercut the very possibility of rational critique. It reduces language to an undifferentiated signifying flux, where discourses compete one against another but afford no prospect of any validating knowledge or grounds of theoretical advance. In Quine's case, the radically *contextual* character of language means that every notion of sense, reference and logic must always be open to conceptual revision if the demands of overall coherence require it. Foucault makes greater allowance for the diverse and conflicting discourses which may coexist within a given historical culture. But he insists, like Quine, on the non-availability of any knowledge that would claim a privileged explanatory power or logical status. And it is *this* strategic refusal, rather than the lack of a 'referential' grounding for language, that creates the sharp divergence between Marxist and post-structuralist theory.

Dummett's critique of Quine has to do with precisely this logical problem about theories that permit themselves no ground on which to stand in pursuit of their own epistemological claims. 'Since any finite sub-theory of the total theory is compatible with any experience whatever, it follows that no one sentence has significance by itself: only a total theory has' (Dummett, p. 593). This holistic conception of language effectively disqualifies any rational critique of its own or any other set of assumptions. Quine's major premises – that 'no experience compels the rejection of any sentence' and that 'no sentence is immune from revision' – create between them a condition of totally disabling undecidability. As Dummett describes it:

> the distinction between periphery and interior disappears, and a total theory must be viewed as confronting experience as a single undifferentiated block . . . the internal structure of the theory, consisting in the interconnection of sentences with one another, is totally dissolved, and the theory becomes a mere featureless collection of sentences standing in no special relations to each other. (Dummett, p. 597)

The same might be said of Foucault's post-structuralist desire to conceive of language as utterly irreducible to any first-order logic of sense or reference. The effect is to liberate a notional

plurality of 'truth-effects' within the various competing discourses of power and knowledge. But this leads to an ultimate
theoretical impasse wherein knowledge confronts its own
powerlessness to escape the relativity of truth. If language is
deprived of any articulate relation between sense, reference
and logic, then it becomes – as Dummett argues – a 'featureless
collection' of indifferent signifying codes.

It may be objected that Frege's is an ideal conception of
language, an account of its logical structure which would only
hold good for exceptionally clear-cut sentences and contexts.
Dummett admits this readily enough, but insists that the
Fregean model is none the less relevant for that. It represents a
workable ideal, he argues,

> just because its interconnections are minimal: there are just
> as many as are needed to confer on our sentences the use to
> which we want to put them. . . . In consequence, the more
> nearly a language approximates to this model, the clearer a
> view we can command of its interconnections and therefore
> of the content of its sentences. (Dummett, p. 626)

Quine's line of argument, on the contrary, has the effect of
reducing all logical distinctions to the level of an undifferentiated signifying mass. It provides for any amount of conceptual change within language, since any given statement will
be 'overdetermined', as Quine expresses it, by a vast number
of related beliefs and suppositions. But this is achieved,
Dummett argues, 'only at the cost of making the principles
which govern change undecipherable' (pp. 626–7). At worst,
Quine's position is thoroughly conservative, since it offers 'no
base from which to criticize whatever is generally accepted'. At
best, the line of argument is merely defeatist, since it 'renders
in principle inscrutable the laws which govern the common
acceptance of a statement as true or its later demotion' (p. 627).
On both counts Quine is to be criticized for making his position
pre-emptively proof against exactly those kinds of rational
critique that philosophy ought to encourage.

A similar case could be brought against Foucault's post-
structuralist variety of discourse analysis. Of course this is not
to argue that post-structuralism needs some positive definition
of 'truth' by which to validate its own interpretative strategies.

Such grounding is no more to be had than the recourse to a straightforward, unmediated notion of linguistic reference. But even the production of truth *effects* requires more by way of explanatory logic than Foucault sees fit to provide. Natural language may typically fall far short of the 'ideal' relations that Frege would establish between sense, reference and logic. But there is no reason to suppose that such concepts are simply irrelevant to the purposes of understanding natural language. As with Frege's treatment of fictional sentences, they form at least a background of normative assumptions against which to interpret the varieties of 'deviant' utterance. Thus the 'ideal' bearing of Frege's model is not, Dummett insists, a limiting condition. On the contrary it offers an argument for viewing that model as a paradigm case towards which language is always implicitly aimed.

IV

To summarize, it would seem that analytic philosophy in the Fregean tradition does have a useful bearing on the problems of recent post-structuralist theory. Its usefulness is clearly not a matter (as some would suppose) of refurbishing a straightforward concept of reference, and thus providing a handy defence against over-sophisticated 'textualist' theories of meaning. There is no support for such a simplified reading in Frege's account of the logic which articulates the complex interdependence of sense and reference. Rather, it is a question of seeing how the *concept* of reference plays an operative role in any adequate theory of language, even where that role is largely defined through its place in a (logically) prior economy of sense. To acknowledge this reciprocal dependence would help to remove some of the self-induced puzzles and perplexities that characterize post-structuralist discourse.

This would clarify, if not resolve, the problematic status of a theory which otherwise tends to resist most available standards of logical accountability. And indeed there are signs that such productive exchange may already be under way. Thus Sollace Mitchell, in his closely argued essay 'Post-Structuralism, Empiricism and Interpretation', remarks very pertinently that 'Derrida (and other post-structuralists) have left language hanging, unanchored to anything that would lend determinate semantic values to its words'.[29] Mitchell's argument ranges widely over the joint terrains of Anglo-American analytic philosophy and Francophile critical theory. Its conclusions differ from my own on a number of basic points, not least in its appeal to the concept of intention (rather than those of sense and reference) as defining the major ground of philosophical dispute. But Mitchell starts out from a similar understanding: that post-structuralism stands in need of certain basic logical distinctions which its own linguistic premisses fail to provide. What is at issue, he suggests, is 'not whether language's *structure* is self-contained, but whether language doesn't relate to the world in some way more direct than significationism is willing to admit'.[30] It is in these terms precisely that post-structuralism needs to re-evaluate the logical standing of its own linguistic concepts and categories. In the process, it could well turn to something like Frege's truth-conditional semantics as a guard against any too easy or premature form of referential agnosticism. And this, as I have argued, is all that philosophy can hope to provide, given the assumption Frege shares with Saussure: that knowledge is in some sense linguistic through and through.

3

Some versions of rhetoric: Empson and de Man

Deconstruction has been seen by some of its opponents as a mere continuation of the 'old' New Criticism by more sophisticated technical means. Both movements, it is argued, arose from a narrow preoccupation with 'the text' which effectively cuts criticism off from a sense of its larger (intellectual and social) obligations. In each case the appeal is to a privileged *rhetoric* – or theory of linguistic figuration – which drives a wedge between textual meaning and the logic of 'normal', communicative discourse. The New Critics made do with a homespun vocabulary of tropes like 'ambiguity', 'paradox' and 'irony', figures that required no elaborate theory by which to back up their ontological claims about the nature of poetic language. Deconstruction developed out of the specialized idiom of post-Saussurean linguistics, coupled to a critique of philosophical concepts far more ambitious than anything dreamt of in New Critical theory. Nevertheless – so the argument runs – this added sophistication cannot disguise the basic continuity of method and aims. Deconstruction merely pushes to its furthest extreme that divorce between rhetoric and reason which the 'old' New Criticism sought to impose. An ultra-refined model of linguistic structure is joined to a thoroughgoing Nietzschean scepticism about the possibility of achieving any knowledge outside the random play of textual meaning. Thus, for all its protestations to the contrary, deconstruction is put down as simply a more exotic, updated version of New Critical dogma.

This view has a certain limited plausibility, especially when applied to some proponents of so-called 'American' decon-struction. The peculiar kinds of licence that were once ex-tended to poetic language – the suspension of logic by a rhetoric of paradox, ambiguity, etc. – are now claimed by critics as rightfully theirs also to exploit. Where New Criticism drew a firm disciplinary line between poem and commentary, deconstruction makes a virtue of crossing that line wherever possible, allowing the critic a speculative style in keeping with the text he or she interprets. Some, like Geoffrey Hartman, have pushed this new-found freedom to the point of dissolv-ing all putative distinctions between 'literature', 'criticism' and 'theory'.[1] The erstwhile structuralist dream of a *science* of literature – an orderly taxonomy of forms and devices – gives way to the joyous post-structuralist assertion that theory is one variety of text among others, and hence no longer subject to the grim paternal law of scientist method. Hartman's pun-ning virtuosity of style goes along with his commitment to a range of hermeneutic models and theories more adventurous than anything allowed for in 'old' New Critical practice. To abandon the protocols of academic criticism – what Hartman calls 'the Arnoldian concordat' – is to come out on the far side of any distinction between 'primary' (creative) and 'secondary' (critical) texts. Henceforth interpretation is to grasp its proper destiny as a free and equal partner in the intertextual dance of meaning. For Hartman, this is the promised land which Arnold glimpsed but failed to possess, interpreting his own as an age of criticism indeed, but one that could only serve as a prelude to some coming creative revival.[2] Such melancholy tonings will seem beside the point, Hartman suggests, if criticism casts off its old inferiority complex *vis-à-vis* the literary text.

Undoubtedly, this is the guise in which deconstruction has made its greatest impact on American literary studies. Its attractions are evident enough, and nowhere seen to more beguiling effect than in Hartman's style of speculative musing on and around the margins of the text. Yet the opponents of deconstruction have a point when they argue that this is, after all, just one more episode in the history of failed attempts to move beyond the confines of 'old' New Critical method. The

liberty that Hartman so brilliantly exploits is still a licence to
interpret texts, albeit in a manner scarcely thinkable to the high
priests of orthodox formalism. W. K. Wimsatt was quick to see
the threat in an essay, published in 1970, which reasserted the
'ontological' argument – the poem as 'verbal icon' – against any
kind of newfangled critical theory which blurred the distinction between text and commentary.[3] A large weight of dogma,
aesthetic and ethical, rested upon Wimsatt's rearguard response. Yet in retrospect it looks as if the threat came not so
much from this textual-libertarian quarter as from another,
more rigorous form of deconstruction which Wimsatt (one
guesses) had yet to encounter.

Of course it is open to debate whether any such distinction
can or should be drawn. If there are, as I am suggesting, 'hard'
and 'soft' varieties of deconstructionist thought, then any such
loaded comparison will quickly be dismantled (or rhetorically
undone) by proponents of the hard-line persuasion. Besides, it
is notoriously difficult to define what should count as argumentative 'rigour' in the context of deconstruction. Certainly
there exist no normative *logical* grounds for distinguishing
rigorous from non-rigorous forms of deconstruction. If philosophy is blind to the rhetorical complications which threaten
its sovereign logic – as Nietzsche argued, and as deconstructionists never cease to point out – then clearly no appeal to
logical consistency will serve to make the needful distinction.
Yet there is, in the texts of a critic like Paul de Man, a power of
'rigorous' or consequential argument which sets them firmly
apart from Hartman's exuberant, virtuoso style. The upshot of
de Man's close readings may be an affront to every standard
notion of logical sense and consistency. But to follow them
stage by stage through the process of his tortuous yet scrupulous argument is to experience something very different from
the heady fascinations of Hartman's writing.

It might seem extravagantly wrong-headed to apply this
same distinction in the case of Derrida's texts. Certainly a
hard-line deconstructor would have ample Derridean warrant
for rejecting any putative difference between 'serious' and
'non-serious', 'rigorous' and 'playful', forms of deconstructionist discourse. That philosophy has always clung to such
distinctions as a self-promoting strategy of true (i.e. 'rigorous')

knowledge is a lesson that Derrida constantly drives home. From Plato on the sophists to Searle on Derrida, it has always been a contest between 'serious' philosophy, aimed at the one, authoritative truth, and on the other hand a rhetoric which knows and exploits its own irreducibly figural status.[4] All the more reason to reject any straightforward distinction, on philosophic grounds, between rigorous and non-rigorous forms of deconstruction. To fall back into that prejudiced habit of thought is to ignore what Derrida's texts most forcefully proclaim: the liberation of rhetoric (or writing) from its age-old subjugation at the hands of philosophic reason.

Clearly there are pressing institutional motives for this readiness among literary critics to accept the broader drift of Derrida's arguments. It is agreeable to be told, after all – and on good 'philosophical' authority – that criticism is not just a poor relation of philosophy but possesses the rhetorical means to dismantle philosophy's claims to truth. But there remains a great difference between Derrida's scrupulous thinking-through of these issues and the way that his *conclusions* are taken as read by many of his American admirers. Again, deconstruction would reject in principle any attempt to discriminate 'original' or first-order deconstructive thinking from its 'derivative', secondary or non-original forms. Such distinctions would merely betoken the lingering hold of an outworn metaphysical prejudice, a harking-back to notions of authority, presence and origins. The slightest acquaintance with deconstructive theory is sufficient to reduce these notions to the status of ungrounded myths or metaphors. So one might gather from reading, for instance, J. Hillis Miller's ingenious meditations on the mazy etymology of 'host' and 'parasite', figuring between them the strange ('undecidable') relation of dependence between 'primary' and 'secondary' texts.[5] Such manœuvres certainly inhibit any talk of first-order deconstructive thinkers on the one hand and mere camp-followers on the other. But it still makes sense – albeit problematically – to single out certain deconstructionist texts for the unsettling power and acuity of their arguments. These texts provoke a sharp and continuing discomfort, a generalized 'resistance to theory' which de Man was quick to diagnose.[6] Unlike the products of mainstream 'American' deconstruction, they hold out against the domesticating pressures which work to assimilate all new ideas to the basically conformist practice of interpretation. In short, these texts stand decidedly apart from the kind of deconstructive activity which – for all its new-found sophistication – still looks increasingly like 'old' New Criticism under a different rhetorical guise.

What creates such acute discomfort in the reading of Derrida and de Man is the disciplined rigour of their arguments, coupled with the seemingly irrational conclusions to which those arguments lead. The New Critics were content to suppose that 'literary' language had its own peculiar logic of paradox, irony and other such safely accommodating tropes. Rational explication was the interpreter's business, but only in so far as he or she respected the saving difference – the radical autonomy – of poetic language. Wimsatt takes his stand on precisely this ground when he argues (against Miller) that criticism needs to maintain a firm sense of the ontological difference between poem and commentary. And it is *this* distinction that de Man most flagrantly transgresses by refusing to separate the logic of commentary from that other, less answerable 'logic' of poetic figuration. For de Man, the mutual questioning of text and critique is pressed to a point where reason itself becomes enmeshed in 'undecidable' contexts of argument beyond its power to comprehend or control. What de Man won't accept is the convenient escape-route which holds that poems just *are* paradoxical and ambiguous, since that is the way that literary language works, as distinct from the language of rational prose discourse. This was the assumption of New Critics like Wimsatt and Cleanth Brooks. It undergoes a radical extension of kinds in Hartman's or Miller's argument that *all* texts are figural through and through, whatever their self-professed 'logical' status. At times this is certainly de Man's position. But along with it – and so closely intertwined as to make this a clumsy way of formulating the difference – there emerges a refusal simply to take refuge in the all-embracing realm of poetic figuration. It is this 'perverse' tenacity of argument which sets de Man apart from critics like Hartman, and which probably accounts for the extreme hostility that his writings often provoke.

A programmatic statement from *Allegories of Reading* may

help to make this point more clearly. The context is de Man's opening discussion of rhetorical questions, as in Yeats's line from 'Among School Children': 'How can we know the dancer from the dance?' In such cases, de Man writes, 'the same grammatical pattern engenders two meanings that are mutually exclusive'.[7] The question simultaneously asks to know the difference and denies (rhetorically) that such knowledge is possible. Yeats's line presents a simple enough case, but it serves to introduce a series of antinomies which de Man exploits to extraordinary effect in subsequent chapters. In particular, it signals his unwillingness to opt – like the 'old' New Critics – for some inclusive rhetoric of poetic figuration which would simply suspend all questions of logical accountability. It is not just the case, de Man writes,

> that the poem simply has two meanings that exist side by side. The two readings have to engage each other in direct confrontation, since the one reading is precisely the error denounced by the other and has to be undone by it. Nor can we in any way make a valid decision as to which of the readings can be given priority over the other; none can exist in the other's absence.[8]

This passage demonstrates the unsettling coexistence, in de Man's critical language, of a rhetoric of textual *undecidability* and a constant demand for *logical* precision. That there is no valid procedure for deciding between readings is a message that Brooks and Wimsatt would happily endorse. A deconstructor like Hartman would be just as much at home with the notion of an open-ended textual 'free play' beyond all governance of critical method. What complicates matters in de Man's case is the insistence that each reading must 'undo' the other, and that meanings cannot simply be conceived to coexist in a peaceful state of aesthetic suspension. There remains an irreducibly *logical* tension between the 'literal' and the 'figurative' senses of language, such that criticism is brought up sharply against the limits of its own linguistic competence.

This is how de Man deconstructs the opposition between 'literary' and 'critical' discourse. It is no longer a question of laying down firm categorical limits within which poetry can safely exercise its penchant for ambiguity and paradox. Text and critique are henceforth involved in a shuttling exchange of priorities which allows of no protective buffer-zone between the two. But neither is it a case – as with Hartman – of simply submerging all limits and distinctions in the undifferentiated play of textuality. De Man may indeed double back and forth across the notional line between 'literature' and 'commentary'. At one moment he will valorize criticism for its power to demystify the 'normative pathos' vested in literary language. At the next, he will elevate the literary text as implicitly *acknowledging* its own rhetorical character, and thus making a dupe of the literal-minded critic who seeks to articulate its truth. But this strategy works to complicate – rather than collapse – the system of tentative checks and resistances set up between text and commentary. It requires, that is to say, a kind of shifting, provisional boundary line, even if the line is constantly blurred by the two-way traffic of interpretative sense that flows across it.

This is why de Man's allegories of reading are enacted in a space which is undecidably both 'in' the texts he interprets and 'in' the deconstructive reading that brings them to light. Simply to collapse that distinction – to merge text and com-mentary in Hartman's manner – would amount to a denial that criticism could achieve any kind of articulate knowledge beyond that provided by literature itself. Such would indeed appear to be de Man's position at a certain late stage of the deconstructive process. But in order to *reach* that stage his argument must undergo the passage through a constant reciprocating dialogue of text and critique which requires at least some residual sense of the difference between them. In the end it may appear, as Barbara Johnson says, that criticism is often 'the straight man whose precarious rectitude and hidden risibility, passion and pathos are precisely what litera-ture has somehow already foreseen'.[9] But on the way to this denouement – and in order to achieve it – theory has to pass through successive encounters with its own 'undecidable' status *vis-à-vis* the literary text. And this entails a certain operative distinction between 'text' and 'theory', no matter how often that distinction is overthrown by the devious logic of intertextuality. On the one hand de Man can argue that 'poetic writing is the most advanced and refined mode of deconstruction'.[10] On the other, he is constantly obliged to set a distance between them, at least as a kind of heuristic device whereby to plot their convergence. Thus:

> It seems that as soon as a text knows what it states, it can only act deceptively . . . and if a text does not act, it cannot state what it knows. The distinction between a text as narrative and a text as theory also belongs to this field of tension.[11]

This passage certainly works to deconstruct any firm categorical distinction between literature and theory. It implicates both within the 'allegory of reading' that constitutes the only possible form of demystified textual knowledge. Yet even here de Man is constrained to make the point by provisionally separating 'narrative' from 'theory' in terms of his own dialectic.

This sets de Man apart from that strain of deconstructionist thinking which breaks with New Criticism only by dissolving all limits to the play of figurative language. He remains, one might say, a *philosopher* of language – a conceptual rhetorician – precisely in so far as his texts resist the drift toward pure, undifferentiated free play. Philosophy may turn out, in de Man's words, as 'an endless reflection on its own destruction at the hands of literature'.[12] But the means of that reflection derive unmistakably from philosophic discourse, that 'labour of the negative' installed within philosophy from Hegel to Adorno. De Man's overriding drive to demystify language goes along with his adherence to the protocols of logical argument, no matter how strange or paradoxical their upshot.

II

It is to William Empson, and not the New Critics, that attention might be turned in seeking a precursor for de Man's kind of strongly interrogative reading. Empson's techniques of verbal analysis were of course taken up by critics like Cleanth Brooks, but not without certain doctrinal reservations. The problem was that Empson insisted on *rationalizing* poetry, not merely seeking out multiple meanings but attempting to fit them into some kind of logical structure. This led the New Critics to view with suspicion Empson's habits of homely prose paraphrase and his constant drawing out of underlying philosophical arguments. Philip Wheelwright suggested that the term 'ambiguity' was partly to blame, since it allowed for a logical 'either/or' response as well as the inclusive 'both/and' of genuine poetic language.[13] 'Plurisignification' was Wheelwright's preferred candidate; 'irony' and 'paradox' likewise served to raise a protective fence around the privileged domain of the poem as 'verbal icon'.

I have argued elsewhere that Empson's kind of sturdy rationalism was especially offensive to the New Critics when he brought it to bear on religious poets like George Herbert and Milton.[14] Poetry and theology both demand respect for their peculiar, uniquely sanctioned varieties of figural language. To read them in Empson's manner – drawing out their logical contradictions – is to open up their mysteries to a secular critique which would threaten that saving autonomy. John Crowe Ransom registered this sense of unease with Empson's method when he spoke of 'the reading of the poet's muddled mind by some later, freer and more self-conscious mind'.[15] To enquire too closely into the logical workings of poetic language is to forget that poetry occupies a separate realm of complex but non-discursive meaning. Thus Ransom remarks, in another context, that any putative 'logic of poetic figure' would always be self-contradictory, suggesting in effect 'a logic of logical aberrations, applicable to the conventions of poetic language'.[16] New Criticism sought to avoid such confusions of realm by drawing a firm categorical line between critical theory and the inwrought structures of poetic irony and paradox. Theory has to do with the broadest questions of interpretative method, and had better not become too closely involved with the actual *reading* of poetry. Thus Brooks legislates flatly that 'the principles of criticism define the area relevant to criticism; they do not constitute a method for carrying it out'.[17]

Empson and de Man have this much in common: they refuse to make any such clear-cut distinction between the structure of poetic meaning and the logic of critical argument. They both insist on pressing their analysis of figural language to the point where it offers a maximal resistance to the habits of straightforward rational thought. But where New Criticism simply suspends those habits – accepting that poetry just *is* paradoxical, and quite beyond reach of logic – Empson and de Man make a point of keeping the logical problems in view. In de Man, this leads to a species of negative hermeneutic which deconstructs the very grounds and assumptions of normative reading. In Empson, it takes a more overtly 'commonsense' form, but runs none the less into regions of textual doubt and self-questioning which often approach the stage of deconstructive aporia. And this comes about precisely through Empson's refusal to let go of logic in pursuit of some other, paradoxical quality invested in poetic language.

The effect is most marked in what Empson classifies as 'ambiguities of the seventh type'. These occur when 'the two meanings of the word, the two values of the ambiguity, are the two opposite meanings defined by the context, so that the total effect is to show a fundamental division in the writer's mind.'[18] *Seven Types of Ambiguity* is a loosely organized book, and Empson makes no claims for any clear-cut, orderly progression of 'types'. There is, however, a marked development of interest which leads from vaguely *inclusive* ambiguities – cases where the mind doesn't need to choose one way or the other – to instances of full-blown logical *conflict*, such as make up the seventh type. Thus Empson can be seen to turn on its head the New Critical idea that poetic ambiguity is properly a matter of 'both/and' rather than 'either/or'. For Empson, the most powerful and productive ambiguities are those that maintain the *logical* tension between two or more 'incompatible' meanings. Like de Man, he resists any premature retreat to a ground of aesthetic reconciliation where opposites can peacefully coexist within a structure of irony, paradox, etc. 'The conditions for this verbal effect', Empson writes, 'are not those of a breakdown of rationality' (*Seven Types*, p. 198).

The most sustained and striking instance of Empson's seventh 'type' comes with his reading of George Herbert's poem 'The Sacrifice'. Here, if anywhere, the method gives reason for those orthodox New Critical fears about the effects of a 'logical' approach to the mysteries of poetry and religion. Empson reads 'The Sacrifice' as riven by internal contradictions, its surface mood of placid acceptance everywhere subject to harsh, self-inflicted ironies. Christ is depicted, in Empson's words, as

> scapegoat and tragic hero; loved because hated; hated because godlike; freeing from torture because tortured; torturing his torturers because all-merciful; source of all strength to men because by accepting he exaggerates their weakness; and, because outcast, creating the possibility of society. (*Seven Types*, pp. 232–3)

These paradoxes are *not* entertained in the spirit of a formalist criticism which would take them (so to speak) on faith, as evidence of poetry's power to reconcile conflicting states of mind. Rather, they are presented as an outright affront to the logic of rational thought, effective as poetry only in so far as reason measures their irrational appeal.

In de Man, likewise, there is an ethical compulsion behind the will to demystify certain predominant poetic tropes and devices. This compulsion is most evident where de Man deconstructs that species of rhetorical bad faith which he associates with Romanticism and its attempts to transcend the antinomies of rational (post-Kantian) thought. These are the stakes in de Man's classic essay 'The Rhetoric of Temporality', first published in 1969. The essay turns on the cardinal distinction between 'symbol' and 'allegory', conceived not so much as two distinct orders of language – since symbol, for de Man, always resolves back into allegory – but as two strategies for *making sense* of linguistic figuration. The rhetoric of symbolism is that which seeks a transcendent, unifying vision atop all the hateful antinomies of subject and object, time and eternity, word and idea. It deludedly hopes that such distinctions may simply fall away in the moment of unmediated, purified perception towards which poetry strives. De Man quotes Coleridge, among others: the symbol is characterized by 'the translucence of the special in the individual, or of the general in the special, or of the universal in the general; above all, by the translucence of the eternal through and in the temporal'.[19]

It is this last claim especially that vexes de Man, and which opens up the gap between logic and rhetoric that his essay proceeds to exploit. Romanticism achieves its moments of delusory transcendence only by ignoring or suppressing the *textual* operations that underwrite its will-to-truth. Refusing to distinguish between experience and the representation of experience, Romanticism seeks to collapse all those awkward distinctions that force an awareness of the secondary, mediating character of language. The ethos of the symbol is precisely this belief that language can attain to a pure ideality where subject and object, mind and nature would at last coincide without the interposition of mere arbitrary signs. And this would also mean – as suggested in the passage from Coleridge – that thought might be momentarily redeemed from its enslavement to the *temporal* condition of language. The 'translucence of the eternal through and in the temporal' is the aim of every discourse founded on the symbol as a means of reconciling logical antinomies. It is the arbitrary nature of the sign – the perpetual slippage between signifier and signified – which enforces the ineluctably time-bound condition of all discursive thought. The language of symbolism seeks to overcome this predicament by abolishing the distance between sign and meaning, between language and the orders of inward and outward experience. With 'the assumed superiority of the Symbol in terms of organic substantiality' (*Blindness*, pp. 192–3), language takes on a new-found conviction of its power to transcend all merely intellectual antinomies.

It is precisely this assumed superiority that de Man sets out to deconstruct by juxtaposing symbol and allegory as rival modes of understanding. He notes how 'the valorization of symbol at the expense of allegory' goes along with the rise of a cult of aesthetic transcendence aimed at securing the radical autonomy of poetic imagination. This process is reversed point for point by substituting 'allegory' for 'symbol' as the ground of all linguistic understanding. Allegory becomes the demystifying trope *par excellence*, the determinate negation of everything claimed on behalf of symbolic transcendence. To interpret allegorically is to read in the knowledge that there always exists, in the nature of language, a constitutive gap between words and experience, between signs and the reality they seek to evoke. Allegory perpetually redirects attention to its own *arbitrary* character, the fact that any meaning there to be read is the product of interpretative codes and conventions with no claim to ultimate, authentic priority. It is thus in terms of allegory – as de Man interprets it – that thought comes to recognize the temporal predicament of all understanding. There is no present moment of self-possessed meaning where signs would so perfectly match up with experience as to obviate the need for further interpretation. Allegory in de Man exerts something like the power of deconstructive leverage that Derrida brings to bear through his key term *differance*.[20] That is to say, it introduces the idea of a differential play within language that everywhere prevents (or constantly *defers*) the imaginary coincidence of meaning and intent. For de Man, this recognition can only be suspended by the workings of a covert ideology – that of transcendental aesthetics – which wills its own blindness to the rhetoric of temporality.

The following passage brings out the underlying ethical dimension of de Man's argument:

> Whereas the symbol postulates the possibility of an identity or identification, allegory designates primarily a distance in relation to its own origin, and, renouncing the nostalgia and the desire to coincide, it establishes its language in the void of this temporal difference. In so doing, it prevents the self from an illusory identification with the non-self, which is now fully, though painfully, recognized as a non-self. It is this painful knowledge that we perceive at the moments when early romantic literature finds its true voice. (*Blindness*, p. 207)

The choice thus posed – 'painful' recognition or mystified, evasive strategy – is cast in terms of an almost existentialist drive toward authentic self-knowledge. For de Man the only truth to be grasped through language is that 'truth' is always non-self-identical, a fugitive knowledge that nowhere coincides with the moment of its own, self-sufficient revelation. Allegorical reading drives this lesson home by constantly revealing the interpretative slide from moment to moment in the chain of signification. Thus 'the prevalence of allegory always corresponds to the unveiling of an authentically temporal destiny', while this unveiling takes place 'in a subject that has sought refuge against the impact of time in a natural world to which, in truth, it bears no resemblance' (*Blindness*, p. 206).

Hence de Man's relentless critique of organicist metaphors in the discourse of post-Romantic thought. Such figures seek to establish an equivalence between processes of natural growth on the one hand and products of spontaneous creativity on the other. Both are conceived as totalizing movements which contain within themselves the shaping principle that assures their intelligible form. For de Man, such metaphors are merely another species of the will to mystify critical discourse, to lift interpretation outside the temporal existence which endlessly defers its own closure. Literary 'form', de Man writes, is 'the result of the dialectic interplay between the prefigurative structure of foreknowledge and the intent at totality of the interpretative process' (*Blindness*, p. 31). Criticism builds its mistaken ontological assumptions on the failure to recognize that metaphors like 'organic form' can never be more than stopgap expedients in the face of an authentically temporal self-understanding. 'Form is never anything but a process on the way to its completion' – a sentence which typically self-deconstructs around its own incompatible terms.

Empson comes closest to a full-dress deconstructive reading in his pages on Wordsworth's 'Tintern Abbey' as the crowning example of fourth-type ambiguity.

> And I have felt
> A presence that disturbs me with the joy
> Of elevated thoughts; a sense sublime
> Of something far more deeply interfused
> Whose dwelling is the light of setting suns,
> And the round ocean and the living air,
> And the blue sky, and in the mind of man;
> A motion and a spirit, that impels
> All thinking things, all objects of all thought,
> And rolls through all things.

To a formalist like Brooks, any logical problems about Wordsworth's poetry can always be turned aside by declaring them strictly irrelevant. 'What Wordsworth wanted to say demanded his use of paradox, . . . could only be said powerfully through paradox.'[21] Empson, on the other hand, holds out against any such willing suspension of logical disbelief. Wordsworth, he argues, 'seems to have believed in his own doctrines', and this makes it only reasonable to interrogate the poetry for 'definite opinions on the relations of God, man and nature, and on the means by which such relations can be known' (*Seven Types*, p. 152).

I wouldn't want to suggest that Empson's kind of sturdy rationalist outlook is just another version of de Man's rigorously negative hermeneutics. Nevertheless, it produces a reading of Wordsworth which leads to some strikingly similar conclusions. Empson shares with de Man a principled mistrust of any totalizing rhetoric which would simply gloss over the elements of strain and contradiction in Wordsworth's inspirational language. He positively wrestles with the poem's syntax and logical connections, only to conclude that they cannot be sorted into any kind of rational-discursive order. In particular, Empson sees fit to resist the heady rhetorical drift which assimilates man and nature to a realm of undifferentiated spirit, with the vague implication that both are subsumed within the mind of God. For Empson, as indeed for de Man, such elisions of the subject/object dichotomy are products of a mystified rhetoric which needs to be questioned, not taken on faith.

I must now quote Empson at sufficient length to bring out the deconstructive bearings of his argument. In the passage from 'Tintern Abbey', he suggests,

> the *something* may possibly dwell only in the natural objects mentioned, ending at *sky*; the *motion* and the *spirit* are then not thought of at all as *interfused* into nature, like the *something*; they are things active *in the mind of man*. At the same time they are similar to the *something*; thus Wordsworth either *feels* them or *feels a sense* of them . . . [so that] man has a spirit immanent in nature in the same way as the spirit of God, and is decently independent from him. Or the *something* may also *dwell in the mind of man*, and have the *motion* and the *spirit* in opposition to it; under this less fortunate arrangement a God who is himself nature subjects us at once to determinism and predestination. (*Seven Types*, p. 153)

In a footnote to the second edition of *Seven Types*, Empson records the objection of M. C. Bradbrook that Wordsworth's logical imprecisions are nothing to the point, since 'his theme is the transcendence of the subject–object relationship'. But Empson rejects this accommodating line, insisting still that 'the more seriously one takes the doctrine . . . the more this expression of it seems loose rhetoric' (*Seven Types*, p. 153).

What Empson is trying to pinpoint here is the tension (or divergence) between logic and rhetoric which de Man will later formulate in deconstructionist terms. In both cases there is a flat refusal simply to go along with the suasive rhetoric and leave the logical antinomies to sort themselves out. Empson protests that he enjoys this poetry, though he clearly feels a nagging mistrust as to the sources and nature of that enjoyment. His case, like de Man's, has ethical implications: poetry may use its rhetorical power to insinuate varieties of plainly irrational belief. In de Man, this suspicion takes the form of an unrelenting will to recall language to its 'authentic' (temporal) condition, rather than permit the tropes to get away with their mystifying work. In Empson, the tone is more frankly puzzled than charged – like de Man's – with a kind of displaced existential pathos. But the object is likewise to resist what Empson sees as the irrational synthesizing claims of Wordsworth's rhetoric. Thus he writes:

> The reason why one grudges Wordsworth this source of strength is that he talks as if he owned a creed by which his half-statements might be reconciled, whereas, in so far as his creed was definite, he found these half-statements necessary to keep it at bay. (*Seven Types*, p. 154)

At one level this reflects Empson's rooted dislike of Christianity and the kinds of officially sanctioned paradox to which such beliefs give rise. But his critique of Wordsworth's 'shuffling' argumentation – 'this attempt to be uplifting yet non-denominational' – also leads into regions of specifically textual contradiction and aporia.

III

De Man wrote admiringly about Empson in an essay called 'The Dead-End of Formalist Criticism' (1956), first published in *Critique* by way of introducing French readers to recent Anglo-

American developments. The 'dead-end' in question was that represented by I. A. Richards's early attempts to put criticism on a 'scientific' basis by reducing it to a matter of applied psychology. De Man finds problems – as might be expected – with Richards's confident assumption that poetry serves to *communicate experience* from one mind to another. On this highly simplified model, the author's task (as de Man describes it) consists in 'constructing a linguistic structure that will correspond as closely as possible to the initial experience'.[22] This 'structure' will exist for the reader as well, so that 'what is called communication can then occur'. Criticism thus has its work cut out describing these kinds of complex experience, determining their modes of verbal organization and removing any obstacles to a full and free response on the reader's part. There may be 'numerous possibilities of error' in the carrying out of these pedagogic aims, but Richards is never in any doubt that 'in every case a correct procedure can be arrived at' (*Blindness*, p. 232).

De Man characteristically denies that interpretative 'errors' can be simply removed by adopting any such straightforward propaedeutic model. Richards's criticism, he writes, can be seen to rest on some 'highly questionable ontological presuppositions', foremost among them the assured idea 'that language, poetic or otherwise, can *say* any experience, of whatever kind, even a simple perception' (*Blindness*, p. 232). Where Richards goes wrong is in failing to recognize the complex mediations and the structures of perhaps *unmasterable* difference that open up within the always error-prone activity of reading. Thus his method assimilates *meaning* to *perception*, and both in turn to a theory of poetic form which likewise ignores its own problematic status. While admitting the attractions of this simplified creed – not least its pedagogical usefulness – de Man is constrained to point out the difficulties in its way. Richards makes do with a commonsense empiricist theory of language that effectively collapses all distinctions between perceptual, aesthetic and critical-reflective orders of cognition. His method runs together the two distinct elements of 'a theory of constituting form' and 'a theory of signifying form' (*Blindness*, p. 232). And this prevents Richards from seeing that errors of interpretative insight may not be simply a matter of corrigible reading habits. As de Man writes:

> It can be said that there is a perceptual consciousness of the object and an experience of this consciousness, but a working out of a *logos* of this experience or, in the case of art, of a *form* of this experience, encounters considerable difficulties. (*Blindness*, p. 23)

These problems, he argues, are constitutive of textual understanding, at least where pursued with sufficient dialectical rigour and hermeneutic tact. Richards can avoid facing up to them because he founds his poetics on a purely *affective* psychology of imputed reader-response. Poetry, according to Richards, deals in varieties of 'emotive' pseudo-statement which give no hold for any logical or cognitive account. Again, de Man sees the usefulness of this as a means of 'saving' poetry for the purposes of humanist edification. But he also insists that Richards's position allows him to sidestep some crucial questions of interpretative theory and practice.

What de Man finds in Empson is a salutary knowledge that criticism cannot sink ontological differences in this brusque and question-begging manner. Empson's 'ambiguity', unlike Richards's 'emotive' language, preserves a keen sense of the problems involved with negotiating the passage from poetry to criticism. To anticipate the language of de Man's later texts, 'ambiguity' finds room for those 'allegories of reading' – or self-reflexive moments of interpretative error – which result from the perpetual non-coincidence of poetic *meaning* and critical *method*. It resists, that is to say, the prematurely totalizing rhetoric of closure that Richards (like his followers, the American New Critics) raised to a high point of principle. The New Critics rejected what they saw as Richards's subjectivist bias, his appeal to psychological states of mind in the reader rather than 'objective' structures of meaning in the poem.[23] But they managed to bypass epistemological problems by simply translating Richards's criteria (of 'complexity', 'equilibrium', etc.) to a notional image of the poem itself as objective verbal construct. Richards thus provided a working model for the basic New Critical strategy of *containing* awkward antinomies by always appealing to a higher, synthetic ground of unified perception. 'Richards', says de Man, 'did recognize the existence of conflicts, but he invoked Coleridge, not without some simplification, to appeal to the reassuring notion of art as the reconciliation of opposites' (*Blindness*, p. 237). This simplification led on directly to the formalist avoidance of those problems about mind and nature, subject and object which idealist aesthetics failed to resolve but refused simply to set aside.

It is at this point that Empson's 'ambiguity' figures as a counter-trope in de Man's dialectical structure of argument. Ambiguity holds out against the synthesizing drive of Richards's poetics and its various formalist offshoots. The source of that resistance, according to de Man, is the sheer impossibility of tracking language back to a moment of self-possessed original *experience* that would serve to ground the communicative process. Richards thinks of poetry as preserving such moments from 'the lives of exceptional people', capturing a state where 'their control and command of experience is at its highest degree'.[24] Empson, on the contrary, shows poetry pressing the signifying potential of language to a point where 'ambiguity' outruns any possible grounding in experience. This lesson is most aptly figured for de Man in Empson's ambiguities of the seventh type, cases where the question of 'conscious' or 'unconscious' meaning becomes lost in a labyrinth of textual undecidability. At this stage, criticism has to acknowledge its powerlessness to halt the figural drift of language in the name of some recuperative humanist ideal. 'All of its basic assumptions have been put into question: the notions of communication, form, signifying experience, and objective precision' (*Blindness*, p. 241). As thought measures up to the problems engendered by linguistic figuration, so it comes to recognize the instability of its own ontological presuppositions. Even within the stronghold of American New Criticism, rhetoric proves more powerful and subversive than anything envisaged by the formalist programme. 'Terms such as paradox, tension and ambiguity abound . . . to the point of nearly losing all meaning' (*Blindness*, p. 241).

Up to now it might seem that de Man's own reading of Empson tends to confirm what I have been arguing here. Certainly it draws some similar conclusions about the inability of formalist criticism to think beyond the terms of its own self-supporting dialectic of method and meaning. It likewise agrees in setting up Empsonian 'ambiguity' as a kind of conceptual stalking-horse whereby to reveal the inbuilt errors and delusions of a prematurely totalizing rhetoric. Ambiguity forces interpretation to the point of an unsettling self-knowledge where 'experience sheds its uniqueness and leads instead to a dizziness of the mind' (*Blindness*, p. 235). It is in this role that Empson serves de Man's argument as a kind of proto-deconstructionist thinker, a conceptual rhetorician willing to forego the easy satisfactions of normative criticism.

But this undoing of naïve ontological assumptions is only one side of de Man's argumentative strategy. Along with it there goes a rather different set of emphases, a rhetoric which treats 'ambiguity' as the product of some deep, aboriginal swerve within the being of language itself. This Heideggerian strain is very marked in de Man's early essays. It is mostly set off against a countervailing drive to demystify the kind of metaphysical pathos which would posit an *authentic* origin or ground, now lost beyond recall through the multiplied errors of linguistic figuration. Where de Man encounters such themes – as in Heidegger's reading of Hölderlin[25] – he interprets them as symptoms of a recurrent delusion, a nostalgic mystique of origins deeply complicit with the history of western metaphysics. Yet the essay on Empson seems oddly disinclined to deconstruct this Heideggerian thematic. It enlists 'ambiguity' as bearing witness to the fundamental split between experience and language that language itself must constantly disguise *and* expose. Clearly de Man is not arguing that there once existed a state of linguistic innocence and grace when no such unhappy condition prevailed. But the rhetoric of his essay often carries such suggestions, if only by way of contesting the simplistic positivist assumptions of a critic like Richards.

Thus de Man writes of Empson that 'he develops a thought Richards never wanted to consider: true poetic ambiguity proceeds from the deep division of Being itself, and poetry does no more than state and repeat this division' (*Blindness*, p. 237). Such formulations are a great deal less circumspect and rigorous than de Man's later idiom in *Allegories of Reading*.

They evoke a Heideggerian ethos of primal authenticity even in the process of denying that condition as a species of impossible and self-deluded dream. This ambivalence is yet more pronounced in other passages. Thus:

> The ambiguity poetry speaks of is the fundamental one that prevails between the world of spirit and the world of sentient substance: to ground itself, the spirit must turn itself into sentient substance, but the latter is knowable only in its dissolution into non-being. The spirit cannot coincide with its object and this separation is infinitely sorrowful. (*Blindness*, p. 237)

This Hegelian dialectic of the 'unhappy consciousness' descends more by way of Kierkegaard than Nietzsche. It carries a charge of existential pathos that is still present – though nothing like as overt – in de Man's later writing. Certainly it seems very remote from the style of 'enlightened' rationalist critique that Empson adopts towards most of his examples in *Seven Types of Ambiguity*. Empson says flatly that his kind of verbal analysis is meant to provide a 'machinery of reassurance' for the reader uncertain how far his or her responses might bear such close inspection. If the results may sometimes seem 'lacking in soul', then that is still preferable (Empson argues) to the attitude that puts up barriers of principled incomprehension between poem and reader. This assurance is important, moreover, since Empson concedes that he is 'treating the act of communication as something very extraordinary, so that the next step would be to lose faith in it altogether' (*Seven Types*, p. 243). De Man, of course, takes this decisive 'next step' when he cites Empson's readings as witness to the ways in which 'true poetic ambiguity' subverts the very logic of communicative language. But in mounting this argument de Man is constrained to read Empson according to a certain predisposed rhetoric of crisis that is by no means self-evident in Empson's text.

The same disposition is at work in de Man's reading of Empson's later book, *Some Versions of Pastoral* (1935). Empson defines pastoral in the broadest possible terms as a matter of 'putting the complex into the simple'. Under this rubric he treats a wide variety of texts – Shakespeare, Marvell, Gray's

'Elegy', *The Beggar's Opera*, *Alice in Wonderland* – as instances of literature's striving to reconcile the claims of a 'complex' imaginative life with the 'simple' requirements of social equality and justice. His opening chapter ('Proletarian Literature') itself gives expression to this 'pastoral' complex of motives by attempting to square the book's line of interest with the current pronouncements of Soviet socialist realism. Now de Man sees clearly that Empson's theme is nothing like as 'simple' as might be thought, either by a Marxist or by a literary scholar of mainstream liberal persuasion. Empson may choose to conduct his argument 'under the deceitful title of a genre study'. What he has actually written, de Man suggests, is a full-scale 'ontology of the poetic', strategically disguised by 'some extraneous matter that may well conceal the essential' (*Blindness*, p. 239).

Here again, de Man's language finds room for metaphysical tonings which his later texts would more rigorously call into question. It winnows the 'essential' from the merely 'extraneous' in the name of an authentically 'ontological' concern which supposedly constitutes the truth of Empson's text. And this truth can only consist, for de Man, in that state of divided or 'unhappy' consciousness theorized by Hegel and endlessly rehearsed in the self-reflexive tropes of poetic language. There is no denying that de Man's preoccupations answer to one – elusive but persistent – line of development in Empson's book. This aspect is most evident in the chapter on Marvell's 'The Garden', which de Man understandably singles out for close attention. Empson reads the poem as a sustained meditation on the antinomies of conscious and unconscious thought, a compressed phenomenology of spirit worked out through successive metaphorical exchanges between 'outward' nature and 'inward' thought.[26] He is plainly more at ease with Marvell's style of wittily discursive 'metaphysics' than with Wordsworth's more earnest and high-toned reflections on a similar theme. And this is what de Man's reading must needs pass over in its desire to harness Empson's versions of pastoral to its own interpretative purpose. De Man seeks out ontological perplexities which will – he assumes – work everywhere to baffle and complicate the aims of normative interpretation. Empson is aware of these deep-seated problems, but treats them as a topic of speculative fancy, finally amenable to some kind of reasoned and more or less persuasive statement.

De Man's account of Empson on 'The Garden' has the effect of reversing this clearly marked preference and reading Empson (as well as Marvell) on distinctly Wordsworthian terms. Empson is quite explicit in drawing the relevant contrast here. Marvell's poem has the pastoral lightness of touch that allows it to suggest all manner of 'transcendent' antinomies and mystical truth-claims without undermining its own witty logic. According to Empson, this also applies to 'Romantic nature poetry' like Wordsworth's, though sometimes the wit is less in evidence and the truth-claims pitched too high.

> A hint of the supreme condition is thus found in the actual one (this makes the actual one include everything in itself), but this apparently exalted claim is essentially joined to humility; it is effective only through the admission that it is only a hint. Something of the tone of pastoral is therefore inherent in the claim; the fault of the Wordsworthian method seems to be that it does not show this. (*Some Versions*, p. 112)

This is the aspect of Empson's criticism that de Man fails to notice through his own preoccupation with the 'deep' ontological problems of poetic language. To borrow de Man's terminology, the 'insights' of his reading are tightly bound up with the 'blindness' it exhibits towards other, less congenial elements of Empson's thought.

The path of this divergence can be tracked with some precision through the course of de Man's argument. His account of Empson on 'The Garden' starts out from a point where he can almost paraphrase *Some Versions* yet manage to imply, in the same form of words, the 'ontological' bearing of Empson's remarks. Thus de Man: 'a reflection is not an identification, and the simple correspondence of the mind with the natural, far from being appeasing, turns troublesome' (*Blindness*, p. 239). By the next paragraph the argument has moved to a somewhat higher level of generalization. 'What is the pastoral convention', de Man asks, 'if not the eternal separation between the mind that distinguishes, negates, legislates, and the originary simplicity of the natural?' (*Blindness*, p. 232). Such language evokes ontological depths and perplexities which belong more properly to what Empson calls 'the Wordsworthian method', rather than Marvell's witty play of self-possessed pastoral conceits.

And then, within a page or so, de Man reaches the point of effectively declaring his revisionary bias. Pastoral figures as the counter-trope to *history*, in particular the Marxist understanding of history as the ground-principle of all interpretation. Empson has a good deal to say about the tensions between Marxist aesthetics (conceived, rather narrowly, as the call for 'proletarian literature') and the different, more complicated workings of pastoral convention. Yet, far from rejecting the Marxist set of claims, he examines their implications in a closely argued chapter, and then goes on to interpret his various texts in terms that always relate – however obliquely – to changing conditions of history and class-consciousness. No doubt *Some Versions* contains many statements which would seem politically suspect or evasive from a Marxist viewpoint. The pastoral strategy of 'putting the complex into the simple' produces a degree of ambivalence which affects both the genre and Empson's sympathetic treatment of it. But there is too much history and class-based analysis in Empson's pages for the book to be read as some kind of cryptic anti-Marxist tract.

Empson comes nearest to explaining his position in some comments on the topic of dialectical materialism. 'I do not mean to say that the philosophy is wrong,' he writes; 'for that matter pastoral is worked from the same philosophical ideas . . . the difference is that it brings in the absolute less prematurely' (*Some Versions*, p. 25). The 'absolute' in question is the grand Hegelian idea of a totalizing movement in thought and history whereby mind would eventually transcend the crass contingencies of time and place. Empson has his doubts about the effect of such idealist residues in Marxist thinking. As with Wordsworth, he resists the synthesizing claims of a rhetoric all too willing to collapse such merely logical obstacles to thought as stand in its way. The virtue of pastoral, Empson suggests, is to handle these claims with a certain ironic 'humility' and tact which saves them from turning into premature absolutes.

De Man is right enough to perceive the tensions that exist

between pastoral and the claims of any hard-line materialist dialectic. But the upshot of his reading is to force Empson's text towards another kind of 'absolute', one that negates historical understanding in the name of a more authentic, 'ontological' concern. It is the great strength of Empson's criticism, de Man writes, that it 'stands as a warning against certain Marxist illusions'. And again, more specifically: 'the problem of separation inheres in Being, which means that social forms of separation derive from ontological and meta-social attitudes' (*Blindness*, p. 240). De Man is able to quote convincingly from Empson to support this ontological reading. But he also has to ignore many passages that allow for no such smooth transition to the realm of metaphysical absolutes. What his reading most actively works to achieve is the subjugation of historical thought to a rhetoric of crisis and division descended from Hegel's 'unhappy consciousness'. As de Man interprets it,

> the pastoral problematic, which turns out to be the problematic of Being itself, is lived in our day by Marxist thought, as by any genuine thought. Marxism is, ultimately, a poetic thought that lacks the patience to think its own conclusions to their end. (*Blindness*, p. 240)

De Man finds this all the more striking for the fact that Empson sets out from a broadly political or sociological set of concerns. *Some Versions* should therefore be read, he argues, as an allegory of modern critical consciousness forced to acknowledge the inherent limitations of its own grounding concepts. Pastoral begins 'under the aegis of Marxism', the better to demonstrate the gulf which opens up between those twin fascinations of present-day theory, poetry on the one hand and politics on the other. Where Marxism holds out positive 'solutions', poetry remains resistant to the point of disrupting all attempts to contain its problematic nature. Empson thus serves de Man's argument in two exemplary roles. Ambiguity is the pretext for a powerful critique of the assumptions underlying any formalist aesthetic of premature reconciliation between language and experience. Pastoral then completes this process by implicitly contesting the truth-claims vested in the Marxist dialectic of history and consciousness.

IV

I have argued that de Man's is a strong misreading of Empson, an appropriative reading deeply committed to its own preoccupations of method and intent. But I also hope to have shown that Empson's criticism presses the analysis of poetic language to a stage where comparisons with de Man are still very much to the point. Empson's attitude of sturdy rationalism makes him far more resistant to the kinds of deep-rooted ontological perplexity which deconstruction discovers everywhere at work. His reading of Wordsworth shows Empson refusing to go along with the poetry and raise metaphysical problems to the level of transcendent (if problematic) truths. The example of Wordsworth, he writes, 'may show how these methods [i.e. those of verbal analysis] can be used to convict a poet of holding muddled opinions rather than to praise the complexity of the order of his mind' (*Seven Types*, p. 154). De Man's is essentially the opposite persuasion: that poetry is 'authentic' only in so far as it reveals the inability of language to disguise its own self-divided and problematic nature.

Hegel, Kierkegaard and Heidegger stand as exemplars for de Man's conviction that knowledge can only be achieved through a chastening of its own positive truth-claims, a *via negativa* of ontological doubt. Empson, on the contrary, assumes that language should always be accountable to some kind of rational argument, even where the process leads – as with Wordsworth – into regions of obscurely paradoxical sense. Rather than equate such obscurity with philosophic 'depth', Empson treats it as a habit of thought which may, on occasion, produce good poetry, but still needs explaining in logical terms. Thus Wordsworth 'sometimes uses what may be called philosophical ambiguities when he is not sure how far this process can tolerably be pushed' (*Seven Types*, p. 151). Such breakdowns in the logic of communicative sense are a symptom of *confusion* on Wordsworth's part, and not – as always for de Man – a symptom of language pushed up against the limits of figural undecidability.

Yet Empson and de Man have a good deal in common beyond the obvious fact that both represent a form of textual close reading that often works to problematize poetic language. They each hold out against the formalist desire to sacralize the poem as a 'verbal icon', a self-enclosed structure of rhetorical devices exempt from the sense-making context and conditions of language at large. In both, there is a will to demystify aesthetics and to press far beyond the kinds of compromise solution which New Criticism sought to impose. In the end, as I have argued, de Man must be seen as espousing a form of negative hermeneutics profoundly at odds with Empson's outlook of enlightened rationalist critique. But in the detailed working-out of these divergent positions they offer some exceptionally interesting grounds for comparison.

4

Transcendent fictions: imaginary discourse in Descartes and Husserl

Philosophers have always been reliant on fiction, and always prone to deny or disguise that reliance. Plato had much to say about the harmful effects of fictional representation, its tendency to substitute plausible myths for the rational pursuit of wisdom and truth. Yet Plato not only made use of illustrative fables but cast his entire philosophy in the form of fictional dialogues, composed with an almost novelistic sense of narrative shape and structure. That he knowingly embraced this patent double-standard is evident from his passages on poetry and fiction in *The Republic*.[1] Fables are bad, says Socrates, if they misrepresent the gods as behaving cruelly, practising deliberate deceits upon mortals or changing shape at whim. Better stifle such influences at source by censoring the poets – even Homer – where they fall into scurrilous nonsense. There remain the good fables, those which Socrates is given to approve for their respecting divinity and the citizenly virtues. Yet Plato makes plain his own attitude of enlightened rationalist scepticism. The myths are little more than handy devices for inculcating piety and obedience among those incapable of rising to abstract philosophic truth.

Thus fictions are devalued by a sovereign philosophy, only to emerge, in Plato's texts, as a constant resort in the face of popular ignorance and superstition. Socratic dialectic aspires to dispense with the props of mere fable and mimetic illusion. Yet the dialogues exploit all the strategies of 'literary' style and

presentation, from seductive local metaphor to full-scale allegory. And this, as I shall argue, is a double tactic – of repression
and covert exploitation – constantly repeated down through
the history of philosophic dealings with fiction. The ideal is a
knowledge of timeless and absolute validity, detached from
the merely circumstantial story of its own creating. Philosophy
at its purest must have no truck with any factual, contingent or
narrative interest, such as might attach to the philosopher's telling of how he arrived at his conclusions. The
danger here is twofold: that philosophy may find itself reduced to an unseemly dependence on accidents of time and
place; and, worse, that such a record might always be construed as a *fiction* masquerading as 'honest' intellectual auto-
biography. History and story can too easily become confused.
The presence of narrative entails the possibility that events – in
this case, mental events – might be so reconstructed as to
maximize interest (or narrative plausibility) at the expense of
straightforward truth. Even Aristotle, in his defence of poetry
against Plato's strictures, made sure to distinguish mimetic
and fictional 'truth' from the strict requirements of logical
reasoning.

On the one hand philosophy, the order of concepts, of
truths as distinct from mere stories or secondhand representations. On the other mimesis in its various forms, whether
dramatic or diegetic (presented directly as actions on a stage or
narrated as events in a story). This distinction is the characteristic gesture by which philosophers have marked off their
own, privileged domain from those of rhetoric, fiction or
literary criticism. Where they have wished, like Aristotle, to
include these latter as components of a unified general system,
it has always been on philosophy's terms, within a hierarchy of
discourses which grants priority to formal logic. Aristotle
doesn't so much contest Plato's premises as shift his argumentative ground so that the limited truth-claims of poetry no
longer get into conflict with philosophic reason. He thus sets
the pattern for a long line of theorists, from Sir Philip Sidney
('the poet nought affirmeth, but everything feigneth') to I. A.
Richards (poetry as 'emotive' language, immune to rational
criticism).[2] Such defences might be said to make little advance
upon Plato's charitable licence: that the poets can carry on

spinning their improbable tales so long as they observe the limits laid down by the guardian-philosopher.

Fiction is thus defined as the determinate *other* of philosophy, a realm of (barely) permissible untruth where the rules of normal, serious discourse are provisionally lifted. This attitude is not too hard to maintain where the 'others' concerned are poets, critics or rhetoricians, happy enough (like Plato's set-piece interlocutors) to play their allotted roles and thus assist in the philosopher's self-elevating act. The problems arise where fiction gets a hold within the very discourse of philosophy. Sir Philip Sidney scored a palpable hit when he remarked that Plato himself was not above using 'poetic' means – metaphor, allegory and myth – in the service of his philosophic arguments.[3] And indeed, the more closely one reads philosophical texts, the more one comes across similar evidence of a covert narrative or fictional strain.

Put simply, the situation seems to be as follows. Philosophy most typically aims at an *a priori* knowledge in possession of which – at its moment of maximal lucidity and grasp – all contingent exposition should simply drop away. The philosopher's life history and previous ideas would belong to the *vita ante acta* of his present achievement, having no part to play in its essential genesis. The act of cognition would be self-guaranteed by the fact of its belonging to this separate realm of clear and distinct ideas. Such has been the persistent faith of philosophers, from Plato to Descartes and thence to such modern schools of thought as Husserlian phenomenology. Plato upheld the transcendent reality of abstract forms or ideas, as opposed to the second-order realm of material appearances (and, of course, the third-order products of artistic mimesis). Descartes strove for a minimal assurance of incontrovertible knowledge, such that the mind could at least presume to rest on a knowledge of its own existence in the present act of taking thought. Thence might be derived – by a kind of collateral deduction – the objective reality of that which the mind was given to contemplate outside itself. For Husserl, this Cartesian gesture was the starting-point for a full-scale phenomenological regrounding of thought in relation to the world of experience. Descartes's experiment in sceptical doubt became a model for the technique of 'suspending' all that might pertain to mere individual perception or subjective awareness.[4] Philosophy would thus gain access to the 'transcendental ego', whose workings could be said to constitute the nature and limits of consciousness in general. This would in turn become the basis of a renewed philosophical and scientific confidence in the mind's power to perceive and comprehend objective reality.

In each of these cases, philosophy wills itself into being by an act of *exclusion*, a gesture which legitimizes its own claims to knowledge by devaluing whatever lies beyond its sovereign conceptual grasp. Husserl wants to suspend every 'fact' of supposedly self-evident experience which might, just conceivably, issue from a merely subjective or distorting viewpoint. Commonsense assumptions may be a species of fictitious beliefs held in place by our need to imagine a shared world of meaning and experience. Descartes is yet more explicit in equating the irrational, the pre-philosophic, with the idea of misleading fables and fictions. Might not the commonsense fabric of our knowledge be spun by some deceiving demiurge with no other purpose than to lead us into error? This *malin génie* of Descartes's creating is close kin to those poets and dramatists whom Plato mistrusted for their power of dissimulating suasion. For Descartes, the fictions are projected from within, like those dreams which leave us hard put to it to distinguish between waking and sleeping.

The first *Discourse* has a passage reflecting on the natural liability of fables to 'make one imagine many events to be possible that are not'. This danger extends furthermore to historical narratives, since these most often work to sustain the reader's interest by selective emphasis on actions and events beyond the common order of experience. Hence the result, according to Descartes, 'that those who base their own behaviour on the examples they draw from it risk falling into the extravagances of the *paladins* of our novels and conceive designs beyond their powers.'[5] Yet, just a few paragraphs before this passage, Descartes may be found putting forward his essay as 'nothing more than an historical account, or, if you prefer, a fable in which, among certain examples one may follow, one may find also many others which it would be right not to copy'.[6] And indeed his philosophical arguments are embedded in a narrative which provides both a context and a seeming rationale for their unfolding. Descartes's career, his practical interests and abstruse researches all converge on the dawning realization of *cogito, ergo sum*. More specifically, this moment is prepared for by the circumstantial details ('Germany . . . the wars . . . the coronation of the Emperor . . . the onset of winter . . . finding no company . . . no cares or passions to distract me . . . shut up in a room heated by an enclosed stove . . . leisure to meditate on my own thoughts') which form the preamble to his crucial Second Discourse.[7] The *cogito* supervenes, so to speak, as the looked-for resolution of a complicated narrative which works to portend precisely such a leap of imaginative thought.

Act or essence?

Jaakko Hintikka has argued, in a well-known essay,[8] that philosophers have mostly been wide of the mark in their attempts to justify (or to criticize) Descartes's central maxim. They have assumed that *cogito, ergo sum*, if valid, must be a product of purely inferential reasoning. In that case the existence of the thinking (first-person) subject would be logically entailed in the act of thought. But, as Hintikka points out, such inference has nothing to do with *thinking* as such, since any ascription of activity (e.g. walking) would likewise entail an existing agent. In fact it was Gassendi, a contemporary of Descartes, who first remarked that *ambulo, ergo sum* was as valid as the *cogito* on these logical terms. Furthermore, Hintikka argues, there is no proving the actual existence of the first-person subject from the fact that logic, in a certain formal mode, necessarily *assumes* it. Such existential presuppositions 'make more or less tacit use of the assumption that all the singular terms with which we have to deal really refer to (designate) some actually existing individual'.[9] But this of course means that the first-person subject of Descartes's formulation is 'proved' to exist only as the empty entailment of a foregone logical conclusion.

So how is the *cogito* to be saved from pure circularity or logical inconsequence? Hintikka suggests that we construe it as a species of *performative* utterance, such that the act of thinking, *so long as it is carried on*, bears along with it a knowledge of first-person agency on the thinker's part. He makes the point as follows:

> The function of the word *cogito* in Descartes's dictum is to refer to the thought-act through which the existential self-verifiability of 'I exist' manifests itself. Hence the indubitability of this sentence is not strictly speaking perceived *by means* of thinking (in the way the indubitability of a demonstrable truth may be said to be); rather, it is indubitable *because* and *in so far as* it is actively thought of.[10]

This succeeds in avoiding the two main pitfalls of Cartesian interpretation. It escapes the logical circularity which undermines any purely inferential link between *cogito* and *sum*. At the same time it avoids having recourse to a purely introspective or intuitive account which would lack any demonstrative force. Descartes's maxim can be justified as expressing the *present impossibility* of doubting his own existence for the thinker actively engaged in the process of thought. Its performative character is the key to its otherwise elusive logical structure.

Hintikka writes of 'thought acts' rather than 'speech acts', though his argument clearly derives from J. L. Austin's distinction between 'constative' and 'performative' modes of utterance.[11] It is, after all, in the *language* of Descartes's philosophic reasoning that the *cogito* achieves its moment of self-vindicating insight. For the commentator likewise, there is no route of access to Descartes's ideas except through the verbal chain, the sequential complex of meanings, wherein they are embedded. Of course there might seem to be a danger here of reading back our modern linguistic preoccupations into Descartes's express concern with 'clear and distinct' ideas. Where philosophers now think in terms of verbal entities – sentences, statements, propositions – the corresponding seventeenth-century interest was in *ideas* as supposedly present to awareness through an act of lucid self-inspection.[12] Descartes adheres to this dominant epistemology in his resolve 'to include in my judgements nothing more than what presented itself so clearly and so distinctly to my mind that I might have no occasion to place it in doubt'.[13] But such passages belong – so Hintikka would argue – to that introspective strain in Descartes's philosophy which makes little sense from a modern, logical point of view. His 'performative' reading of the *cogito* is intended to redeem it, for philosophic purposes, from the various confused ideas which sometimes attend its exposition.

This requires, in effect, an act of *translation* by which to bring out the contemporary import and relevance of Descartes's argument. The 'linguistic turn' in modern philosophy involves a distinctly selective treatment of whatever it is given to interpret. This emerges from Hintikka's reading in the fact that the *ergo* of Descartes's maxim must appear misplaced or merely redundant if it turns out to serve no logical or inferential function. Deprived of its apparently deductive force, the statement might just as well run *ego cogito, ego sum*. Such translations into a different context of relevance are always possible, as much with philosophical as literary texts. Thus Kant, for example, is selectively reread to bring his transcendental deductions into line with the appointed limits of modern (linguistic-analytical) thinking.[14] Hintikka pursues a similar course in his 'performative' reading of Descartes. He attends, that is, to what the argument requires its language to perform, or – more to the point – how language affects the very tenor of the argument, given that thought is indissolubly linked to the performative act which determines its bearing. Descartes's 'ideas' are thus translated into the latter-day conceptual idiom of linguistic philosophy.

It then becomes a question of how such readings can claim validity and not appear to license an endless free-for-all of rival updatings. Hintikka adopts a familiar technique, that of the selective appeal to tradition. He points out that the *cogito* of Descartes was anticipated both by St Thomas and St Augustine, but that only St Thomas seems to have grasped its true, performative character. This followed from the central Aquinan premiss that 'the intellect knows itself not by its essence but by its act'. Of course there is an element of circular reasoning here: the precursor is picked out to support the very reading of Descartes which makes him (Aquinas) the favoured candidate. But some such appeal to tradition seems necessary

if philosophy is not to give way before the relativism always
implicit in acts of revisionist interpretation. The 'performative'
turn is especially threatening in this respect, since it translates
out of an original idiom of 'clear and distinct ideas', and *into* a
much more pragmatic discourse based on varieties of plausible
intent. Thus Hintikka's argument ultimately comes down to
what Descartes *must be construed* as having meant, according to
the currently most cogent (or persuasive) reading.

The danger is, to repeat, that this will seem just one more
interesting construction placed upon Descartes's elusive text.
As we have seen, it is characteristic of philosophy to eschew
such mere 'interpretation' in the interests of arriving at a
demonstrable truth immune to further vagaries of meaning.
That philosophers might be in the business of improvising,
rather than constructing *a priori* valid arguments, has remained unthinkable (for most of them) since Socrates laid
down the rules of the game. Yet what are we to make of
Descartes's statement – however disingenuous – that the
Discourse may be read as 'fable' or 'history' if the reader is of a
mind to take it that way? What again of his remark, in the First
Discourse, that 'I shall say nothing about philosophy', since its
problems have been debated 'by the very best minds which
have ever existed over several centuries', and yet not one of
them settled or placed beyond reasonable doubt?[15] 'Philosophy' would seem to represent, for Descartes, a subject less
clear and distinct than the ideas which supposedly provide its
indubitable grounding. The irony is oddly compounded by his
employment of such eminently Cartesian language ('the very
best *minds* which have ever *existed*') by way of casting doubt on
philosophy's claims to knowledge. The effect is to place a
certain critical distance between the self-sufficient *cogito* of the
Second Discourse and the framing narrative which serves to
introduce it. The prehistory of Descartes's opinions and development threatens to displace – or at least somewhat to
complicate – the ground-rule of Cartesian method.

Hintikka offers a performative reading of the isolated formula *cogito, ergo sum*. Despite his anti-essentialist arguments,
this is still to take it on trust that the maxim contains the
central, contestable element of Descartes's philosophy – that to
which everything else in the text must be considered strictly

subordinate. This assumption works to keep a hold on the *Discourse* as fit material for *philosophic* treatment, as opposed to mere 'interpretation'. It functions, that is to say, as a kind of disciplinary check on the otherwise threatening possibility that Descartes's text may prove of more interest as a narrative, or even (in some degree) as a *fictional* construct. Yet Hintikka is obliged to tell a complicated story of his own in order to make good sense of Descartes's crucial formulation. The story involves a speculative reconstruction of the influences, motives and possible confusions which went into the making of Cartesian discourse. It takes in not only precursors like Augustine and Aquinas, but also those subsequent commentators (down to Hintikka himself) whose interpretative problems with Descartes are construed as having figured, however obscurely, in his own consciousness. Thus Descartes is presented as hoping to 'jump' from one to another of the different interpretations that Hintikka places on the *cogito*. What we are offered, in effect, is a complex narrative of mental events recounted from a standpoint – like that of the omniscient narrator – capable of seeing both *into* and *beyond* the thoughts of his central character.

This emerges most clearly from the following passage, where Hintikka entertains – only to reject – the 'inferential' reading of Descartes's dictum.

> I do not want to deny that it expresses *one* of the things Descartes had more or less confusedly in mind when he formulated his famous dictum. But it is important to realize that this interpretation is defective in important respects. It does not help to elucidate in any way some of Descartes's most explicit and most careful formulations. It is at best a partial interpretation.[16]

'Partial', one may ask, in comparison with what? Hintikka's reading is undeniably partial in the sense that it needs to overrule *de jure* those other formulations which he regards as belonging to Descartes's more 'popular', hence less rigorous attempts at explaining his ideas. Nor is the 'dictum' itself quite free of the confusions which apparently beset the whole enterprise of which it purports to be the crowning statement. The *cogito*, whatever its 'performative' status, is riven by doubts as to how it might connect with the governing purpose of Descartes's writings. It is, after all, a very striking turn of argument when Hintikka is forced to conclude that Descartes had various things 'confusedly in mind' at the very moment of formulating the *cogito*. Within the sovereign gesture of philosophic thought – of consciousness claiming to secure and comprehend its own existence – there appears the shadow of a complicating doubt. And this doubt possesses a curious contaminating power. It spreads itself, not only through Descartes's writings, but through the texts of those, like Hintikka, who seek to overcome or dispel it.

Fables of identity: Descartes, Hamlet, Beckett

Hintikka keeps such doubts at bay by supposing that the 'thought act' of Cartesian reason can at least in principle – or on occasion – coincide with the verbal proposition which expresses it. He may take leave to question whether Descartes ever attained a full understanding of the 'proper' interpretation required by his cardinal insight. On the other hand he needs to assume – if his reading stands up – that the *cogito* involved an 'existential' (or thought-act) commitment on the philosopher's part which left small room for the alternative (inferential) reading. Descartes is represented as struggling, however 'confusedly', to achieve a valid knowledge atop all these shifts of logical perspective. Yet this, as we have seen, is precisely the kind of cognitive assurance which Descartes's text not only fails to sustain but actively calls into question.

The performative character of *cogito, ergo sum* depends on its *not* being *merely* a performance, a staging or rehearsal of the philosophic move which Descartes has planned all along as a climax to his well-turned narrative. Austin's notion of speech-act 'felicity' requires that the speaker *mean what he or she says* as well as observing the appropriate conventions in saying it. Austin expressly denies that these conditions can be met by such 'parasitical' or pseudo-performative instances as speech acts spoken in jest, uttered on the stage or merely invented (as of characters in a novel). These exclusions create the rather obvious problem that performatives are *always* in a certain sense 'parasitical', since their force derives from their properly conforming to standard protocols of utterance. Speech acts are purely conventional, not only in deviant cases (by default of good faith), but because they necessarily work by respecting a reiterable verbal formula.

Austin's rejection of narrative or fictional speech acts has a bearing on the problems of interpreting Descartes's dictum. That the *Discourse* might indeed be taken as a 'fable' is sufficient to threaten the integrity of the *cogito* at precisely that point where genuine knowledge is required to take over from mere 'introspection'. Hintikka demands, like Austin, that speech acts (in this case, propositions) correspond to the thought acts which should properly accompany them. Such is the 'existential presupposition' which saves the *cogito* from falling into logical vacuity or circular argument. Hence the decisive importance of *thinking* as a proof of the thinker's participant existence in the self-present act of thought. As Hintikka puts it:

> This performance could be described only by a 'verb of intellection' like *cogitare*. For this reason, the verb *cogitare* was for Descartes a privileged one; for this reason nothing could for him belong to his nature that was 'something distinct from his thinking'.[17]

But what if the *cogito* – to take up Austin's point – were encountered in the course of a fictional narrative, or quoted in some other context? What remains of Descartes's inaugural thought act if one cannot be certain that his words correspond to any clear or distinct cognition? It might be the case that *cogito, ergo sum* is not so much a valid 'existential' proposition as a kind of narrative denouement, skilfully led up to through a sequence of fictional pretexts. And indeed it is impossible to rule this out *de jure*, since Descartes's text itself entertains the notion. If philosophical reasoning is a species of performative utterance, it remains to be asked: what *kind* of performance, and within what authenticating order of discourse?

It seems at least arguable, on the evidence so far, that the *cogito* partakes as much of narrative as of logical or indeed 'existential' necessity. This would apply, not only to Descartes, but to any text which attempted to draw a line between the rational self-evidence of philosophy and the merely contingent record of how that knowledge was arrived at. One need not invoke the *malin génie* to make the point that such texts can always be read as products of narrative contrivance. This is merely to remark that philosophers write, not only in response to abstract problems, but in order to make at least provisional sense of their own preoccupations and history of thought. Some element of narrative shaping, or selective reconstruction, goes along with any attempt to clarify the process by which a starting-point in 'hunch' or intuition leads on to the achievement of an argued philosophical case. The unwritten assumption is that reason will discriminate the core propositions or content (*cogito, ergo sum*) from those parts of the text which merely provide a kind of narrative setting. And it is precisely this assumption that begins to look shaky if one asks – like Descartes – how far we can distinguish philosophical from fictional discourse.

Hintikka offers an example from Shakespeare to demonstrate the uselessness of a purely inferential reading of the *cogito*. 'Hamlet did think a great many things; does it follow that he existed?'[18] The point, of course, is that *cogito, ergo sum* has genuine performative status only when uttered by the first-person subject whose existence as agent of thought is thereby guaranteed. The ascription of such thought acts to fictional characters fails to meet the strict Austinian requirements of performative validity. Yet there is a sense – and no very perverse or paradoxical sense – in which Hamlet has quite as good a claim to 'exist' as the author of the *Discourse on Method*. That Hamlet is a character in a play, and Descartes the first-person subject of a philosophic text, may induce us to weigh their arguments according to different criteria. But there is nothing to prevent us from attaching a similar philosophical import to Hamlet's *words*, had he (or, rather, Shakespeare) hit upon the same 'existential' formula. Conversely, there is nothing in Descartes's text which would render the *cogito* radically proof against a narrative or fictional reading. Historical record warrants our belief that Descartes was once an existent individual and Hamlet (at least, the Shakespearian Hamlet) never more than a product of the dramatist's art. But the fact remains that they are both of them known to us only by means of our construing the *texts* wherein their thoughts take 'performative' shape.

Hamlet is an obvious example for Hintikka to choose, since its brooding soliloquies strongly suggest a Cartesian obsession with the puzzles of existence and identity. One could, however, multiply comparisons to enforce the general point. Samuel Beckett, for one, exploits the Cartesian predicament of characters who retain a lucid self-awareness while reduced to the utmost of physical privation. Critics have shown the extent of Beckett's reading in Descartes and those of his successors, like Geulincx, who arrived at a yet more extreme version of the mind–body dualism. John Pilling explores this Cartesian connection in a fine chapter on Beckett's intellectual sources.

> However much his body may disintegrate, no Beckett character doubts that, at least for the duration of the fictional work which calls him into existence, he is engaged in the act of thinking.[19]

This amounts, Pilling argues, to a *reductio ad absurdum* of Descartes's doctrine that thinking alone provides evidence of the physically existent world, and then only for the individual thinker who effectively wills it into being.

Beckett's is plainly 'philosophical' fiction which achieves its curious mixture of comedy and pathos by exploiting these uncannily suggestive ideas. But the reverse is also true, in the sense that Descartes presses philosophical scepticism to the point where its arguments enter the domain of fictional imagining. Pilling recounts a cryptic exchange between Beckett and Joyce which nicely illustrates the point. 'How could the idealist Hume write a history?' Joyce apparently asked; to which Beckett replied: 'A history of representations.'[20] The end-point of epistemological scepticism is a radically constructivist viewpoint which reduces all knowledge to a species of fictional projection. The Cartesian *cogito* is no longer immune to the nagging suspicion that its very existence may be a product of narrative contriving. Far from acting as a rock-bottom guarantee for the existence of a reality outside itself, the mind is thrown back upon an endless series of ungrounded 'representations'.

Returning to Hintikka's *Hamlet* comparison, it thus becomes possible to ask what grounds there might be for accepting his crucial distinction. Textual mimesis, or representation, plays a part in the unfolding of Descartes's arguments, as it does – more acceptably – in the tragical history of Hamlet, Prince of Denmark. There is no good reason for allowing a genuine 'performative' force to the *cogito*, while denying that similar consequences flow from Hamlet's 'To be, or not to be . . .' Hamlet's reflection may lack the appearance of deductive form (which in any case, according to Hintikka, is not the philosophical heart of Descartes's argument). If what counts is the 'thought act' supposedly entailed by reflective uses of language, then Hamlet's soliloquy might just as well serve as evidence of Hamlet's self-conscious 'existence'. At this level of argument the fact of his being 'merely' a character in a play need pose no additional problems. With Descartes likewise, we have only his word for it that thought act corresponds to speech act, or present awareness to its verbal representation. In each case the operative form of words carries as much – or as little – 'existential' significance as one cares to attribute to it. The first-person subject of the *cogito* is as much a figment of language as Hamlet himself.

Suspending judgement: fictions in Husserl

It is not by chance that phenomenology includes, as one of its prominent subdisciplines, a large body of work on literary theory and interpretation. Such criticism aims at uncovering the distinctive structures of consciousness which characterize different authors, texts or habits of reader-response. This approach is most often identified with the so-called 'Geneva School' of critics, among whom Georges Poulet is perhaps the best known.[21] It claims to operate at a level beyond the linguistic surface of the text, seeking out patterns of perceptual experience and meaningful order which yield up their secrets only to such an inward, phenomenological reading. Thus Poulet explores the different modalities of internal time-consciousness as these affect the writings of Montaigne, Pascal, Descartes and others.[22] The object is always to isolate those qualities of consciousness and imaginative experience which leave their unique impression on what is loosely called 'structure' or 'style'.

Other critics, like Wolfgang Iser, focus their attention on the ways in which the *reader* comes to recognize or interpret these facets of the literary text.[23] Iser points to those narrative 'gaps' or elements of thematic 'indeterminacy' which demand that the reader flesh out the text by various acts of interpretative insight. Such openings become the more frequent, he shows, as novelists develop ever more subtle techniques for placing their own omniscient authority in question. Iser's applied phenomenology of reading thus aims to heal the breach between formalist theories of the literary text and subjective accounts of the reader's (more or less private) response. It claims to transcend such hateful autonomies by locating the experience of an answerable reading precisely *within* the possibilities opened up by the text itself.

It could be argued that these 'literary' uses are alien to the grounding rationale of Husserlian thought. In his later writings, Husserl became increasingly insistent that the method of phenomenological reduction should lead back beyond such subjectively variable layers of experience to the constitution of a 'transcendental ego', implied by every possible act of consciousness or perception. The *Cartesian Meditations* of 1929 are the major source for this rigorous understanding of Husserlian precept and practice. The following passage is representative:

> It would be much too great a mistake, if one said that to follow this line of research is nothing else than to make *psychological descriptions* based on purely internal experience, experience of one's own conscious life . . . a great mistake, because a *purely descriptive psychology of consciousness* is *not itself transcendental phenomenology* as we have defined the latter, in terms of the transcendental phenomenological reduction.[24]

This would certainly disqualify much of what currently passes for 'phenomenological' criticism, in so far as the interpreter's main concern is with describing (like Poulet) those qualities peculiar to the individual author or work in hand. Iser's project perhaps comes closer to Husserl's specification, since its findings can be generalized into something which resembles a universal grammar of reflective reader-response. Still it might be argued that *aesthetics*, rather than criticism, is the proper domain of phenomenological theory – its aim being not to interpret individual works but to isolate the defining or constitutive elements of literary response in general. Roman Ingarden is true to this rigorous Husserlian project in his analysis of the many-levelled 'intentional' structure of literary works of art.[25]

We may remark a certain pattern of Cartesian origin repeating itself here. Descartes had a principled mistrust of fictions but was unable to exclude them absolutely from his philosophic reasonings. The *cogito* emerged as the upshot of a narrative which cannot (as I have argued) be simply set aside in the interests of a higher, self-authenticating truth. Philosophy entertains fictions at the risk of finding its homeground invaded by their numerous progeny. The literary offshoots of Husserlian method exemplify a similar process at work. And the problem cannot be contained by simply ruling *de jure* that such applications are not to count as 'genuine' phenomenological research. For the fact is that fictions play a prominent and highly ambiguous role in Husserl's own writings. At the heart of phenomenological enquiry is the same suspicion which Descartes admitted, though always with a view to outflanking or containing its ultimate subversive effects.

Husserl devotes a great deal of complex argument to the matter of distinguishing the 'actual' from the 'fictional' as modes of mental experience. He begins by drawing another, preliminary distinction: between this pair of terms and the couplet 'real'/'unreal', which he takes to refer to a wholly different order of judgement.

> Predicates of existence, which have their counterparts in negations of existence, must not be confused with predicates of actuality, which have their counterparts in predicates of nonactuality, of fiction.[26]

The non-existent can only be conceived as negation, as devoid of the predicative status which attaches to all genuine (i.e. real or conceivable) objects of consciousness. Fiction, on the other hand, *does* possess an aspect of 'reality' in so far as it relates to representations which undeniably have their place in our waking thoughts. At the outset we have no need for such distinctions. Reality is comprised in the 'natural' or pre-reflective attitude where experience is simply 'pre-given' or assumed as a matter of straightforward commonsense perception. The non-existent supervenes as an abstract negation of this naturalized realist ontology. Fiction belongs to a different dimension since it represents or *simulates* the real so as to produce its own distinct form of imaginative credence. Talk of the 'actual' (as opposed to the 'fictional') is only called for when we come to recognize this further distinction. It is clear enough (to adopt Austin's sexist metaphor) which concept wears the logical trousers here. 'Actuality' is brought into service by way of supplying a positive counterpart to the realm of imaginative fictions.

Lest this summary seem impossibly abstruse, let me quote – in all fairness – a passage from Husserl which follows out the same line of argument. (I quote at some length so as to give a firm hold for subsequent discussion.)

> It is only when we imagine, and, taking a position beyond the attitude which characterizes life, we pass to actualities given in the attitude of imagination (the attitude of quasi-experience in its different modes), and when, in addition, going beyond the occasional isolated act of imagination and its objects, we take them as examples of possible imagination in general and of fictions in general that there arise for us the concept of fiction (or imagination) and, on the other hand, the concepts of 'possible experience in general' and 'actuality'.[27]

Again, it seems a case where the negative concept wears the logical trousers. 'Actuality' figures in our consciousness only as opposed to 'fiction', which thus becomes the ground – according to Husserl – of all 'possible experience in general'. Hence his reiterated argument that fictions are *not* the 'negation' of reality, but in some sense compose a separate order of judgement with its own distinct claims to eidetic consistency and truth.

This argument has two distinct consequences for the general

unfolding of Husserlian phenomenology. Its avowed *purpose* is to mark out a conceptual space for the activities of imagination, while preventing them from interfering with the primary business of phenomenological enquiry. Thus 'fictions' are opposed to 'actuality' by a gesture of containment which denies that they can properly get into conflict with 'the real'. Philosophy is confirmed in its prior commitment to acts of consciousness which bear upon objects or events in the existent life-world. At the same time it is able to accommodate fictions as strictly second-order or derivative phenomena. 'Only he who lives in experience and from there "dips into" imagination, whereby what is imagined contrasts with what is experienced, can have the concepts of fiction and actuality.'[28] To this extent the imaginary is firmly held in place by a primary concern with lived experience.

So much for Husserl's express categorical purposes. Yet, returning to the above-quoted passage, one remarks how the concept of fiction can nevertheless tend, in its very formulation, to upset the terms by which its secondary status is supposedly maintained. 'Actuality', we have seen, is an idea derivative from 'fiction', a conceptual counterpart brought into being by the need for some corresponding opposite term. Yet actuality is equated by Husserl with 'possible experience in general', a dimension which can scarcely be held distinct from the normal speculative range of phenomenological enquiry. In the opening sentence, likewise, the act of imagining is treated analogously with that of 'taking a position beyond the attitude which characterizes life'. Again, this description might just as well apply to the generalized method of 'phenomenological reduction' which suspends our 'natural' or commonsense assumptions in pursuit of purely *a priori* knowledge. It thus becomes increasingly difficult, on a close reading of Husserl's text, to distinguish reality from fiction, or first-order phenomenological thought from that subsidiary discipline which deals with imaginary constructs. Husserl may speak of 'quasi-experience', or the 'as if' attitude of provisional credence which characterizes fictional experience. But the logic of his argument raises doubts whether the imaginary can really be prevented from leaving its impress on the very foundations of phenomenological certitude.

Worlds out of time: Husserl and Derrida

Shall we conclude, as with Descartes, that fiction pervades every attempt to raise philosophy to the self-respecting status of an absolute knowledge? Husserl, of course, cannot countenance such an argument. He therefore sets about providing a form of transcendental deduction which would clearly distinguish the real from the fictional as modes of reflective awareness. The passage once again needs quoting at length:

> In between the lived experiences of the perceptive intention of objects in the actual world there can appear – without connection with them – lived experiences of imagination, which are directed toward fictions, toward objectivities intended as fictions. These have *no connection with the perceptions*; this means: while all perceptions with regard to the objects intended in them are joined together in a unity and have reference to the unity of a single world, the objectivities of imagination fall outside this unity; they do not join together in the same way.[29]

Fictions, in short, stand apart from the various tacit continuities of knowledge and experience which we depend upon (however unconsciously) for our sense of waking reality. Most important of these, for Husserl, is the element of time-consciousness which always relates the first-person individual to an 'absolute present', a temporal position uniquely his or hers to occupy. Time may be *represented* in the imagination – even, Husserl says, 'intuitively represented' – but it remains a kind of 'quasi-time', a floating temporality without any present anchor-point. Fictions are therefore apprehended as distinct from the lived continuities of everyday experience. They exist or unfold in a *virtual* time which cannot be confused with its real counterpart.

This applies both to fictional entities like centaurs and to products of the narrative imagination. In each case we are aware, according to Husserl, that the representation belongs to a realm where occurrences are unrelated one to another by any self-present moment of experience.

> The centaur which I now imagine, and a hippopotamus which I have previously imagined, and, in addition, the

table I am perceiving even now have no connection among themselves, i.e., they have *no temporal position in relation to one another*.[30]

With fictional narratives likewise, the temporal sequence is purely internal (a matter of interrelated tenses), and at no point coincides with the lived present of experience. Yet Husserl has to recognize that there *is* in fact a unifying consciousness at work when we read narrative texts. Despite the 'essential disconnectedness' of imaginary events, their narration brings about a continuity of interest, on the reader's part, which effectively sustains the fictional illusion. Such unity is always possible, Husserl argues, in so far as 'in all imaginings . . . there is constituted a single *quasi-world*, partly intuited, partly intended in empty horizons'[31] – 'empty' in the sense that such imaginary 'horizons' are viewed from no particular or privileged position, their limits being those of a virtual space, like the virtual time of fictional narration. Yet Husserl here seems very close to admitting the ultimate convergence of the real and the imagined, since both come about through a unifying act of mental presentation.

Husserl takes as his generic example the fairy-tale, a species of fiction as remote as possible from the everyday, natural world. Such 'free imaginings' are grasped under the aspect of a narrative flow which carries the reader along by creating the conditions for sustained, active involvement. As Husserl describes it, the process resembles that 'willing suspension of disbelief' which Coleridge defined as the chief source of pleasure in certain forms of narrative poetry. Fairy-tales figure for Husserl as pre-eminent examples of a 'quasi-actuality' that keeps its imaginary distance from the real precisely by virtue of its self-enclosed fictional world. Such products of fantasy create their own simulated time-span, a temporal rhythm of memories and anticipations which the reader comprehends *by analogy* with lived experience. There remains, however, this decisive difference between actual and fictional worlds: that the latter involve no anchor-point of reference to the real-time continuum of past–present–future within which we all necessarily live. Fictional time is a highly provisional modality which nowhere relates to the singular experience of the self-present ego.

But again one might ask: how is that experience guaranteed proof against the imaginary constructions which it so much resembles? Take the following passage, where Husserl describes the temporal ordering of imaginary (fairy-tale) events:

> Each new stretch is linked to the preceding one by an obscure horizon, but one capable of further development, whereby the obscure memories are for me, the continuing reader of the tale, actual memories of what I have already read and which have been imagined by me, while in the course of my engagement with the tale the linkage takes place in 'memories in imagination', which are themselves quasi-memories.[32]

The processing of narrative thus reduplicates, at an imaginary level, the experience of time as registered in our real-life waking thoughts. The latter are characterized by Husserl (in *The Phenomenology of Internal Time-Consciousness*) as a complex amalgam of present awareness, past memories and future anticipations.[33] Memories can in turn be classified into two distinct types, according to their temporal placing in relation to the present moment. 'Retentions' are the memories of just-past events whose traces linger on into the present and constitute a kind of momentary retroactive linkage. As these events recede into the subject's prehistory, so they take on a definitely *past* significance, henceforth to be marked as *representations* of that which once took place. Husserl finds a similar distinction at work in the forward-looking character of consciousness. He uses the term 'protention' to describe the moment-to-moment anticipative character of present experience. Quite distinct from this, and beyond the grasp of immediate, intuitive awareness, is the knowledge of a future as yet unrealized except as indefinite possibility. Each of these dimensions, past and future, has reference to the privileged existential moment of self-present thought.

It will be seen that this account of internal time-consciousness has much in common with Husserl's phenomenology of narrative, as summarized above. The temporal predicament of reading is akin point for point to that of lived experience, except for such terms as 'quasi-memory' which register its imaginary status. Otherwise the 'possible worlds' of fictional creation are subsumed under the same phenomenological description as applies to their 'actual' counterparts. They are distinguished only by the sense of open possibility which removes them from any definite grounding in time or place. In the actual world, 'nothing remains open; it is what it is'. In fictional worlds, on the other hand, things are what they are 'by grace of the imagination'. Here we encounter a 'complex of imaginings' which 'never comes to an end' but always leaves open 'the possibility of a free development in the sense of a new determination'. Yet even then, Husserl maintains, such freedom is inherently limited by the 'unity' required of each imaginary world, the 'encompassing form of the time of imagination pertaining to it'.[34]

I have attempted to convey the extraordinary lengths of argumentation to which Husserl seems forced in his effort to distinguish fictional from lived experience. Like Descartes, he needs to make good this distinction if philosophy is to carry through its primary endeavour, that of interpreting the world from the standpoint of a sovereign or 'transcendental' consciousness. That this standpoint might itself be the product of a *radical fiction* is of course a possibility which Husserl cannot seriously entertain. Yet what is the 'method' of phenomenological reduction if not the imagining of a possible world inhabited by intelligences pure enough to perceive their own constitutive workings? Husserl characterizes the fairy-tale as a work of 'unencumbered imagination', conceived in an ideal freedom from real-life laws and constraints. For all his strenuous arguments to the contrary, it is a similar movement from the real to the 'actual', and thence to a realm of ideal imagining, that typifies the moment of Husserlian meditation.

Jacques Derrida makes the point rather differently in his deconstructive reading of Husserl's major texts.[35] Phenomenology requires a transcendental grounding in the self-present acts of a consciousness turned in upon its own momentary workings. To this end Husserl sets up a whole series of distinctions between primary (authentic) and secondary (derivative) orders of meaning and experience. For internal time-consciousness, the present – as we have seen – is the privileged moment whence derive our various dependent gradations of pastness and futurity. When it comes to language, Husserl discriminates 'expressive' from 'indicative' signs, the former endowed with intentional meaning, the latter signifying only by routine convention and possessing no authentic expressive force. Derrida deconstructs these oppositions to remarkable effect. The notional 'present' of Husserlian time is an imaginary construct which can only be conceived as existing in the hiatus, the differential gap between past and future, 'retention' and 'protention'. Meaning in language is likewise dependent on pre-existing structures and relationships which prevent any appeal to originary acts of 'expression' on the part of individual speakers. Language is *difference* through and through, an articulated network of signifying elements where signs can never be assumed to coincide with a pure, self-identical meaning. Such is the 'indicative' character of language which everywhere forestalls and implicitly questions the 'expressive' potential which Husserl would claim for it. Temporality and language are both decentred in relation to the self-present subject of Husserlian philosophy. The transcendental ego turns out to be an empty subject-position, an imaginary construct incapable of playing its required phenomenological role.

Derrida's reading lends further support to my argument that *fictions* are everywhere present – even when apparently contained or marginalized – in Husserl's reflections on mental life. Like Descartes, he thinks to admit the imaginary only on his own special terms, but finds it rewriting those terms to the point where crucial distinctions begin to break down. The 'quasi-' prefix comes to seem little more than a saving resort in the face of this unlooked-for convergence of real and imaginary. It becomes increasingly clear that 'the temporal unity of lived experience' finds a duplicate realm – and not merely a secondary analogue – at the level of narrative imagining. And this points in turn to the act of *imaginary* suspension which Husserl posits as the opening move and most characteristic gesture of phenomenological enquiry. To relinquish the 'natural' (or commonsense) attitude is prerequisite, Husserl would argue, to a grasp of *a priori* thought acts and judgements. Yet a similar gesture appears to characterize that fictional 'suspension' of the natural world which permits imagination to work

its unifying effects. The 'possible worlds' of imaginary experience are closely related to the philosophic quest for those
structures of awareness which mark out the limits of possible
experience in general.

Dreams of reason: fiction in philosophy

What we find in Husserl (as in Descartes) is the philosophic
scandal of fictions which move from the periphery of knowledge to its operative centre. The more rigorously thought
attempts to isolate its own essential workings, the more closely
it approaches a fictive realm where 'possible worlds' are
created in accordance with a self-sustaining imaginary logic.
The primordial continuity of lived experience is rivalled by an
alternative world-making power of comparable scope and
consistency. There may not, after all, be much to distinguish
Husserlian 'transcendental' phenomenology from the uses
that are made of it by critics like Poulet, more interested in the
fictive *varieties* of experience than its *a priori* cognitive claims.

Poulet's essay on Descartes (in his *Studies in Human Time*)
strikingly exemplifies this shift of emphasis. It looks to the
'dark side' of Descartes's imaginings, the dream-life which he
recorded in detail during that same period of intense intellectual activity which produced his revolution in thought. Poulet
describes the alternating rhythm of 'cyclothymia' which manifests itself – to increasingly drastic effect – in Descartes's
passage from reason to unreason, waking clarity to dreaming
terror and confusion. 'Supreme moment in which one arrives
in the full light of day, but a moment surrounded by a ring of
darkness. For it is not without danger that one lifts oneself to
the summits of the mind.'[36] The pursuit of pure reason exacts a
painful toll of repressed instinct and psychic disorder. In the
sublimated narrative of Descartes's dreams – with their ima-
gery of violent wounding, outcast wandering, physical revulsion – Poulet reads the unconscious history of Cartesian
reason. The *cogito* thinks to grasp its own genesis in a moment
of perfect self-knowledge which transcends human time and
attains an ultimate objectivity beyond either change or doubt.
Time ceases to exist for Descartes's waking consciousness.

And yet, says Poulet, 'if the affective part is neglected, the time that reigns there in some way intensifies its power and multiplies in us the changefulness which is its essence'.[37] Such is the pattern of disintegrating consciousness that Poulet discovers in Descartes's dreams. The initial twofold split (between reason and instinct) gives way to an 'infinite multiplication' of momentary selves, an unending sequence of 'ephemeral personalities' which bear no necessary temporal relation one to another. 'There is no longer anything more than affective instants, each one experienced for itself alone and lived in isolation.'[38]

Poulet's is finally a redemptive or consolatory reading of Descartes's predicament. He sees the third dream as holding out images of a reconciliation – between time and eternity, man and God, instinct and reason – which Descartes will henceforth strive to maintain in his philosophic thinking. In this dream we witness 'a genuine reintegration of the instant in time, and a sort of construction of duration'.[39] As temporal continuity reasserts its hold, so a certain equilibrium is established, a promise – at least – that reason may continue its clarifying work unthreatened by the dark side of instinctual self-knowledge. Such, according to Poulet, is the lesson to be read in those 'decisive hours' of and around 10 November 1619.

> It is by contact with episodes like these that one can better grasp the affinities which exist between the anxieties of the soul and the speculations of the mind, and that there comes to be illuminated that out of which a philosophy is formed: a work not only of the purely intellectual part of one's being, but of the entire being.[40]

Of course it may be argued that Poulet is merely offering a more or less plausible fiction of his own on the basis of texts (the dream narratives) which are in any case marginal to Descartes's philosophic claims. But this would be simply to reiterate the well-worn Platonic prejudice which elevates 'philosophy' by asserting its independence of fiction or 'literature' in general. That prejudice, as we have seen, takes various forms, notably in the efforts of Descartes and Husserl to relegate the imaginary to a secure minor province of mental representation. But the effects of such repression remain clearly visible in the breakdown of firm, categorical distinctions which so often occurs in their writing.

Philosophy is inescapably bound up with fiction, no matter how philosophers may resist the idea. If Poulet indeed has a story to tell, it is the story of how Descartes, caught within a fiction of his own unconscious creating, was led to construct a form of *counter-narrative* to hold his fears at bay. Even without the collateral evidence of Descartes's dreams, the *cogito* would still seem involved with a fictive mode of presentation which works to undermine all the grounds of philosophical assurance. The transcendental standpoint of Husserlian method is likewise a speculative construct, unable to break altogether with the realm of imaginary thought acts which makes up its illusory counterpart. That realm turns out to exist not so much alongside as *within* the same privileged zone that Husserl marks out as 'lived experience'. Philosophy can only repeat to itself the comforting assurance that truth and reality must finally bear witness in its favour, against all the subtle beguilements of fiction. Meanwhile, the 'evil spirit' of Descartes's devising – that lord of eidetic misrule – continues to haunt the innermost recesses of philosophic reason.

5

Aesthetics and politics: reading Roger Scruton

I

Aesthetics is the prime example of a subject discipline that exists purely by virtue of its own self-generated problems. That art needs explaining, or that such explanations possess some distinctive philosophical interest, is self-evident only in terms of that discourse which produced 'aesthetics' as a largely autonomous order of knowledge. This is not to say that the discipline is a fraud or that its arguments have no possible use or relevance. There have indeed been those – like I. A. Richards[1] – who dismissed aesthetics *tout court* as a species of mystified word-magic, and sought to replace it with a 'scientific' study of what goes on psychologically when we respond to works of art. But this kind of bluff empiricist gesture ignores the very real *conceptual* problems which have grown up – for better or worse – around the categories of 'art' and 'aesthetic experience'. These issues may be wholly self-induced by the discipline which sets out to explain or resolve them. But the same is true to some extent of any branch of knowledge that defines its subject area by singling out questions of especial theoretical interest. Even the 'hard' sciences construct a selective domain of research and, with it, a certain heuristic model of the objects, problems or phenomena under investigation. To suppose otherwise is to fall, like Richards, into an unreflecting positivism devoid of theoretical content or grasp.

Aesthetics is not, then, a mere pseudo-discipline simply because it deals with problems which arise out of its own self-constituting interests. Rather, its peculiarity lies in the constant need to define its juridical claims *over and against* other subject disciplines, notably those of criticism and politics. Aesthetics has to carve out its own proper region of conceptual validity precisely by excluding those other kinds of interest which threaten to encroach on that sovereign domain. Thus Kant legislates that aesthetic experience should have nothing to do with the urging or promoting of specific political ends. Works of art may be partisan in various ways – may serve as vehicles, even, for overt political propaganda – but this can have nothing to do with their value *as art* or as objects of strictly aesthetic enjoyment. Hence the widespread assumption since Kant that 'genuine' art must aspire to an ideal of impersonal detachment, of disinterested contemplation. Any doctrine which argues otherwise – for instance, the philosophy of 'socialist realism' – is held to be a gross betrayal of 'art' to the interests of mere propaganda. The fortunes of aesthetics as a proper subject discipline are closely bound up with these claims for art as a separate, autonomous realm of experience.

Thus political interests are excluded *de jure* from the discourse of aesthetic understanding. A drastic polarization of values is brought into play, whereby 'art' and its attendant ideology can be insulated safely from the pressures of political commitment. Other threats from 'outside' the aesthetic domain are dealt with in a similar, if rather less frontal, manner. Thus *criticism* of the arts – appreciative or even theoretical criticism – is allowed its place as a valid activity so long as it respects the superior status of aesthetic judgement. Critics are considered to overstep the mark if they presume to answer such questions as: What is literature? What is the structure of literary understanding? or, more pressingly, What need for aesthetics if criticism has answers to questions like these?

The aesthetician's line of argument would typically run as follows. Criticism does its job most effectively where it confines itself to describing, interpreting or analysing the distinctive features of individual works of art. Of course it can also put forward evaluative judgements and point to those details of structure or style which supposedly justify its claims. What it *cannot* do – the aesthetician will argue – is provide any ultimate ground of appeal in the form of generalized statements about the nature of art and aesthetic understanding. This is the business of philosophers, however they choose to interpret their task. Aesthetics stands to criticism in much the same way that ethics stands to the detailed practicalities of everyday moral choice. That is, it seeks to clarify the larger context of implicit assumptions within which all such issues must finally be adjudicated.[2]

Idealist philosophers in the Kantian tradition found two principal ways of meeting this demand. On the one hand they could ask 'ontological' questions about the status of the work of art, its mode of existence, and the kinds of distinctive truth-claim that might be made on its behalf. On the other they could ask, with Kant, what must be the structure of aesthetic understanding for such claims to be borne out in our experience of art. Both lines of argument proceed from the assumption of a transcendental grounding, either in the special cognitive properties of the art-work itself or in the faculty of aesthetic judgement which calls them into play. It is in this respect that modern (analytic) philosophers depart from Kantian precedent. Rather than seek out transcendent structures of aesthetic cognition – whether 'in' the work of art or 'in' our understanding of it – they prefer to analyse the conceptual framework (or 'logical grammar') within which such judgements are typically couched. Aesthetics still claims a certain regulative role *vis-à-vis* the practice of criticism. It no longer looks to provide a full-scale ontology of art or a firm categorical grounding for the exercise of critical judgement. What it offers instead is a 'logical' account of how perceptions, reasons and evaluative judgements hang together in a well-conducted sequence of critical argument. Wittgenstein is of course the main authority for this view that philosophy is best (or least misleadingly) occupied in sorting out the kinds of conceptual 'fit' between language, logic and the varieties of experience.

For Wittgenstein, famously, philosophy 'leaves everything as it is'. Philosophers are deluded and, worse, betray others into needless delusion if they think to give complicated answers where no real problem existed in the first place. The best they can do is patiently unbuild the edifice of mystified verbiage which others of their trade have so long been piling up in pursuit of illusory, self-generated puzzles. Among these distracting pseudo-problems are the issues of aesthetics as posed in the terms of traditional (Kantian) philosophy. A 'theory' of aesthetics is no more to be had than a 'theory' of mind, of knowledge, of representation or any other candidate for first-place philosophic honours. Rather it is the case, Wittgenstein would say, that we do have certain (adequate and intelligible) ways of discussing these things, and philosophy can only create confusion by inventing 'problems' and a specialized jargon to cope with them. Our talk about art-works can be usefully tidied up by occasional attention to the logical 'grammar' of the concepts it habitually uses. And this is the legitimate business of aesthetic philosophy, once it climbs down from those vertiginous realms of abstraction which have so far rendered it worse than useless.

It is clear enough that certain kinds of criticism – and, more particularly, certain forms of critical *theory* – would be judged invalid according to these criteria. Any attempt to isolate the defining characteristics of 'literature' – perhaps after the formalist manner, in terms of predominant stylistic and structural traits – will be rejected as lying beyond the competence of criticism as such.[3] Aesthetics alone can provide some answer, since 'literature' is a concept whose manifold entailments and logical 'grammar' require understanding in philosophic terms. Still less can aesthetics countenance any theory which sets out to 'explain' literature with the aid of concepts and methods imported from another discipline. Marxist approaches to criticism are usually the favoured target here. Roger Scruton puts the case with maximum brevity and point. It is characteristic of Marxist 'doctrine', he writes,

> that it will always deny the autonomy of any activity to which it is applied, while the subject of aesthetics arises directly from the perception that the significance of art is inseparable from its autonomy – inseparable, that is, from our disposition to treat art as bearing its significance within itself. (p. 8)[4]

This passage neatly demonstrates the 'logical' move by which aesthetics underwrites its claims to determine what shall *count* as valid critical argument. Those claims depend directly on the assumed 'autonomy' of art, its resistance to theories which would seek to account for it on non-aesthetic (Marxist or other) grounds. Given that the work of art 'bears its significance within itself', this argument is self-confirming and aesthetics thus justified in its legislative role.

But of course that same statement will appear merely vacuous if one rejects the twin propositions (1) that art is indeed an 'autonomous' activity, and (2) that aesthetics must have the last word since it alone respects that sovereign autonomy. To raise such questions is to reverse the terms of Scruton's argument and move *beyond* aesthetics to criticism. One would then be led to ask what interests are at work in the move to subjugate 'critical' to 'aesthetic' modes of reason. And this would point back to that displacement or repression of *political* themes which has often, since Kant, gone along with such talk of aesthetic autonomy. It is no coincidence that Scruton should deploy such arguments specifically against the Marxist claim to demystify aesthetics from a socio-political standpoint. The same applies in lesser degree to those other kinds of 'theoretical' criticism – stylistics, structuralism, decon-struction – which likewise challenge the conceptual autonomy of aesthetic understanding. Theory is suspect in so far as it raises questions which aesthetics must either rule out of court or treat as possessing a strictly limited, second-order interest. Otherwise it would yield up its title to insist on those first-order principles – like the autonomy of art – which in turn lend support to its own intellectual claims.

II

Clearly there are large issues of cultural politics behind Scruton's effort to promote aesthetic reason above all forms of critical theory. It is of more than anecdotal relevance that Scruton is one of the 'Salisbury' group of younger right-wing intellectuals who have set out to revive the 'conservative' tradition of political and philosophic thought. His aesthetics is very much a part of that programme, for all its appeal to a Kantian rhetoric of principled detachment and disinterest. The *purpose* of that rhetoric is precisely to deflect any criticism which might raise awkward questions about the ideological underpinning of Scruton's arguments. A Marxist might well put forward a diagnostic reading of those arguments in terms of the current political situation and Scruton's elective role as right-wing philosopher and ideologue. This reading would focus on the mystified concepts of culture, tradition and 'aesthetic understanding' which Scruton – like many conservative thinkers, from Burke to T. S. Eliot – sets beyond reach of criticism. It would also point out some interesting convergences between Scruton's ultra-conservative image of a just society and his views on the subordinate place of critical 'theory' in relation to aesthetics. What these arguments have in common is the desire to set firm limits to the criticism of existing values and institutions. Any theory that claims to adopt a more intelligent, enlightened or progressive standpoint must always be written off as misconceived and incoherent.

Thus Scruton takes Raymond Williams to task for thinking to explain the provenance of art in terms of a Marxist 'base-and-superstructure' model. First he reduces that model to a crudely mechanistic causal version which bears not the least resemblance to anything in Williams's writing.[5] Then he goes on to acknowledge that there *have* been more 'subtle' versions, 'conceived within the broad spirit of Marxian materialism'. But these refinements (and Scruton nowhere troubles to describe them) are, as it turns out, equally beside the point. For it is, Scruton argues,

> not *subtlety* that is required in order to make the theory of history relevant to aesthetics; the question of its relevance can be decided only from the standpoint of aesthetics, and is not a question for the theory itself to answer. (p. 8)

The argument is again self-confirming if one accepts the 'aesthetic' viewpoint, and vacuously circular if one rejects it. By 'subtlety' Scruton presumably means the kind of theoretical refinement which would make more plausible the Marxist claim to have provided a historical understanding of art on other than purely 'aesthetic' terms. Such claims must at all costs be resisted, as must any argument that seeks to account for aesthetic *philosophies* by reference to their background of ideological production.

What is centrally at issue in this whole debate is the power of reason to stand back and *criticize* existing forms of cultural life. Conservative philosophers like Scruton wish to deny this possibility. They take their cue from Wittgenstein in arguing that causal 'explanations' are not to be had, since genuine understanding involves a due deference to the habits, traditions and cultural forms which make up the tacit dimension of all such knowledge.[6] On this view *reasons*, not causes, are what count as valid evidence in the interpretation of cultural and social institutions. Reasons have to do with motives, meanings and the human intentions which animate social practice. Causal explanations ignore such sources of insight, or treat them as highly unreliable, since tied to subjective (or merely culture-bound) states of belief. Most deluded of all are those forms of ideological criticism which claim to lay bare the varieties of *misrecognition* at work in the self-understanding of human individuals and communities. According to Scruton's Wittgensteinian argument, such modes of explanation are beside the point because they substitute causes for reasons in a discipline (that of the 'human sciences') where only reasons possess any kind of conceptual validity. To break with the self-understanding of a cultural tradition is to give up any hope of interpreting its customs, traditions or characteristic art-forms. Interpretation depends upon a shared possession of the relevant criteria (or standards of judgement) required to make sense of experience. The most that philosophy can do is elucidate the underlying 'grammar' of concepts which supports those tacit criteria.

'To imagine a world purged of aesthetic preoccupations', writes Scruton, 'is to imagine a world with neither concepts nor eyes' (p. 188). This – on the face of it – extravagant claim may help to explain why aesthetics has so often come to seem a crucial testing-ground for the encounter of rival ideologies. For Kant, the critique of aesthetic judgement was an indispensable means of passage from experience to concepts, a bridge (as Scruton puts it) 'between the sensuous and the intellectual'. The categories of pure reason could only be given empirical *content* by way of this mediating theory. Aesthetic understanding was henceforth installed within philosophy as the problematic stage of transition from a purely cognitive to a practical realm. Paul de Man states the case as follows:

Aesthetic theory is critical philosophy to the second degree, the critique of the critiques. It critically examines the possibility and the modalities of political discourse and political action, the inescapable burden of any linkage between discourse and action. The treatment of the aesthetic in Kant is far from conclusive, but one thing is clear: it is epistemological as well as political through and through.[7]

Aesthetic philosophy since Kant has therefore been presented with a choice of possible paths. On the one hand it can take up the Kantian challenge, accepting (that is to say) the need for some articulated theory of aesthetics, politics and knowledge, though conscious of the difficulties that stand in its way. This path must inevitably lead *beyond* aesthetics as such to a critical accounting of interests and truth-claims which would undermine its role as an autonomous discourse. On the other hand philosophers can choose (like Scruton) to shore up that autonomy by simply declaring it out of bounds so far as politics and 'theory' are concerned. In this case they will make the obvious appeal to aesthetic 'disinterest', to what Kant expressly *stated* about the character of art, rather than what the whole structure of Kant's philosophy *constrained him to imply*.

This returns to the question of *how* – by what conceptual right – criticism can set aside certain express meanings and values in favour of another, perhaps more recondite explanation. Such would be the move by which a critic might challenge both Kant's doctrine of aesthetic disinterest and Scruton's insistence that we treat it as conceptually binding. The critic would then go on to ask, reversing the rhetoric, just what specific *interests* are served by the detachment of art from politics on the one hand and critical theory on the other. In Scruton's case those interests are clearly political, and none the less so for their taking on the mantle of Kantian autonomy. There are two main reasons why conservative philosophy should now wish to capture the high ground of aesthetic debate. First, and most obvious, is the existence of a powerful opposing tradition: a line of aesthetic philosophers – from Schiller to Marcuse – who have stressed the emancipatory character of art, the critical charge that may always be released by the contrast between 'real' and 'imagined' worlds. This tradition of left-Romantic thought has taken various latter-day forms. It issues in the 'negative dialectics' of a thinker like Adorno, as well as in the humanist Marxism of early Lukács. But aesthetic philosophy also has its uses as a counter-revolutionary creed, and it is here that one finds the second major reason for right-wing attempts to recolonize the subject.

This is the thrust of Scruton's argument against 'theory' and the various forms of ideological criticism. Such thinking, he says, 'refers things with which we are intellectually at ease, to a hypothesis (both unproven, and in all probability unprovable) which implies that we do not really understand them' (p. 170). In other words, it threatens to disrupt or subvert the placid continuity of tradition, the self-understanding that reconciles a culture to its own (past and present) conditions of life. As Scruton conceives it, aesthetics is the discipline which demonstrates most clearly how society can dispense with any critical ideas which challenge that conservative self-understanding. Of course there are precedents in plenty for the use of a generalized aesthetic creed to suppress or marginalize political themes. Coleridge provides the most striking example, attempting to defuse the radical implications of his own early thought by erecting a conservative church-and-state mythology on the basis (or ruins) of his organicist poetics.[8] T. S. Eliot travelled a similar route to much the same political end.

What these philosophies have in common is the need to elide or ignore the problematic relation between aesthetics, theory and politics. That this problem, so evident in Kant, should now be pushed out of sight is clearly an ideological reflex and not just a sign that debate has moved on since then. Nor is it hard to identify the characteristic move by which Scruton's aesthetic manages to bypass the Kantian critical legacy. It is a move which consistently translates from the 'sensuous' to the 'intellectual' realm, but not by way of any critical reflection that might raise the issue of their practical (or political) bearing.

More than once, in making this move, Scruton refers to John Casey's book *The Language of Criticism*, another Wittgensteinian account of the 'logical' concepts governing aesthetic judgement.[9] Again it should be noted that Casey is

currently an active proponent of conservative views on edu-
cation and matters of cultural politics. His book is concerned
with the philosophic status of evaluative terms like 'sincerity',
'truth' and (their negative counterpart) 'sentimentality', as
they function mainly in the language of literary criticism. F. R.
Leavis is the critic whose use of such terms most often engages
Casey's attention. Leavis himself had small patience with the
claims of 'philosophic' criticism, refusing (in a well-known
exchange with René Wellek[10]) to argue any kind of theoretical
case for his own evaluative judgements. Casey, however,
believes that there *is* a Wittgensteinian warrant for the way
that Leavis deploys his key evaluative terms. That 'sincerity' in
verse should preclude 'sentimentality' – that the unselfcritical
indulgence of emotion is simply incompatible with 'mature'
creativity – is a matter (Casey argues) of *logical* conviction, and
not just the way things happen to be. Scruton agrees, and
sums up the argument by claiming that 'Leavis's conclusions
are, if true, necessarily true, and reflect an insight into the
concepts of sincerity and sentimentality' (p. 6). In Wittgensteinian terms, such judgements possess a logical 'grammar' whereby their application, though in no sense rule-
bound, is provided with good and sufficient criteria.

This line of argument is seen as justifying Leavis's refusal to
'philosophize' in matters of literary-critical judgement. There
is no need actually to spell out those logical interconnections
which make up the grammar of a genuine, convincing argument. This task is at any rate one for the philosopher, while
critics like Leavis had best get on with the sensitive (but largely
untheorized) business of interpreting and evaluating texts.
Once again, it is in the logic of Scruton's position that certain
kinds of critical intelligence are effectively bypassed or declared
superordinate, so that only the aesthetic philosopher need
trouble to tidy up their grammar. And the tidying-up, as might
be expected, includes a sanitary clearing-out of all 'theories'
which transgress the proper limits of aesthetic understanding.
On Casey's terms, as Scruton puts it, 'criticism would be an
extension of conceptual analysis, covering those important but
elusive areas of the human mind which art makes peculiarly
vivid to us' (p. 6). His argument thus moves directly from the
'vivid' contingencies of experience to the realm of abstracted

philosophical concepts. It strategically avoids that dangerous middle-ground where theory might raise questions about the *interests* at work behind this conceptual underwriting of Leavis's critical practice.

Scruton, however, is not entirely satisfied with Casey's way of addressing these issues. His reservations might even be taken to imply that Scruton does, after all, see a role for 'theory' within the project of a larger, philosophical aesthetics. Thus he comments that Casey's kind of conceptual analysis 'redeems art for philosophy' only by jumping over certain crucial grounds of argument, and by seeing in criticism 'only instances of more general philosophical concerns' (p. 6). Yet more surprising is Scruton's subsequent assertion that 'of course, it is not an accident that literary criticism forces its practitioners to confront . . . fundamental questions in the philosophy of mind' (p. 6). But it soon becomes clear that these seeming concessions are very much a part of Scruton's argumentative strategy. They are designed to pre-empt any critique of his position which might point to the inherent narrowness and conservatism of present-day analytic philosophy. Scruton concedes that this charge has a certain force. He even goes so far as to agree that 'this reluctance to engage in the activity that Matthew Arnold (noting its overwhelming importance for the German mind) called "criticism", is rightly to be condemned as philistine' (p. 7). Arnold, of course, was distinctly ambivalent in his attitude to those new strains of German critical thought. On the one hand he berated the English middle classes for their philistine indifference to such matters. On the other he made sure to contain their more radical implications – especially with regard to religion – by expounding them always in the context of a broadly conservative cultural politics. And this is precisely Scruton's motive for shifting tack on occasion to engage with the claims of Marxism and critical theory. These continental movements, unlike (British) analytical philosophy, clearly possess both 'a large appetite for culture' and a programmatic claim 'to incorporate art directly and centrally into their conceptions of philosophic method' (p. 7). Their arguments must therefore be confronted, but only (as we have seen) on the terms laid down by Scruton's aesthetic ideology.

III

Casey's book appeared in 1966, during a period of broad-based consensus politics when ideological differences were comparatively low-key. The implicit conservatism of his argument is likewise a kind of compromise formation, a loose policing of conceptual bounds which – in true Wittgensteinian form – 'leaves everything as it is'. Scruton's latest writings on aesthetics are the product of a very different ideological formation. They reflect the emergence of a self-styled 'radical' conservatism anxious to establish hegemonic power in every sphere of political and cultural thought. Hence Scruton's determination to take on the left at those points of maximum ideological investment where theory contests the inertial force of tradition. Hence also his polemics against structuralism, semiotics, deconstruction and other present-day manifestations of that same critical spirit which Arnold both welcomed and strove to contain. 'We should remember', he writes, 'that the study of what is right and appropriate does not lead to *theoretical* knowledge' (p. 187). This denial is the heart of Scruton's aesthetic enterprise, as of many previous attempts to annex the domain of critical reflection on behalf of conservative ideology.

One last example – of a rather more specific character – may help to focus these arguments. Scruton has an essay on 'Photography and Representation' (pp. 102–26) which argues that photographs (or images on film) are aesthetically quite distinct from paintings. There is a strictly *causal* relation between photograph and subject, such that the image inherently attests to its subject's having *actually existed* at a certain moment in time. In the case of paintings the relation is *intentional*, our interest being focused on the artist's creative activity and not (or not merely) on the object represented. 'The photograph is a means to the end of seeing its subject; in painting, on the other hand, the subject is a means to the end of its own representation' (p. 114). This means that photography and film are *in themselves* devoid of aesthetic (or representational) interest. Where they *do* possess evident artistic merit, it is rather to be sought in the subject arrangement (dramatic action in the case of film; composition of detail in the photograph) which necessarily precedes the moment of technical capture. Thus, in Scruton's words, 'the representational act, the act which embodies the representational thought, is completed before the photograph is ever taken' (p. 110). Our properly 'aesthetic' interest in a painting is closely bound up with our interest in grasping the painter's constitutive intentions. In the case of photographs, such interest is conceptually misplaced, since there exists no such necessary link between intent and representation.

The importance of this distinction for Scruton's philosophy lies in the hold it gives for a further insistence on the principle of aesthetic 'disinterest'.

> For unless it were possible to represent imaginary things, representation could hardly be very important to us. It is important because it enables the presentation of imaginary scenes and characters toward which we have only contemplative attitudes: scenes and characters which, being unreal, allow our practical natures to remain unengaged. (p. 109)

It is vital for Scruton that aesthetic understanding should be held categorically distinct from 'theory' on the one hand and 'practical' engagement on the other. Photography and film threaten to blur these distinctions, since they hold out the clear possibility that certain conscious productive *techniques* may determine the very nature of aesthetic experience. And this translation of theory into practice can in turn be used for directly persuasive (political) ends. It is significant that Scruton should refer specifically to Eisenstein's techniques of cinematic montage by way of arguing this point. In such cases, he writes, we respond to the effects of 'striking visual metaphors' which 'startle us into a recognition of the underlying thought' (p. 125). Thus the artistry of Eisenstein's films – in so far as we are obliged to acknowledge it – consists in the 'intentional juxtaposition of unconnected images', and not in any notional 'aesthetic' quality of the cinematic medium itself.

Of course this throws a sizeable paradox into Scruton's distinction between film and painting. It is no longer clear just why photography should exclude the kind of 'intentional' meaning which supposedly attaches to genuine aesthetic experience. All that's left of Scruton's initial *de jure* argument is the stress on that 'causal' relation between photographic subject and image which (it is claimed) leaves no room for 'intentional' significance. But this argument is self-deconstructing once it turns out to make an exception of highly 'imaginative' films like *The Battleship Potemkin*. Why should this count as a special case on the grounds (as Scruton argues) that 'the causal relation between image and subject is replaced by an intentional one'? Are not cinematic cause and intention *always* thus related, even (one might say, though the jargon is redundant) as part of the 'logical grammar' that enables a proper understanding of film? And, if this is the case, then surely it follows that photography and painting are *not* to be distinguished on aesthetic grounds, since each is the product of certain techniques which invite various kinds of analytical approach, depending on one's angle of interest. That this imaginary distinction should figure so importantly for Scruton is a sign of his ideological commitment to a mystified aesthetic philosophy.

What these arguments work to promote is a notion of artistic 'truth' cut off from all reference to theory and practical interests. 'Those thoughts which animate our perception when we see the realistic painting with understanding are true thoughts' (p. 108). True, that is, to a vaguely defined concept of intentional experience which insulates aesthetic understanding from other, less conformable kinds of knowledge. Scruton's ideas about photography and film are designed to reinforce this dogmatic separation of realms. He ignores all those manifold choices of productive technique that intervene not only before but *during* and *after* the moment of capturing a photographic image. These include the selection of lens and filters, the decision as to aperture and speed, and the various techniques of processing and printing (as well as cutting and editing in the case of film). Scruton is obliged to pass over these complicating factors in the interest of maintaining his distinction between 'aesthetic' experience and other, merely technical forms of cultural production. There is an interesting comparison here with Walter Benjamin's well-known essay 'The Work of Art in the Age of Mechanical Reproduction'.[11] Photography, according to Benjamin, is one of those modern, essentially *reproducible* art-forms which must soon bring about a drastic modification in our concepts of aesthetic experience. Traditionally it has seemed that great works of art were unique, each possessed of an individual meaning and significance which set it apart from mere second-order 'imitations'. This quality – 'aura', as Benjamin calls it – can only be progressively eroded with the advent of new and ever more efficient means of mechanical reproduction. The artist as solitary genius gives way to a distinctly Brechtian figure: the artist as *producer*, concerned not merely with creating new 'works' but with opening up new and revolutionary forms of mass culture.[12] This activity rejects the traditional distinction between 'art' and 'criticism', as indeed between 'original' works and the various kinds of changes, updatings and revisions to which they can always be subject. Innovation in the sphere of cultural production necessarily entails major changes in the concept of aesthetic 'authenticity'. And to understand such changes is to engage, like Brecht, in a constant reciprocal practice of art, criticism and (so to speak) media technology.

Benjamin's essay is touched with a certain ambivalence on these questions of cultural politics. One detects a lingering attachment to tradition and the 'aura' which once invested its most cherished artistic touchstones. Nevertheless he is clear enough about the practical choices involved. Right-wing ideologists will attempt to 'aestheticize politics', to project a blandly homogeneous cultural tradition modelled, like T. S. Eliot's, on the 'timeless' proprieties of art. It is thinkers on the left who must challenge that projection, work to understand its self-interested motives, and *theorize* the mystified concepts upon which it rests. 'Does art have a history?' asks Scruton, and answers that indeed it does, but only when approached with a due respect for its 'autonomous' character. 'Purposeless' institutions like art allow of no causal explanations which would show them to unfold in an historical, progressive or 'rational' way. Rather it is the case – as Scruton writes, echoing Eliot – that 'the aesthetic order may undergo a shift which changes the aspect of all that has preceded it' (p. 178).

This 'imaginary museum' idea of art history has its obvious political analogue in Scruton's conservative image of a just and self-regulating social order. Take the following passage where

he develops the contrast between 'purposeful' and 'purposeless' institutions. The history of war, Scruton argues,

> moves in an orderly way, in accordance with the progressive
> sophistication of means, and the consequent simplification
> of ends, among our conquerers, while the history of that
> most purposeless of all human things, peace, remains un-
> fathomable. (p. 176)

What interests might actuate this curious choice of analogy?
For one thing, there is Scruton's conservative view that the
chief common goods of mankind form a timeless order of
permanent truths, beyond reach of mere 'political' theory and
practice. This connects with Scruton's argument (in *The Meaning of Conservatism*) for a stable, traditional order of society
wherein most individuals would accept their role without
need for abstract legitimation. Other, more specific interests
are at work in the rhetoric that assimilates *peace* to the category
of 'purposeless' and 'unfathomable' blessings. That Scruton is
a prominent spokesman for right-wing opposition to current
anti-nuclear protest groups is very much in keeping with his
argument here.

Of course, from the standpoint of aesthetic 'disinterest',
such connections would seem anecdotal at best, another case
of politics intruding its irrelevant concerns into the subject
domain of a properly 'autonomous' discipline. This argument
can best be turned back by a close and consequent critique of
Scruton's aesthetics. In particular, it would show how real and
pressing are the ideological interests that conceal themselves
behind such talk of principled autonomy. As Scruton comments in another connection, it is a mark of 'intellectual
imperialism' that certain ways of thinking should attempt to
establish 'conceptual beachheads in all territories at once'
(p. 174). This hegemonic drive is nowhere more evident than
in the discourse of conservative aesthetic philosophy.

6

Philosophy as a kind of narrative: Rorty on post-modern liberal culture

I

Philosophy seeks the truth, while literature is content with mere invention and pleasing fables. Such was Plato's view of the matter, and so it has remained – with minor local adjustments – down through the history of western thought. Sometimes the distinction gets blurred and philosophers find themselves compelled to insist on a proper demarcation of interests. At present they are coping with one such problem, in the form of a deconstructionist literary theory which denies the very grounds of that distinction. Philosophy, it is argued, stakes its claim to rationality and truth only by *forgetting* or constantly *repressing* its own rhetorical character. A whole tradition of philosophic thinking – Derrida's 'logocentric' epoch – rests on this unconscious refusal to acknowledge the kinship of philosophy and literature. Hence, as Nietzsche was first to proclaim, the root dissimulation of philosophic reason: the pretence that its truths have an absolute validity independent of the metaphoric ruses and devices that bring them into being. The salient fact of its *textual* constitution is what philosophy has to ignore in the interests of preserving its pure conceptual regime. That truth should be indeed, as Nietzsche maintained, a product of sublimated textual figuration is a threatening possibility scarcely to be dreamed of in 'serious' philosophic discourse.

Nowadays this quarrel takes the form of a split within philosophy itself, a widespread disagreement about what should *count* as competent, rational argument. On the one hand there are those in the 'analytic' camp, working to clarify traditional problems by the use of more up-to-date logical and linguistic idioms. Although the emphasis has changed since Kant – roughly speaking, from philosophy of mind to philosophy of language – the central issues remain much the same. Where Kant pinned his hopes to a theory of knowledge arrived at by rigorous 'transcendental' deduction, the modern philosopher prefers to analyse the terms in which such arguments are typically couched. There is still a broad consensus as to which are the problems worth raising and how one should logically set about providing answers. On the other hand there exists a counter-tradition of speculative thought whose major representatives (say Hegel, Nietzsche, Heidegger, Derrida) by no means offer such a settled agenda for debate. Far from engaging in a common, rational enterprise, these thinkers each tend to redefine the concept of 'reason' in keeping with their own, more radical and heterodox claims. Rather than conceive of language as a literal, transparent medium – a vehicle for clear and distinct ideas – they deliberately exploit all manner of stylistic devices to problematize the relation between signifier and signified, word and concept. To the promise of 'constructive' solutions held out by analytic philosophy they respond with a deconstructionist will to undermine or radically transform the relations of knowledge and truth.

That the two 'traditions' are worlds apart is evident enough in their few brief and baffled exchanges to date. Thinkers in the 'other', broadly continental line are dismissed by analytical philosophers with a kind of pitying fondness, as simply having failed to learn the current rules of the game.[1] Deconstruction is regarded with particular distaste because it appeals in the main to literary intellectuals who – so the argument runs – lack the rigour and discipline of a 'proper' philosophic training. Thus there develops a kind of uneasy truce in which literary theorists hang on to those thinkers (the Nietzsche–Derrida succession) whom their analytic counterparts anyhow regard as scarcely worth rescuing. Deconstructionists continue to snipe from the sidelines at a mainstream philosophy which clings to its deluded belief in truth, logic and sufficient reason. Analytic philosophers content themselves with occasional sallies – book reviews, mostly – which deplore the muddle-headed presumption of their literary colleagues. The latter then respond by arguing that 'philosophy', thus narrowly conceived, is blind to crucial aspects of its own textual make-up, and forced to ignore whole tracts of its own prehistory. From one side of the fence the quarrel is between tough-minded *genuine* thinkers and woolly-minded literary hangers-on. From the other, it is a case of unlocking the prisonhouse of concepts which has rendered philosophers incapable of *reading* – properly, intelligently reading – the major texts of their tradition.

Richard Rorty is one of the few philosophers who have attempted, if not to straddle this gulf, then at least to peer across from both sides and communicate the effect of double vision. Rorty's career and his three books to date are likewise emblematic in this respect. He has lately moved from the Philosophy Department at Princeton to become Kenan Professor of Humanities at the University of Virginia. In 1967 he edited *The Linguistic Turn*, an influential anthology of essays in the ordinary-language and analytic mode.[2] Yet in his preface to that volume Rorty was already facing up to the idea that certain conflicts of approach *within* the prevailing (analytic) tradition were such as to call its more confident claims into doubt. These differences, he argued, could only be repeated – not resolved – since they surfaced so insistently throughout the debate. The most obvious example was the issue between those (like J. L. Austin) who reposed their trust in the commonsense wisdom of 'ordinary language', and those others – in the line of Russell and Carnap – who sought stricter forms of logical expression. In the face of such dilemmas, Rorty maintained, philosophers might have to accept that their differences were best argued through in a spirit of ongoing dialogue, rather than a quest for onesided ultimate answers. This turn towards a more 'conversational' ethos for philosophy suggests at the same time a mood of chastened confidence, a turning away from positivist rigour and truth-claims.

The result, Rorty argues, is to change the self-image of philosophy from a specialized, technical discourse to one that would share significant concerns with adjacent 'disciplines' like literary criticism. At best this development might yet produce a revival of the pragmatist outlook espoused by thinkers like Dewey and William James.[3] This would be a matter of accepting, in James's words, that truth may be defined for all practical purposes as 'the name of whatever proves itself to be good in the way of belief'. It would therefore mean abandoning the project of philosophy as conceived by thinkers in the western tradition from Plato, through Kant to the modern analytic school. What impels that project throughout its long history is the quest for epistemological certitude, for a truth not merely 'good in the way of belief' but good for all time and all possible modes of experience. It is this tradition that Rorty sets out to deconstruct in his book *Philosophy and the Mirror of Nature* (1980). Conceiving of itself as an ultimate, 'foundational' discipline – a knowledge grounded in clear and distinct ideas – philosophy is destined to an endless rehearsal of its age-old problems and perplexities. Hence the present need, as Rorty sees it, for a healthy infusion of 'old-fashioned' pragmatist ideas.

One consequence of this change would be to reverse the Platonic prejudice which elevates philosophic truth above the merely diverting, storytelling interests of literature. What if it turned out that philosophers had *always* been in the business of constructing plausible fictions, even when convinced most firmly that their object was the one, inviolable truth? Such, after all, was the line of counter-argument adopted by poets like Sir Philip Sidney in the face of Plato's philosophic strictures. It was largely by means of fictions, parables and set-piece scenes of imaginary dialogue that Plato pressed home his case against the poets. Metaphor and simile were likewise deployed in texts (like the *Phaedrus*) which ostensibly warned against their dangerous, irrational character. Rorty is not the first to turn the tables on philosophy by asking whether its own privileged truth-claims might also be products of the figurative realm. It is, he writes, 'pictures rather than propositions, metaphors rather than statements, which determine most of our philosophic convictions'.[4] The pragmatist is in a position to acknowledge this fact and get along with it comfortably enough. More important to raise the right questions and keep the conversation going than to fret about the non-availability of rational foundations. For the pragmatist's 'analytic' counterpart, on the other hand, philosophy is nothing if not possessed of a firm epistemological grounding. The suspicion that this might be merely a species of enabling *metaphor* is for that reason scarcely to be entertained.

It is consistent with Rorty's pragmatist outlook that he should want to give a full-scale *narrative* account of how philosophy arrived at its present situation. The outline of his story can be summarized roughly as follows. Modern philosophy took a wrong turn when Descartes (and subsequently Kant) defined its main task as that of providing an answer to the problems of knowledge and epistemological doubt. A dominant metaphor took hold, picturing the mind as a 'mirror of nature' and philosophy as the discipline whose business it was to examine, polish and more accurately *focus* that mirror. The picture was vague enough to leave room for some (apparently) crucial differences of view. Empiricists and idealists could still disagree over how to interpret the metaphor: whether, for instance, the mind was merely the passive recipient of a given, objective reality, or whether it played a more essential role in actively *shaping* that reality. With a slight shift of standpoint the image could be changed, as M. H. Abrams has shown,[5] from 'mind as mirror' to 'mind as lamp'. And this, broadly speaking, is the textbook history of philosophic arguments as seen from *within* the continuing tradition to which Descartes and Kant gave rise.

Rorty's point is that these differences of view are quite minor compared with the single, overriding prejudice that unites them. Philosophers, whether 'idealist' or 'empiricist', were agreed at bottom on the following articles of faith:

1 that philosophy was best and most properly engaged in a quest for its own rational or logical foundations;
2 that these foundations would reveal themselves to a mind specially trained in the business of lucid self-knowledge;
3 that philosophy would thus become a 'science' *primus inter pares*, since it promised an ultimate, objective grounding for all other modes of thought.

It is this idea of philosophy as a 'foundational' or first-order discipline that Rorty thinks we should now be willing to abandon. On pragmatic grounds he would presumably have to admit that it has been valuable at least as a highly productive and (to some extent) co-operative effort of thought. But that use-value has now been outlived, he believes, and philosophy is long overdue for the kind of radical overhaul that can best be brought about by a pragmatist recasting of its central questions.

On Rorty's diagnosis, this revision is already under way, spurred on by certain recent developments in the 'analytic' camp. Philosophers like Quine are in the process of dislodging the Kantian 'problem of knowledge' by denying that any firm distinction can be drawn between purely logical (analytic) truths and those arrived at by experience or observation. This programme of 'radical empiricism' rejects all the forms of surplus conceptual baggage entailed by traditional post-Kantian philosophy. Thus, according to Quine, the 'structure of knowledge' at any given time is best pictured as a fabric of manifold related propositions, some of which (those near the centre) seem to possess *a priori* status, while others (nearer the periphery) are open to empirical adjustment.[6] Knowledge is always provisional to this extent: that experience may *conceivably* require us to modify the most cherished ideas of hard-core 'logical' truth. In Quine's terminology, the whole complex fabric is 'underdetermined' by its boundary conditions, so that radical changes can always come about in what counts as veridical *a priori* truth. This would have far-reaching consequences, not only for any neo-Kantian philosophy of mind, but also for its latter-day offshoot in the form of linguistic analysis. Quine's empiricism leaves no room for abstract regularities assumed to underlie the surface varieties of language use. It denies the resort to ideas of semantic analyticity designed to substitute for Kantian notions of pure *a priori* knowledge. Sentences may be 'stimulus-analytic', or so constructed as to win assent from all members of a given language-community. But this betokens only that they seem *for all present and practical purposes* beyond reach of empirical refutation. There is no categorical guarantee that they will retain this status through all the varieties of possible 'fit' between language and experience. Thus Rorty can look to Quine for confirmation of his view that analytic philosophy has come up against the limits of its own more rigid conceptual assumptions.

This position lines up with the pragmatist viewpoint which Rorty finds developed by earlier thinkers, Dewey and Wittgenstein included. It is an outlook which treats the perennial problems of traditional philosophy as largely self-induced through obsessive adherence to unworkable metaphors of knowledge and truth. As these metaphors begin to loosen their hold, so philosophy takes on a larger freedom and looks, once again, beyond its technical sphere to questions of a wider cultural significance. Thus the story that Rorty wants to tell is one that explains 'how philosophy-as-epistemology attained self-certainty in the modern period'. Its denouement is summarized in the claim

> that to think of knowledge that presents a 'problem', and about which we ought to have a 'theory', is a product of viewing knowledge as an assemblage of representations – a view of knowledge which, I have been arguing, was a product of the seventeenth century.[7]

The moral to be drawn, he concludes, is that, 'if this way of thinking of knowledge is optional, then so is epistemology, and so is philosophy as it has understood itself since the middle of the last century'.[8] To question this specialized self-image might create (as indeed Rorty has) some flutterings in the professional dovecot. But it would have the more important advantage of reopening philosophy to interests outside its present narrow range of concerns.

II

Like most such stories, Rorty's is one that takes its main bearings from the present, reviewing tradition in the light of contemporary problems and concerns. What is more unusual about Rorty's tale is the idea that philosophy can *do no more* than make plausible sense of its own prehistory by treating it in broadly narrative terms. That the tale leads up to where we stand at the moment doesn't mean that thought is any closer to resolving the problems that have always vexed it. There is no question here of a grand Hegelian synthesis, though Rorty admires the kind of 'naturalized' Hegelianism – freed, that is, from its epistemological trappings – which he finds in Dewey and the pragmatists. Nor is it a matter of technical advances which might claim, like the logical positivists, to have shown up the confusions in traditional philosophy and solved its longstanding problems once and for all. The gist of Rorty's tale is that solutions are not to be had, at least while philosophers continue to seek them on the terms laid down by traditional debate. What remains is the business of demystifying philosophy by treating it as a series of productive wrong turns; productive, that is, of philosophical discourse, but incapable of answering its own most fundamental questions.

One further consequence of Rorty's view is that no *final* narrative is likely to turn up, such as might close the conversation by offering a God's-eye view of all previous episodes. Like the post-Jamesian novel, philosophy is to give up the privilege of omniscient narration in exchange for a livelier, more flexible sense of its manifold possibilities. The quest for a master-plot, a story to end all stories, is another of those inveterate delusions that philosophers are prone to entertain. The last grand attempt, according to Rorty, was the logical-positivist project of rewriting the history of western thought as a series of more or less failed approximations to logical rigour and method.[9] The trouble with such meta-narratives is that they have to assume a godlike perspective atop all the previous confusions of plot. They claim to have arrived at definitive solutions while in fact they are simply rehearsing old problems from a different standpoint and with different narrative ends in view. In place of these masterly constructions, Rorty thinks, we should now learn to live with more provisional accounts of how things hold together from a certain cultural perspective. Philosophers would still have a special interest – even an acquired expertise – in describing the various ideas and vocabularies which made up this 'post-philosophical' culture. What they *wouldn't* need to claim any longer is access to a privileged order of truth which they, and they alone, were equipped to understand. They would be people, in short, 'who had no special "problems" to solve, nor any special "method" to apply, abided by no particular disciplinary standards, had no collective self-image as a "profession"'.[10] Their role would resemble that of the present-day literary 'intellectual', rather than the tenured academic philosopher.

Rorty himself fulfils this role in various interconnected ways. He speaks up, not only for a 'literary' culture beyond the narrow enclaves of professionalized philosophy, but also for thinkers in the speculative line whom philosophers ignore in the interests of keeping their discipline 'pure'. This alternative tradition has its uses, for Rorty, in contesting the hegemonic claims of mainstream (Anglo-American) philosophy. On the one hand he is prepared to give serious attention to those, like Heidegger and Derrida, whose texts represent a standing affront to the norms of 'rational' argumentation. On the other, he wants to challenge the existing distinction between 'serious' (= analytic) and 'non-serious' styles of philosophic writing. The appeal of a 'textualist' position like Derrida's lies in its avoidance of the deep-laid conceptual traps which thought seems endlessly to prepare for itself. Rorty is not interested in deconstruction as a theory, method or species of negative metaphysics. This would reduce it to simply another diverting episode in the grand epistemological tradition which it was ultimately destined to rejoin. For Rorty, as a pragmatist, its virtues are those of a spirited refusal to play the old game on rules laid down by that outworn tradition.

This means arguing that the present-day 'textualists', whatever their mistaken aspirations to theory, are in fact all heading – wittingly or not – towards their own versions of pragmatism. Thus Nietzsche, as Rorty reads him, offers a critique of nineteenth-century philosophical assumptions parallel to William James's attack on the tenets of metaphysical idealism. James's 'version' is preferable, furthermore, since it 'avoids the "metaphysical" elements in Nietzsche which Heidegger criticizes, and, for that matter, the "metaphysical" elements in Heidegger which Derrida criticizes'.[11] Nor is Derrida exempt from this criticism, as Rorty argues in his generally admiring essay 'Philosophy as a Kind of Writing'. His point is that textualists go a long way – but perhaps not quite far enough – towards dissolving the illusory concepts and truth-claims of traditional philosophy. The bad side of Derrida, for Rorty, is that which fastens on to terms like *trace* and *differance* as a kind of negative theology, one that replaces the absent God with the non-existent Transcendental Signified. The good side is that which occasionally transforms him from a last-ditch metaphysician into someone who can acknowledge that philosophy 'is just the self-consciousness of the play of a certain kind of language'.[12] From this point it is no great distance to the pragmatist position where knowledge is conceived as the ongoing process of reflective adjustment between various cultural needs and interests. Only their residual attachment to theory prevents the modern 'textualists' from following this argument through to its appointed conclusion.

All the signs, therefore, point to pragmatism as the upshot and looked-for denouement to Rorty's tale. It is a story which unfolds through its own long phases of advancement and arrest, while its protagonists may or may not fully grasp the role they are allotted to play. Some, like James and Dewey, possess a sure grasp of the way things are tending and therefore cease to vex themselves with pointless, insoluble problems. The rest are divided between seekers-after-truth who have not yet seen the pragmatist light, and halfway converts (the 'textualists' among them) who are stumbling towards it from various directions. On this view, as Rorty expresses it, 'James and Dewey were not only waiting at the end of the dialectical road which analytic philosophy travelled, but are waiting at the end of the road which, for example, Foucault and Deleuze are currently travelling.'[13] If this argument sounds suspiciously Hegelian, Rorty can reply that the pragmatist upshot is enough to discountenance any kind of teleological reading. What remains is that element of 'naturalized' Hegelianism which allows that philosophy may voice the main concerns of its own cultural epoch without thereby setting itself up as a master discipline of knowledge and truth.

Yet this answer must in turn provoke further questions about the *kind* of cultural self-interest bound up with Rorty's pragmatist viewpoint. There may, as he argues, be real benefits in telling a story of western philosophy which requires no epistemological grounding or ultimate narrative authority. Omniscience may be just another fiction, decked out with such imposing disguises as 'clear and distinct ideas, sense-data, categories of the pure understanding, structures of pre-linguistic consciousness, and the like'.[14] Rorty's pragmatist outlook is shrewdly on guard against premature abstractions like these. But it does carry along with it a strongly marked complex of cultural motives and interests which play their part in shaping the story he has to tell. Rorty writes as – in his own careful phrase – a 'postmodernist bourgeois liberal', which position he equates with the present self-awareness of American intellectual culture at large. That is to say, he regards the benefits of pragmatism as working not only to save philosophy from needless mystification, but also to bring it into line with his idea of what a 'liberal' society ought to be. This connection is made, expressly or implicitly, in several of Rorty's more recent essays. It throws some needed light on that relationship between social and intellectual values which Rorty is always quick to point out.

III

In the phrase 'postmodernist bourgeois liberal' it is the word 'postmodernist' that probably most needs explaining. Rorty's usage comes partly from the generalized currency of literary-critical debate, but also – more pointedly – from Jean-François Lyotard's book *La Condition postmoderne* (1979).[15] Lyotard describes the present state of knowledge – scientific and cultural alike – as marked by a break with traditional forms of legitimating 'truth' and authority. More specifically, he backs up Rorty's contention that there exists no transcendent discourse or generalized theory that would serve to 'ground' such authority once and for all. This issue is conveniently focused in the debate between post-modernists like Lyotard and others – notably Habermas – who want to preserve some ultimate appeal to norms of rational belief. For Habermas, this grounding takes the form of an imagined 'ideal speech situation' where language and thought would no longer be distorted by effects of power, self-interest or ignorance.[16] It remains very much a utopian projection but also, he argues, an end-point implicit in every communicative act. What Habermas seeks to defend, in distinctively modern terms, is the classic liberal (Kantian) position which conceives of reason as the final guarantee of human morality and freedom. It is from this point of view that he criticizes 'relativists' (like Foucault and Lyotard) for their willingness to abandon the hard-won gains of enlightened rationality.

In keeping with his pragmatist outlook, Rorty rejects this line of attack and argues for a 'post-modern' liberalism willing to dispense with such Kantian props and devices. He cites approvingly Lyotard's distinction between 'narrative knowledge' (or 'popular narrative pragmatics') and those other kinds of truth-claim which invoke some higher, meta-narrative authority. Habermas is seen as clinging pointlessly to a quest for legitimizing principles which are simply not to be had if one accepts, with Rorty, the essentially culture-bound character of all such beliefs and ideologies. In fact, the very term 'ideology' needs to be questioned, or suitably modified, in the light of this pragmatist critique. It belongs to that 'enlightened' tradition of thought which imagines that theory can rise above the conditioned assumptions of its own time and place, the better to explain or reform them. This is what links the 'meta-narrative' stance to the Kantian image of human beings as autonomous, free-willing agents, constrained only by the sovereign dicates of rational obligation. For Rorty, such notions are redundant at best, and their eclipse a welcome sign that post-modern liberal culture can dispense with that whole shaky edifice of self-promoting abstract endorsements.

This would place Marxism squarely in the company of those other meta-narratives, from Kant on down, that Rorty would have us abandon. On his pragmatist account, it is impossible for thought to get the kind of detached critical leverage required to emancipate consciousness from its own cultural values and presuppositions. Still less can there exist a 'revolutionary vanguard' whose privileged access to the master-plot of history allows them to predict and hasten its outcome. Rorty would seem to concur with Foucault in viewing Marxism as merely one symptomatic episode in the sequence of delusive totalizing systems set in train by Kant and Hegel. The virtues of 'post-modern' liberalism include its refusal to invest any faith in large-scale explanatory programmes, such as (in Lyotard's words) 'the dialectics of the Spirit, the hermeneutics of meaning, the emancipation of the rational or working subject, or the creation of wealth'.[17] These are seen as displaced emanations of the old preoccupying quest for absolute knowledge. In its place would be set the pragmatist assurance that cultures generate their own kinds of story which require no legitimating back-up of abstract principles. These stories define, in Lyotard's words, 'what has the right to be said and done in the culture in question, and since they are themselves a part of that culture, they are legitimated by the simple fact that they do what they do.'[18] Thus for Rorty the project of dismantling traditional philosophy goes along with an express commitment to the ethos and values of present-day American society. Old-fashioned meta-narratives – Kantian, Marxist or whatever – are rejected as simply irrelevant to the purpose of carrying on this privileged communal enterprise. Rorty makes the point plainly enough when he distinguishes the *good* kind of bourgeois liberalism ('the attempt to fulfil the hopes of the North Atlantic bourgeoisie') from its dubious 'philosophical' counterpart ('a collection of Kantian principles thought to justify us in having those hopes').[19] The latter, it is implied, cannot possibly legitimate – and may indeed actively hinder – the workings of a genuine bourgeois liberal culture.

It is therefore an important part of Rorty's project to rescue the word 'liberal' from some of the chronic ambiguities and confusions surrounding its present-day usage. This he wants to achieve by narrating the relevant background in such a way as to give the word a properly supportive historical and cultural slant. Since no other form of justification would count – there being no appeal, as Rorty insists, to universal or abstract definitions – this procedure is assumed to carry its own criteria along with it. Such 'narrative knowledge', Lyotard writes, 'does not give priority to the question of its own legitimation, and . . . certifies itself in the pragmatics of its own transmission without having recourse to argumentation and proof'.[20] Rorty has two such edifying narratives to recount. One is the story of post-Cartesian philosophy, its self-induced dilemmas and the progress toward a wished-for pragmatist issue out of all its afflictions. The other, distinctly consonant with this, is the story of American 'liberal' institutions and their continuing cultural vitality.

Both tales are interspersed with regrettable swerves and

temptations from the path so clearly marked out. Among philosophers there has grown up a counter-pragmatist movement (Rorty calls it 'technical realism') which attempts once again to ground knowledge and truth in a privileged relation to the real. Thus Saul Kripke argues a hard-line realist philosophy of language and reference, one that treats the world (in Rorty's summary) as 'already divided not only into particulars, but into natural kinds of particulars and even into essential and accidental features of those particulars and kinds'.[21] Part of Rorty's business is to argue that such revisionist concepts do nothing to resolve traditional problems. Thus Kripke's 'technical realism' (for instance) amounts to little more than a terminological updating of the old 'intuitive realism'. Similar moves are afoot, Rorty thinks, on the wider front of contemporary ethics and moral philosophy. When pragmatists argue that a society is 'just' if its laws are in accordance with the shared self-understanding of its members, there will always be opponents – neo-Kantians of various colour – to reject their viewpoint as mere unprincipled 'relativism'. Such arguments take it as axiomatic that morality is founded on something more accountable than prevailing social convention.

Rorty interprets this anti-pragmatist 'backlash' as a product, in part, of the moral revulsion felt by many intellectuals over America's involvement in the Vietnam war.[22] The breakdown of consensus created a desire for moral judgements to be grounded in a validating framework independent of transitory local opinion. Intellectuals came to define their status – as so often in the past – not *within* but *against* the communal self-image of their times. The same would apply to those nineteenth-century movements in the wake of Kant and Hegel which looked to a systematizing philosophy as the bulwark of reason against mere collective prejudice. In Rorty's view such movements are usually reactive, symptomatic of the need to invent meta-narratives where the primary sense of cultural involvement is for some reason forced out of joint.

It will be evident by now that Rorty's 'liberal' assumptions have a great deal in common with 'conservative' thinking on issues of culture and politics. The ambiguity of such terms is notoriously hard to unravel, especially when it comes to translating them from an American to a British context. At any rate, the 'liberalism' that Rorty appeals to has the following pre-eminent features:

1 a mistrust of programmatic theories which claim to transcend and criticize the culture they spring from;
2 a corresponding stress on the cultural rootedness of ideas and values;
3 a kind of intellectual free-market outlook which wants to have done with all restrictive or legitimating checks and controls.

In fact, Rorty uses the word 'liberal' in a sense more akin to current economists' parlance than to anything the mainstream humanist is likely to understand by it. Certainly there is little enough in common between Rorty's ideas and those of either a 'liberal' activist like Chomsky or a 'liberal' culture critic like Lionel Trilling. The one would assert a rationalist critique of language, culture and politics alike; the other a voice of ironically tempered humanist dissent which defines itself squarely against the self-images of the age. Both run counter to Rorty's pragmatist faith in the virtues of American (or 'North Atlantic bourgeois') society and culture as it presently exists. From the viewpoint of Rorty's conservative liberalism, theirs would seem merely a belated showing of the old nineteenth-century drive to meta-narrative transcendence.

Rorty insists that this renunciation of legitimating grounds is in no sense a species of moral or intellectual relativism. To urge that any reasons adduced for a given line of argument are valid *only within the culture which holds them justified* is, he points out, very different from urging that any argument is as good as any other.[23] If truth is – as the pragmatist would have it – a matter of 'warranted assertability', then at least there must be good cultural warrant for the argument in question. But this evades the more crucial problem of how one could criticize *any* system of belief if the only means of properly understanding it was on its own implicit terms of cultural justification. This Wittgensteinian argument is familiar enough and finds perhaps its best-known defence in Peter Winch's book *The Idea of a Social Science*.[24] It lines up with Rorty's pragmatist position in denying that cultural facts can be interpreted except by giving reasons which would count as valid arguments with a member of the culture concerned. Sociologists, philosophers and others must therefore be deluded if they think to explain some alien system of belief in terms supplied from their own conceptual stock. Again, it is the nineteenth-century outlook of progressive 'enlightened' opinion that philosophers like Winch and Rorty are most anxious to disavow. Rorty's liberalism runs directly counter to the Whiggish varieties he finds still active among many modern intellectuals.

IV

It is scarcely surprising that Rorty's ideas have been welcomed more by literary critics and theorists than by philosophers of a 'technical' or analytic mind. It is, after all, a main plank in his argument that philosophy should let up on its narrow, specialized concerns and rejoin the kind of communal sense-making enterprise which criticism chiefly carries on. For deconstructionists there is further encouragement to be had from Rorty's insistence that philosophic texts have no monopoly on reason and truth, but are there to be *interpreted* along with all the others that make up a cultural tradition. If philosophy is about to give up its privileged role, then criticism is ready to step in – as Rorty suggests – with its own, less grandiose story to tell.

There are, however, certain conditions to be met if this transfer of power is to bring the kinds of benefit the pragmatist has in mind. For one thing, literary critics had best give up the idea that philosophy (or 'theory') is capable of solving any problems created by their own interpretative practice. That this notion is still current among certain critics (not least the camp-followers of deconstruction) is a sign, Rorty thinks, that they have yet to work through and beyond the grip of classical theories of knowledge. Thus critics look to philosophy for arguments designed to prop up their own more workaday, practical assumptions about meaning, validity or authorial intent. In this they are mistaken, in Rorty's view, because no kind of 'theory' has the power to dictate what should or should not count as valid interpretation.

There are those – 'strong textualists', Rorty calls them – who accept this situation, abandoning the quest for ultimate truths without a trace of guilty nostalgia. Then again there are others, 'weak textualists', who fall back on theories of meaning and method as a form of halfway compromise solution.[25] These latter, Rorty argues, are the heirs of nineteenth-century idealist philosophy, having merely substituted language for mind as their object of investigation. For Kantians and weak textualists alike there has to be some notion of invariant structure – whether mental or linguistic – to replace the lost foundations of epistemological truth. Otherwise there would just be the random play of ungrounded knowledge and representation. It is their willingness to face up squarely to the latter possibility that the strong textualists share with thinkers like James and Dewey.

These critics have at last caught up with the fact that explanatory systems (structuralist, New Critical, neo-Aristotelian or whatever) are just so many *texts* on an equal footing with those other, less presumptuous texts they seek to interpret. While the weak textualist continues to believe 'that there is really a secret code and that once it's discovered we shall have gotten the text right' – assuming, in short, that the critic's business is 'discovery rather than creation' – the 'strong misreader' (like Foucault or Bloom) is happy to let go of this illusion. He no longer cares, as Rorty puts it,

> about the distinction between discovery and creation, finding and making. He doesn't think this is a useful distinction, any more than Nietzsche and James did. He is in it for what he can get out of it, not for the satisfaction of getting something right.[26]

So this is what Rorty chiefly demands of the 'post-modern' literary intellectual. It is a matter of seeing that the best way to build bridges between philosophy and literature is to stop treating the former as some kind of privileged discourse. What most often prevents this realization is the tendency in literary critics 'to think that literature can take the place of philosophy by *mimicking* philosophy – by being, of all things, *epistemological*'.[27] Once rid of this chronic delusion – still there, Rorty thinks, in the 'philosophic' rigour of theorists like Paul de Man – criticism can take its place as an equal partner in the unfolding dialogue of post-modern liberal culture.

On the face of it this proposal should prove attractive to literary critics. After all, it very neatly turns the tables on that condescending attitude which philosophers, from Plato to the logical positivists, have displayed toward poets and critics alike. Nevertheless it might be well to look more closely at the practical options that Rorty holds out. What *kind* of story would critics have to tell if they followed his injunction to dispense with theory and stick to 'natural' or first-order narrative pragmatics? More specifically: how would this alliance work out for critics who wanted to question some of Rorty's more conservative ideas about language, ideology and cultural politics? Perhaps it is the case, as Rorty argues, that

> pragmatism is the philosophical counterpart of literary modernism, the kind of literature which prides itself on its autonomy and novelty rather than its truthfulness to experience or its discovery of pre-existing significance. Strong textualism draws the moral of modernist literature and thus creates genuinely modernist criticism.[28]

But this creates problems, not least because Rorty is here collapsing his own distinction between 'modern' and 'postmodern' attitudes. What he (like Lyotard) usually means by the former is a standpoint of 'enlightened' reason which looks for grounding principles or a source of meta-narrative justification. It is the *post-modern* outlook that breaks with this supposedly fruitless quest and contents itself with adding a further, interesting chapter to the story of western liberal bourgeois culture. Perhaps this is simply a case of terminological slippage brought about by the difficulty of transferring labels from one vocabulary to another. It does, however, suggest a certain ambivalence about Rorty's understanding of present-day literary culture.

Literary critics have a fair working notion of the difference between 'modernist' and 'post-modernist' writing. Like all such distinctions it is highly contestable, but it does at least serve to pick out two contrasting ideas of how narratives work their effect.[29] The difference could be stated roughly as follows. 'Modernist' writers like Joyce, Woolf or Lawrence saw themselves as creating a new and better form of realism, one that discarded the circumstantial trappings of Victorian fiction and rendered the truth of subjective experience. Having done with the otiose machinery of mere description was a stage toward achieving that rapt intensity and heightened perception which these novelists took for their goal. The idea of 'realism' was thus redefined in keeping with a shift from broadly objective to more 'psychological' or inward criteria. This is something like the pattern of changing priorities that Rorty traces down through the history of western philosophic thought. Empiricists may quarrel with idealists, but both seek the same kind of ultimate knowledge, in the one case as grounded in external reality, in the other as somehow built into our transcendental faculties. Literary 'modernism' could therefore be seen as a further variation on the terms laid down by this traditional debate. 'Post-modernists' on the other hand (Pynchon, Fowles, Barthelme and others) have no such recuperative end in view. They accept that reality is made, not found, and that novels had better draw attention to their own fictive devices, rather than trying to pass themselves off as chunks of real-life experience. Post-modernism finally dispenses with the notion that literature can give us a privileged view, whether of the world outside the book or of the mind's interior workings.

Now it may be, as I said, that Rorty is just adopting a handy conflation of terms when he equates literary 'modernism' with the pragmatist turn in philosophy. On the other hand it is striking that the story he tells about philosophy and its present situation is more like a traditional well-made plot than a piece of post-modernist invention. It is a tale of obstacles finally surmounted, of problems brought about by a sequence of errors and resolved by an effort of clarifying hindsight. This is the whole point of Rorty's insistence that we stick to a first-order 'natural' perspective, rather than seeking forms of meta-narrative justification. The story then reads as a straightforward persuasive account of how we (the bourgeois liberal intelligentsia) have put away the problems of traditional thought and emerged at last as decent commonsense pragmatists. Much the same moral is to be found in any number of nineteenth-century narratives concerning deluded presumptions of mastery and the saving virtue of sensibly accepting the limits of human nature. Such exemplary fictions treat their protagonists in the manner that Rorty regards his philosophers from Descartes to Dewey. It is a tale which disclaims meta-narrative authority in the interest of conveying the pragmatist outcome to which all its episodes lead up. But this means adopting an implied teleology, a grasp of its unfolding narrative logic which does, in effect, lay claim to superior insight. Rorty might respond that this objection is misconceived: that he is *not*, after all, seeking to have the last word but precisely to continue the open-ended dialogue which thrives in a liberal-pragmatist culture. But this, once again, begs the question *how* – by what shaping of narrative intent – the story turns out as it does. That everything points so clearly to a pragmatist denouement implies a strategy with its own secure standing atop all the partial views on display.

There is, I would argue, a sharp distinction between Rorty's avowed 'post-modernist' attitude and the kind of story he tells by way of backing it up. In literary terms, the main point of post-modernist narratives is to challenge, subvert or paradoxically exploit the conventions in play when we make sense of texts. This involves a high degree of self-conscious contrivance and, by implication, a manipulative stance outside and above the story-line flow of events. In this sense, contrary to Rorty's argument, post-modernism carries along with it a strong 'meta-narrative' tendency which precisely *undermines* the naïve habit of trust in first-order 'natural' narration. As novelists (like critics) grow increasingly aware of the conventions that govern their genre, so fiction moves away from a naturalized 'realist' mode and begins to exploit its more remote possibilities. Thus one could argue that post-modern literature is *not*, as Rorty would have it, caught up in a widespread movement of revolt against forms of meta-narrative constraint. On the contrary, it manifests a will to demystify realist conventions and – accessory to that – a highly self-conscious, manipulative dealing with plot and narration.

That Rorty draws the opposite moral is a consequence of his always assuming that intellectual history *must* be heading towards the looked-for pragmatist and bourgeois-liberal conclusion. It is a framing assurance which inevitably leaves its mark on the shape and structure of Rorty's narrative. What is more, it exemplifies precisely the kind of naturalizing gambit which post-modern writers treat with such evident suspicion. Like the typical nineteenth-century novel, it raises a specific set of cultural values – those of bourgeois liberalism – to the status of a wholesale teleology and universal ethos. As a pragmatist Rorty can readily concede that his is just one story among many, to be picked up, developed or abandoned according to its present and future utility. But of course this wouldn't prevent it from having the last word against anyone who wanted philosophy to be *more* than just a story – who resisted, that is, the pragmatist upshot of Rorty's tale. Under cover of its liberal-pluralist credentials, this narrative very neatly closes all exits except the one marked 'James and Dewey'. The rejection of a meta-narrative standpoint goes along with a refusal to entertain any serious alternative account of what philosophy ought to be. It is this use of a liberal rhetoric to frame an authoritative message which marks the real kinship between Rorty's pragmatism and nineteenth-century narrative forms.

Hayden White raises some relevant points in the context of modern historiography.[30] Seeking to explain the current disrespect (as he sees it) for history as an intellectual discipline, White finds a reason in its failure to exploit a full range of *narrative* modes and options. More specifically, he argues that historians are still content to work, by and large, within the 'old' nineteenth-century conventions of plot and chronological sequence. By ignoring the alternatives provided by modern (and post-modern) literary texts, historians have effectively consigned themselves to a marginal position in contemporary culture. White is repeating what Nietzsche had to say about the uses and abuses of history, especially its function of suppressing creative thought by preserving a bland, homogeneous notion of 'tradition'. The following passage communicates the spirit of White's polemical argument:

> When many contemporary historians speak of the 'art' of history, they seem to have in mind a conception of art that would admit little more than the nineteenth-century novel as a paradigm . . . they seem to mean that they are artists in the way that Scott or Thackeray were artists. . . . While often displaying the works of modern nonobjective artists

on their walls and in their bookcases, historians continue to
act as if they believed that the major, not to say the sole,
purpose of art is to tell a story. . . . It is of course true that the
artist's purpose *may* be served by telling a story, but this is
only one of the possible modes of representation offered to
him today, and it is a decreasingly important one at that, as
the *nouveau roman* in France has impressively shown.[31]

From this it is clear how different are White's and Rorty's views
on the type of narrative paradigm required by a genuinely
'post-modern' culture. For White, the need to 'tell a story' is no
longer the main consideration, at least in terms of what Rorty
would call 'first-order natural pragmatics'. The advent of
alternative, challenging forms of representation has rendered
such storytelling not perhaps redundant, but certainly open to
meta-narrative experiment.

Seen in this light, Rorty's pragmatist assumptions take on a
more restrictive, even doctrinaire aspect. They work to legitimize a fairly narrow view of what philosophy (or criticism)
ought to regard as its proper cultural role. Having a story to tell
about that role and its background may represent a more
'liberal' option than merely turning over the same old problems of language, logic and truth. But any freedom in the
manner of telling is strongly overdetermined, for Rorty, by the
need to arrive at a suitable (i.e. liberal-pragmatist) conclusion.
The constraints of this narrative may not announce themselves
in the form of theory or principle, but they are none the less
compelling for that.

One such tale is that which runs from Plato, through Kant
and Nietzsche to Heidegger and (as its crowning episode)
American pragmatism. Up to Kant it is a history of misapplied
reason, of metaphors taken for concepts and philosophy side-
tracked into various forms of epistemological dead-end. With
Nietzsche these illusions begin to lose their power and to seem
mere fictions created in pursuit of an errant western metaphysics. Heidegger is left to declare a final break with that whole
tradition; to insist that we give up the search for a grounding
epistemology and ask instead the more fundamental questions
of Being and authentic existence. Heidegger is among the
heroes of Rorty's narrative, but only up to a point.[32] Rorty

applauds his turning away from the idea of knowledge as a form of correspondence, a matching-up between truthful propositions and the facts they represent. That logic should provide a set of infallible criteria for judging the accuracy of assertions – a language that would 'cut nature at the joints' – is seen as the root delusion of Western epistemology. All this Heidegger tells us, along with the message that thinking consists in a kind of productive brooding on language more akin to poetry than logical argumentation. It is in the choice of a 'final vocabulary' that philosophers stake their claim to truth, and not in the mere conceptual juggling with abstract schemes of correspondence. But Heidegger (according to Rorty) betrays this promising insight by failing to press the argument through to its destined pragmatist conclusion. He links the critique of rationalist tradition with a wholesale dismissal of modern, technological culture. Pragmatism he views as the vulgar philosophic counterpart of a science which perverts all thinking into forms of instrumental reason. Thus Heidegger's 'final vocabulary' is a language of nostalgia for lost authenticity, one that refuses all commerce with the ongoing narrative of western civilization.

But Heidegger is mistaken, Rorty thinks, in his reading of the present-day cultural signs. His mystified language of primordial Being goes along with a wilful blindness to the virtues and viability of bourgeois liberal institutions. Where Heidegger tells a story of irreparable loss – of the constant falling-away from truth and authenticity – Rorty responds with a utopian or science-fiction narrative hopeful of good things to come. Such, he argues, is the vision vouchsafed by Dewey's pragmatist faith in the continuing productive dialogue of science, society and cultural need. When Heidegger turned his back on this American portent, he effectively condemned his own philosophy to a condition of marginal relevance and helpless mystification. Had he but grasped the pragmatist upshot towards which his arguments were heading, Heidegger would also have seen that liberal democracy, American-style, was the saving hope of science and philosophy alike.

V

It is thus fair to say that Rorty's whole account of western philosophy, past and present, rests on his distinctively 'American' view of pragmatist cultural politics. Underlying his version of Heidegger is the argument that America now represents – as once did Greece or Germany – the source of all that is best and most productive in modern thought. This westering movement is imagined as a kind of *translatio imperii*, a turning away from classic 'European' preoccupations in order to set the American experience in its own distinctive cultural context. Literary critics like Geoffrey Hartman have a similar end in view when they insist on the freedom to adopt an interpretative style more adventurous than anything sanctioned by classical precept.[33] Hartman is clear enough about his motives in this. It is an effort to rescue American literary culture from the stifling influence of T. S. Eliot and his strongly Anglophile ideas of 'tradition' and critical decorum. Rorty seeks to do the same for philosophy, though in his case the ideological commitment is more plainly spelled out. 'Postmodernist bourgeois liberalism' is the end to which philosophy must always have aspired if America is now to be the brave new world of intellectual progress and freedom. To tell the story differently, as Heidegger does, is to miss the whole point of this edifying narrative.

It is quite natural, given these socio-political commitments, that Rorty should so construct his case as to exclude *de jure* any possibility of an 'enlightened' counter-critique. His idea of a post-modern pragmatist culture is deeply wedded to the hegemonic values of present-day American society. It reverses the traditional assumption – common to most thinkers from Plato to the present – that philosophy concerns itself with reasons and truths independent of mere opinion. This opposition between *logos* and *doxa*, reasoned argument and popular prejudice, no longer has a place in Rorty's philosophy. Opinion becomes the very element wherein societies discover their self-image and the stories by which they choose to live. Pragmatists and liberals can afford to acknowledge this absence of legitimating theory. Life goes on, the story unfolds, and their business is to make it hang together as interestingly as possible. Others – notably Marxists – may claim to criticize that story from a higher, 'meta-narrative' standpoint. But they, like Plato, can be taken as speaking for a culture which has not yet arrived at the pragmatist stage of mature self-acceptance.

One might argue that Rorty is excessively sanguine about the prospects of American civilization. In the light of recent history it is difficult to share his rosy view of the benefits stored up for society at large through the wise application of modern technology. Nor does it take a very cynical observer to remark that American 'liberal' ideology has proved itself adaptable to meanings and purposes not always in keeping with the highest intellectual virtues. But this is to challenge the pragmatists on their own chosen ground, since it amounts to rejecting their preferred version of events and simply putting another, rival interpretation in its place. An effective counter-argument would need to do more than this. It would have to insist at every stage that enlightened critique is *not* a concept disposed of by pragmatist arguments; that cultural forms of life *can* be understood and criticized on terms not their own; and that the powers of theoretical reflection are *not* exhausted in the recounting of first-order myths and narratives. Only thus could it seriously challenge the perfect (if circular) consistency of Rorty's pragmatist outlook.

One line of argument is put most forcefully by Alasdair MacIntyre in his essay 'Rationality and the Explanation of Action'. MacIntyre sets out to controvert the idea that actions and motives can be accounted for only according to the cultural 'rules' or criteria that implicitly govern them. Such, as we have seen, is Winch's argument against any form of judgement which adopts a critical standpoint *outside* the system of beliefs in question. Criticism is thus deprived of its power to question ideologies or, at the limit, to distinguish 'rational' from 'irrational' modes of thought. MacIntyre cites the case of historians who reject the smug rationalism of nineteenth-century 'progressive' opinion. They, like Winch, make it a point of principle not to judge past or alien cultures by present-day 'enlightened' standards of reason. But, as MacIntyre points out, they are prone to argue that certain beliefs (e.g. in witchcraft) are best explained in social-diagnostic terms, while others (like minority scientific views) have their own kind of justifying logic. As MacIntyre puts it,

> To characterize a belief as irrational is to characterize the intellectual procedures and attitudes of those who hold it. It is to say in effect – at least in the extreme case – that the believer is invulnerable to rational argument. . . . For the explanation of rational belief terminates with an account of the appropriate intellectual norms and procedures; the explanation of irrational belief must be in terms of causal generalizations which connect antecedent conditions specified in terms of social structures or psychological states – or both – with the genesis of beliefs.[34]

This is to argue, as against Rorty, that there *are* situations in which one system of thought may find itself compelled to explain, or 'rationally' criticize, another. That this should be so is a logical necessity built into the very structure of causal explanation.

Philosophers like Winch would rebut this argument by claiming that *reasons*, not causes, are what explain human actions and social arrangements, so that all explanations of a psycho-social kind are simply beside the point. MacIntyre's response is to argue, again, that the self-understanding of a culture or its individual subjects may not be the *real* – or may perhaps be only a *partial* – explanation of motives and actions. To think otherwise is to give up distinguishing adequate from inadequate explanations. And this principled agnosticism can only lead to a quite untenable relativist position. Some kind of meta-narrative claim is implicit in all attempts to reach a genuine understanding of alien belief-systems. As MacIntyre points out, 'the concept of ideology can find application in a society where the concept is not available to the members of that society.' And the fact that the concept is applicable – that it serves an explanatory purpose – implies furthermore 'that criteria beyond those available in the society may be invoked to judge its rationality'.[35]

MacIntyre's arguments indicate one line of resistance to the pragmatist position, coming as they do from a squarely opposed philosophical standpoint. Another, I have suggested, is the very different sense which attaches to the term 'post-modern' when used to describe certain textual strategies of ideological demystification. Rorty's reading of Derrida is similarly open to challenge. Deconstruction is not – or not only – a handy ruse for dismantling the truth-claims of philosophers from Plato to Heidegger. Nor is it a kind of halfway house on the road to pragmatist wisdom, prevented from getting there (as Rorty would argue) by its lingering obsession with a phantom 'metaphysics of presence'. Deconstruction is most importantly a textual activity that works to undermine the kinds of consoling self-image given back by a dominant cultural tradition. Up to a point, of course, Derrida and Rorty seem to be engaged upon a similar project. Both see the turn towards epistemology as marking a specific aberration in western thought, the result of certain (mainly visual) metaphors being promoted to the status of sovereign concepts. Both set out to deconstruct that tradition by exposing the ruses it has to adopt in order to maintain its authority. But where Rorty draws his pragmatist moral, content to let old problems fall away, Derrida insists on thinking them through to a radically disruptive end. Deconstruction is in this sense the closest 'philosophical' counterpart to that strain of unsettling meta-narrative experiment found in post-modernist fiction. That is to say, it interrogates not only the concepts of western tradition but the usual ways of fitting them into a sequence, a history, a well-formed narrative. This is where deconstruction runs counter to Rorty's pragmatist requirements.

There is no doubting the current appeal – among American intellectuals – of this sophisticated update of Deweyan pragmatism. Like the 'end of ideology' argument propounded in the 1950s, it holds out the prospect of a new social order based on widespread consensus and no longer needing to criticize its own ideological assumptions. Basic to that earlier movement was the premiss that real social conflict had come to an end, so that now there was simply no reason for mounting any kind of radical critique. Consensus was sufficient guarantee that majority interests would be well looked after. But the 'end of ideology' was itself a very potent ideological myth, one which helped sustain the current self-image of American society. It ignored, for one thing, the differences of interest between those within and those outside the established dominant consensus. Like Rorty's 'postmodern bourgeois liberalism', it was very much the creed of an intellectual class with the leisure to interpret society according to its own cultural lights.

MacIntyre argues forcefully against the idea that philosophy can simply identify its interests with those of a prevailing (no matter how 'liberal') consensus. His reasons for rejecting it are linked to his reasons for denying the 'end of ideology' thesis. That tensions should exist between philosophy and ideology is not just a symptom of local maladjustment but an inbuilt necessity of rational thought. It is, he writes, 'one of the signs . . . that an ideology is living and not dead, that it should actually breed conflict both with the philosophy and with the empirical science of its day.' Without the possibility of such conflicts developing, thought would be deprived not only of its critical capacity but also of its practical incentives. Consequently, MacIntyre argues,

> any situation in which an ideology has no problems of conflict with philosophy or human or natural science is characteristically a sign, not that the ideology in question has triumphantly solved the intellectual problems of the age, but rather that the ideology has become empirically vacuous and won its freedom from conflict at the cost of becoming empirically and perhaps practically empty.[36]

Rorty's pragmatist outlook is in danger of succumbing to precisely this condition of unresisting passive ideology. The story as he tells it has definite attractions, combining a grand historical sweep with a fine sense of having come out on top of all the age-old intellectual problems and conflicts. But it rests, as I have argued, on a narrative ploy – joined with a reading of the 'post-modern' situation – which philosophers and critics had best not accept on its own persuasive terms.

7

Suspended sentences: textual theory and the law

I

Jurisprudence is becoming a fashionable source of arguments and analogies for literary critics. Debates about the nature of legal reasoning, the laws of evidence and the politics of juridical discourse are seen as bearing directly on issues in literary theory. At present these overtures are distinctly unilateral, with students of law showing little interest in returning the compliment. Occasionally it is recognized, in passing, that what goes on in a court of law is often rather like what happens in novels. 'Hard' cases of various kinds have their obvious analogues in fictional terms. Where motive is in question, the process of arriving at a just or equitable verdict may strike the observer as something like the experience of reading a complex 'psychological' novel. Other cases – those where the background situation needs piecing together from circumstantial clues – might resemble a piece of detective fiction. But these are just loose and strictly onesided analogies, based on the assumption that law is 'for real' and literature at most a source of illustrative fancies. Furthermore, it is the traditional well-made plot – the kind where everything hangs together, at least when one has turned the last page – that always underlies these analogies. It is hard to imagine any student of law being told to read Kafka or Robbe-Grillet as adjuncts to a training in legal interpretation.

In this chapter I am not so much concerned with such broad analogies between law and the novel. Nor do I intend simply to reverse those assumptions, treat the law as a species of elaborate narrative fiction, and argue (like Barthes, in a famous essay from *Mythologies*) that bourgeois 'justice' most often takes the form of a wholesale novelistic frame-up.[1] My concern is more with those questions of language and interpretation that preoccupy certain critical theorists and legal philosophers alike. What I *do* want to challenge is that notion of a one-way flow of authority, such that 'the law' (as sovereign discourse) seems to offer some kind of legitimating ground for interpretation in general. In fact, as I shall argue, debates in modern jurisprudence have stopped far short of the questions opened up by contemporary critical theory. In this they are constrained by the need to preserve the authority of law as a discourse immune to any form of antinomian critique. Legal philosophers may go a long way towards acknowledging that law is always and everywhere a product of interpretation, a reading of the evidence based in turn upon statutes, precedents and other sources of (written or textual) authority. But to push beyond such token recognition to a full-scale deconstructive treatment of the law is clearly to challenge every source of its legitimating power.

We can begin on firm legal ground with the seemingly straightforward distinction between statute law and case law. Statutes are handed down in the form of definitive rulings arrived at by an authorized legislative body and applied wherever their specific provisions permit. In principle at least their terms are unambiguous and their range of application clearly defined by the care and precision with which those terms are framed. They aspire, in short, to the condition of straightforward declarative *statements* embodying a definite decision procedure to be followed strictly according to rule. Case law, on the other hand, applies to instances where no such clear-cut rules are available, since there exists no statute whose provisions would cover the case in hand. The judge must then have recourse (in the words of H. L. A. Hart) to

> particular precedents or past decisions of courts which are treated as material from which legal rules may be extracted although, unlike legislative rules, there is no authoritative or uniquely correct formulation of the rules so extracted.[2]

Hart goes on to give a brief (and rather sceptical) account of the reasoning that is often assumed to underlie this application of 'rules' to particular cases. Where the law is clear-cut, any judgement will be 'exclusively a matter of deductive inference', the product of a syllogism in which the major premiss is the rule concerned and the minor premiss the established facts of the case in hand. Where the appeal is to precedent, this argument can then be turned round so as to keep the idea of 'rules' in play but introduce a measure of interpretative latitude. With case law it is a matter of treating 'the courts' extraction of a rule from past cases as inductive reasoning, and the application of that rule to the case in hand as deductive reasoning' (Hart, p. 99). Thus both types of case can be represented as rule-governed, with the difference that no fixed form of words may exist to settle what *counts* as the relevant rule. Nevertheless it is assumed that any appeal to past decisions in case law will be governed by implicit norms and procedures with a kind of unwritten prescriptive force.

It is not hard to find parallels between case law and the business of interpreting literary texts. Both activities arguably depend on a generalized grasp of the 'rules' which govern their particular discourse. Both, on the other hand, resist any attempt to erect those rules into a clear-cut system of articulated theory or principles. The critic gets along with a sense of the various regulative 'contexts' to which he or she can appeal in the face of some especially baffling or ambiguous passage. Where meanings threaten to get out of hand – or where deconstruction lets language run riot in the endless 'dissemination' of sense – the interpreter can always recall us to sanity by insisting on 'context' as a principle of order. This appeal takes various forms, according to the critic's predilection. It may be the context of the work as a whole, conceived as exerting a pressure to conform on its various constituent meanings. Or it may be the larger historical context which scholar-critics most often call to witness by way of keeping the plurality of sense within tolerable limits. Or, again, it may take the form (currently enjoying a certain revival) of a downright appeal to authorial *intention* as the final determinant of literary meaning. Each of these viewpoints has its present-day upholders, and all of them unite to reject what is seen as the total disrespect for contextual restraints displayed by the deconstructionists.

This threat has a twofold aspect. On the one hand, it is a matter of critical *theory* overstepping the limits of intuitive sense and presuming to doubt where (as 'reason' would have it) no doubt can sensibly be raised. On the other, it is the fear of a textual 'free play' which seems to overrun all boundaries of context and thus to dissolve the very distinction between text and commentary, 'literature' and 'criticism'.[3] On both counts the deconstructors appear open to the charge of betraying their trust as faithful interpreters of the text. Nor, of course, would they wish to rebut that charge, since to them the very notion of a 'faithful' reading is the product of arbitrary rules (like the appeal to 'context') whose validity is always subject to doubt.

It might seem unlikely that theorists of jurisprudence could afford to entertain such a sceptical argument. Yet here also there are those who adopt a thoroughgoing conventionalist position, such that the 'rules' of juridical procedure amount to nothing more than a set of arbitrary protocols, incapable of truly 'deciding' a case one way or the other. At its most extreme this doctrine would claim that judges in effect *make law* every time they go beyond the explicit provisions of a clear-cut judicial precedent. And this would apply not only to obvious 'hard cases' but to just about *every* case in practice, since (as Hart observes) 'rules cannot provide for their own application, and even in the clearest case a human being must apply them' (p. 64). On this view there is no firm distinction to be drawn between the one kind of reasoning (supposedly 'deductive') which argues logically stepwise from premises to judgement, and the other ('inductive') approach which arrives at its conclusions by a more roundabout route. Even the distinction between statute and case law begins to look rather shaky. No matter how carefully framed to meet all contingencies of future application, a law still has to be *interpreted* in light of each particular case. This makes it possible to argue that judges are never constrained by existing law but exercise an ultimate freedom of decision, even where they *choose* to think themselves so constrained. In this case they are acting in accordance with precedent but *not* with some binding legal obligation which prevents them (in law) from acting differently.

Hart calls such scepticism simply 'unacceptable' but does concede that it serves to emphasize how difficult it is 'to give any exhaustive account of what makes a "clear case" clear or makes a general rule obviously and uniquely applicable to a particular case' (p. 64). The sceptic's problems result, he argues, from an overreaction against the kind of narrow formalism which takes deductive reasoning as the only way to arrive at valid conclusions. Such reasoning would fit the facts as required only in the ideal case of an actual situation whose every last detail was explicitly provided for by the law in question. Otherwise the facts and the 'rules' which cover them must always leave room for some looseness of fit in the way those rules are applied. For the rules to work at all there must, Hart says, be 'a core of settled meaning'. But as soon as those rules are applied there will also be 'a penumbra of debatable cases in which words are neither obviously applicable nor obviously ruled out' (p. 63). The sceptic's mistake is to think that the only cases where the law truly holds are those in which a clear-cut piece of legislation matches up directly with a plain set of facts. This ignores the obvious problem, as Hart points out, that

> fact situations do not await us neatly labelled, creased and folded; nor is their legal classification written on them simply to be read off by the judge. Instead, in applying legal rules, someone must take the responsibility of deciding that words do or do not cover some case in hand. (pp. 63–4)

To conclude from this that all cases are strictly undecidable – the sceptic's conclusion – is to ignore the range of 'penumbral' applications that any given law must somehow cover. It assumes, that is to say, an impossibly high standard of conceptual 'fit' between laws and cases, such that no working system could ever live up to the notional ideal.

A similar charge is often brought against deconstructionist literary critics.[4] Deconstruction starts out (so this argument runs) from a wholly unworkable idea of how words and things are supposed to match up in a one-to-one scheme of representation. Having shown that this 'theory' fails to work – that reference comes about only by virtue of a complex signifying system – deconstruction then swings to the opposite

extreme, declaring that reference is in any case strictly impossible, since reality is 'textual' through and through. Such polemical arguments possess little force, working as they do with a
grossly simplified and distorted idea of what 'deconstruction'
is about. But they offer a useful point of entry to the line of
counter-argument which Hart adopts against sceptical philosophies of law. In both cases the saving resort is to a commonsense position which denies that there was *really* any problem
in the first place, the issue having been conjured up by a false
idea of what counts as an adequate explanation. Thus Hart
rejects scepticism – or the notion that judges 'make' law – in
favour of a generalized assurance that valid inferences do in
fact occur, though often on the basis of complex judgements
which cannot be reduced to any hard-and-fast 'rule'. Otherwise, he argues, law would give way to the 'nightmare' vision
of a free-for-all system where judges could invoke any
governing principles that happened to suit their own
interests.

Again, this argument will sound familiar to anyone who has
followed recent debates in literary theory. Stanley Fish is most
prominent among those who would contest the sceptical
rigours of deconstruction by arguing that texts make sense
according to powerful conventions underwritten by communal agreement.[5] What shall *count* as a valid interpretation is
not to be decided by appealing to authorial intentions or any
other kind of first principle. Rather, it is a question of seeing
how the relevant conventions work to legitimate certain
readings and exclude others which fail to conform to the
prevailing standards of interpretative competence. Critics can
afford to let go of the idea that there must be some single right
reading – at least as a matter of working faith – on which their
whole enterprise stands or falls. The only such constraint,
according to Fish, is the set of tacit norms and conventions by
which the appropriate community decides which readings are
to count as 'competent'. Such decisions emerge from a kind of
professionalized collective unconscious, a process of selection
which decides (among other things) which student essays are
up to the mark or which books are sufficiently good to merit
publication. There exists, in short, a whole powerful set of
institutional norms and expectations which fix certain limits to

the licence accorded to competent readers. Deconstruction would thus seem to miss the point in its startled discovery that meaning is 'merely' the product of arbitrary codes and conventions. It would figure as the latest, most sophisticated version of the error to which all sceptical philosophies are prone: the false trail that leads from the non-availability of absolute truth to the idea that truths are always and everywhere a species of radical fiction. According to Fish, such doubts are best laid to rest by a clear understanding of the role played by *institutions* – or communities of knowledge – in the production and maintenance of meaning.

Fish has lately drawn attention to the close similarities between legal and literary acts of interpretation.[6] Both take rise within a complex system of values and assumptions, the 'rules' of which can never be established to the point of subsuming all relevant cases. To interpret is always to understand a text or document in the light of conventions that effectively decide which *aspects* of the case are to weigh most heavily in reaching a final judgement. There are no hard facts that exist outside this context of governing assumptions. When the critic reads a novel, or the judge reviews a case, they are both engaged in a communal enterprise which makes it impossible to wipe the slate clean and start out from self-evident factual grounds. The critic will begin with a working idea of the various generic constraints which mark off fictional language from other kinds of prose discourse. The formalist might want to argue that the text itself provides all the necessary cues and indications as to how it must be read. Thus a poem will exploit certain formal devices which focus attention on its language, while a novel may involve such distinctive features as the so-called 'fictional preterite', rarely found in other contexts. But these are just conventional markers which only make sense – according to Fish – if one knows how to read them aright and relate them to a larger background of tacit interpretative norms. There are no brute facts or straightforward descriptive data which suffice to define this or that text as a poem or novel. In the same way, there is no kind of legal reasoning from facts or precepts which doesn't involve a generalized sense of judicial fitness. There is always already an interpretative context, a background of pre-understanding without which legal judgements would have no force or institutional validity.

Fish offers this argument as a means of avoiding the two main errors to which (as he reads them) legal theorists are prone. On the one hand is the 'positivist' attitude which insists that laws are statements of *fact* whose binding character can always be established by a careful construal of their terms and provisions. On the other is the so-called 'realist' outlook which reacts against this narrow positivism by declaring that laws are open-textured and judges therefore free to interpret them as they will. Fish sees the same false dichotomy at work in the field of literary criticism.

> Just as there are those in the legal community who have insisted on construing statutes and decisions 'strictly' (that is, by attending only to the words themselves), so there are those in the literary community who have insisted that interpretation is, or should be, constrained by what is 'in the text'; and just as the opposing doctrine of 'legal realism' holds that judges' 'readings' are always rationalizations of their political or personal desires, so do proponents of critical subjectivity hold that what a reader sees is merely a reflection of his predispositions and biases.[7]

The only way out of this trap, Fish suggests, is to recognize that neither version leaves room for the background of tacit *institutional* norms and assumptions which enter into every act of judgement. The positivist ignores this background in thinking that the legal 'facts' will speak for themselves, so that any interpretation is strictly a matter of secondary glossing in this or that context. The realist ends up in an equally untenable position by assuming that laws are totally devoid of determinate sense and therefore open to a radical new interpretation each time they are applied.

Fish's objection to the latter line of argument resembles his case against deconstruction. Such extreme forms of linguistic scepticism arise, he argues, from a failure to appreciate the extent to which all understanding depends on the acceptance of communal norms. The literary critic (even the deconstructionist) has to suppose that his or her text will be construed by a reader who genuinely wants to make sense of it. And not just *any* kind of sense, furthermore, but a meaning as nearly as possible in line with those other, more specialized forms of constraint that operate in various professions or disciplines of study. There is no theory of interpretation so resolutely anti-nomian that it asks for its own arguments to be systematically misread. Deconstructionists may offend against just about every established norm of interpretative tact and relevance. Yet the *force* of such readings must always depend on the existence of strong but elastic conventions which can stretch around even the more extreme varieties of sceptical attack. Otherwise the texts of deconstruction would simply languish unread, or – what amounts to the same thing – be read without the least regard for their sense or purpose.

Fish takes the same argumentative line against the legal 'realists', those who would have it that judges always impose their own will under cover of applying some established law. As he remarks,

> a judge who decided a case on the basis of whether or not the defendant had red hair would not be striking out in a new direction; he would simply not be acting as a judge because he could give no reasons for his decision that would be seen *as* reasons by competent members of the legal community.[8]

Again, the analogies with literary theory come readily to hand. Even the most striking of new departures – like the 'anti-novel' or *nouveau roman* – presuppose all manner of established conventions against which to measure their radical intent. Critical theories are likewise constrained to make sense of themselves *and* the texts they read by showing at least a residual respect for the conventions of critical debate. The out-and-out sceptic and the hard-line traditionalist are each falling victim to the same delusion. They are both taking it for granted that the only valid reading is one that comes equipped with good legitimating grounds *beyond* those provided by communal sanction. The sceptic discovers that such grounds are unobtainable, and therefore decides that reading must henceforth be a game of randomly competing strategies. And this false reasoning also infects the opposition, those who would 'save' their discipline from the threat of mere anarchy loosed upon texts. 'In searching for a way to protect against arbitrary readings', the conservative, according to Fish,

> is searching for something he already has and could not possibly be without, and he conducts his search by projecting as dangers and fears possibilities that could never be realized and by imagining as discrete, entities that are already filled with the concerns of the enterprise they supposedly threaten.[9]

Such paranoid defensive postures would come to seem merely beside the point if it were accepted (by lawyers and critics alike) that meaning is an *institutional* affair, created and sustained by communities of knowledge.

II

I have presented Fish's arguments in detail because they state very clearly and (within limits) persuasively the case for what might be called a consensus view of interpretative reason. Hart takes a broadly similar line in rejecting the extremes of 'positivist' and 'realist' doctrine. Like Fish, he rests his argument squarely on the idea of law as a corporate institution with its own (often unstated) 'rules' as to what makes sense in juridical terms. He also looks to speech-act philosophy as a way beyond the deadlocked antinomies of recent debate. Legal theorists have too long been bogged down in attempts to define the logical standing of abstract entities like the 'state', 'corporation' or 'rights'.

> Some say . . . that the things for which these legal words stand are real but not sensory; others that they are fictitious entities; others that these words stand for plain fact but of a complex, future or psychological variety. (Hart, p. 32)

What they had much better do, Hart suggests, is examine the varieties of language use in which these expressions play a role. It would then become clear that language in its legal application is most often *performative* in character, being used not so much to state facts about the world as to register various kinds of promise, obligation, commitment, and so on. This would help to show where those theorists go wrong who see nothing but a choice between positivism (factual self-evidence) on the one hand and realism (the sceptic's retreat) on the other. It would also explain the otherwise puzzling fact that 'it is possible to create obligations, to transfer rights, and generally to change legal situations merely by using language' (Hart, p. 276). Rather than ascribe some species of 'legal alchemy' to words, this power can be accounted for simply by examining the various contexts and customary tokens of performative utterance. Thus legal philosophy is delivered from many of the artificial problems forced upon it by theorists who work with a narrow (or purely 'constative') idea of language.

Speech-act theory has also been invoked by literary critics (Fish among them) as a means of resolving such overworked issues as the problem of authorial intention and the cultural relativity of meaning.[10] Literary texts – so the argument runs – have their own special place in the range of distinctive linguistic practices recognized by any culture. Confronted with a poem or novel, the reader knows straight away that certain commonplace functions of language (e.g. that of simply conveying information) are henceforth suspended, while other, more specialized 'literary' functions are brought into play. Such adjustments are part of the literary 'competence' which readers acquire early on and refine through successive encounters with texts. They have seemed to some critics a sufficient basis for rejecting the fruitless antinomies which vex literary theory. On the question of 'intentions' Fish returns a confident response. Interpretation has to do with meanings implicit in the nature of the literary 'enterprise', and not with meanings uniquely present to some individual consciousness or other. It is hard, he says,

> to think of intentions formed in the course of judicial or literary activity as one's own, since any intention one could have will have been stipulated in advance by the understanding of what activities are possible to someone working in the enterprise.[11]

According to Fish, this serves to rule out the more extreme forms of subjectivist theory, like those advanced in the name of 'creative' reader-response. But it also helps to show what is wrong with formalist appeals to 'the text itself' as a hedge against interpretative freedom. Objectivity of this kind is no more possible than the opposite extreme of total anarchic licence. Both sides to this dispute are ignoring the fact that texts always come to us heavily laden with assumptions about how we should best – most productively – read them.

Fish takes a clearly conservative stance in regard to what he calls the 'institutional' context of literary studies. His essay was written in response to an article by the legal philosopher Ronald Dworkin, a piece which (on the face of it) agrees pretty much with his own position.[12] Dworkin likewise insists that law is pervasively a matter of *interpretation*; that positivists and realists confuse the issue by ignoring this fact; and that valid judgements neither have nor require an 'objective' basis in logic or fact. Yet Fish finds Dworkin perpetually losing sight of these sound ideas and slipping back into bad old habits of thought. In particular, he criticizes Dworkin's claim that, in 'hard cases', it will often be on grounds of *principle* – or conscientious choice – that judges must finally decide. Dworkin sees ample evidence of this in the widely varying interpretations placed on statutes like the Equal Protection Clause in the American Constitution. Nothing, he argues, could demonstrate more clearly the fact that there exists, in the law as in every institution, a range of *political* values and commitments whose effect must often influence the thinking of those who administer justice. Conservatives, liberals and radicals will frequently discover very different meanings in a clause which contains no obvious 'ambiguities' of phrasing or terminology. The well-attested history of visions and revisions on crucial points of constitutional law is evidence enough, Dworkin thinks, that this is what happens very often in practice.

Dworkin is addressing these issues specifically in the light of American legal history. The main difference between American and English law is the power exercised by the Supreme Court, giving it (as Hart observes) 'a role and a status unlike that of any English court and indeed unlike any courts elsewhere' (p. 124). This situation has arisen through two distinctive turns in the course of American judicial history. The first was the Supreme Court's own decision that 'it had the power to review and declare unconstitutional and so invalid enactments of Congress as well as of the State legislatures' (p. 124). The second was the principle that certain Amendments – those bearing on fundamental matters of life, liberty and individual rights – could be applied by the courts not only to questions of 'form and procedure' but also to the *content* of any legislation. As a result, judges came to exercise a power of decisive intervention on matters of social and political concern, a power far beyond the normal conventions of juridical practice. 'To an English lawyer's astonishment', Hart writes,

> even a statute of Congress of impeccable clarity, passed by an overwhelming majority and conforming to all procedural requirements specified in the Constitution, might still be held invalid because its interference with individual liberty or with property did not satisfy the requirements of a vague undefined standard of reasonableness or desirability, a doctrine which came to be called 'substantive due process'. (p. 125)

Thus the American courts were 'set afloat on a sea of controversial value judgements', and the principle was enshrined – as Dworkin's essay makes clear – that 'hard cases' may finally come down to a choice of ethical commitments.

This helps to explain why the issue between Dworkin and Fish has a particular sharpness and resonance in the context of American legal history. Fish is quite willing to concede that moral and political values have a role to play in the ongoing dialogue that makes up the communal 'enterprise' at large. What he *won't* acknowledge is the force of Dworkin's argument that judges may often strike out in new directions which amount to a 'strong rewriting' of legal precedent. This doctrine seems to Fish just another, and in some ways more desperate, version of the sterile dispute between positivists and realists. That is to say, it sets up a wholly artificial distinction between the plain, uninterpreted 'facts' of legal history on the one hand, and the judge's scope for decisive interventions on the other. Of course, as Fish concedes, there is always a degree of revisionist activity in any attempt to fit existing laws to some new and unique case in hand. 'Paradoxically', he writes, 'one can be faithful to legal history only by revising it, by redescribing it in such a way as to accommodate the issues raised by the present.'[13] But this activity turns out to have sharp limits, since it remains – according to Fish – a 'function of the law's conservatism' that cases must always be related not only to past decisions but also to the tacit communal norms by which those decisions were governed. Any talk of 'striking out in a new direction' is thus to be rejected as false to the nature of legal understanding.

Of course there is a kind of flat good sense about Fish's proposals. It is surely true, as he says, that no interpretation can break completely with existing conventions except by giving up all claims to *make sense* within its own community of knowledge. Nor can one object to his general argument that revision – or the process of continual 'rewriting' – is essentially a part of the communal enterprise and not (in Fish's words) 'the willful imposition of a personal perspective on materials that have their own proper shape'. But there is clearly more at stake in his quarrel with Dworkin, as becomes apparent when they turn expressly to the politics of interpretation. On Fish's consensus view it is possible to accommodate the sharpest differences of principle by reducing them to so many shifting perspectives within the broad community of judgement. 'One man's found history will be another man's invented history, but neither will ever be, because it could not ever be, either purely found or purely invented.'[14] The judge who takes a stand on some principle of politics or conscience will always be governed by consensual ideas which precede and inform his reasoning.

Dworkin and Fish are largely in agreement to this. Fish can trump Dworkin's arguments only by taking the conservative line which insists that political differences are really *nothing more* than variations on a communal theme. His 'institutional' theory of meaning translates very easily into a species of disguised apologetics for the legal and political status quo. Dworkin, on the other hand, reverses that order of priorities by arguing that principles may actually *determine* what counts as a 'just' interpretation in any given case. Debates about the Equal Protection Clause would have had more point, he suggests, 'if it had been more widely recognized that reliance on political theory is not a corruption of interpretation but part of what interpretation means.' And again: 'the history of the last half-century of constitutional law is largely an exploration of exactly these issues of political morality.'[15]

'Institutional' theories can therefore be seen to carry their own specific weight of ideological assumptions. As a literary critic Fish seems committed to much the same kind of levelling consensualist position. Interpreters work within the broad constraints established by a sense of professionalized literary 'competence'. Any reading which sets out deliberately to *flout* those constraints will be either assimilated by a complex process of adjustment or rejected out of hand as a piece of unintelligible whimsy. Once again, the argument moves across imperceptibly from a 'neutral' descriptive stance to a stress on those aspects of the critical enterprise that set firm limits to dissenting views. This would apply as much to deconstructionist readings as to those which claim a Marxist or other political provenance. Such approaches are not, of course, simply ruled out, but their validity is seen as wholly dependent on the governing consensual norms. Deconstruction would be welcomed back into the 'enterprise' on terms laid down by that very consensus whose ruling conventions it calls into doubt. Political readings would likewise be subject to the generalized requirement that they *make good sense* according to the dominant sense-making norms.

The emphasis falls very differently in Dworkin's argument. What we need to consider, he suggests, is the complex relationship between politics, theory and interpretation. One could ask, for instance,

> whether liberalism can indeed be traced back into a discrete epistemological base, different from that of other political theories, and then ask whether that discrete base could be carried forward into aesthetic theory and there yield a distinctive interpretative style.[16]

On Fish's account there is simply *no room* for such far-reaching questions of interpretative theory. They could be of relevance only in so far as the enterprise consented to view them on its own institutional terms. This would effectively rule out any serious critical engagement with principles or theories which challenged that consensus. 'The politics of theory' would thus be construed in such a way that politics took second place to a generalized notion of interpretative competence. And 'theory' itself would be demoted to the role of a discourse, like Fish's, designed to maintain the existing institutional arrangements.

III

In the rest of this chapter I propose to look at other, less conservative uses of the analogy between law and literary theory. In particular I shall raise the question how things might stand for the philosophy of law if one treated some of its more problematic claims from a deconstructionist viewpoint. We have seen how the distinction between 'clear' and 'hard' cases begins to break down once it is recognized how much interpretation is involved in applying even the most perspicuous laws. By the same token it becomes more difficult to assign distinct 'rules' or decision procedures to statute- and case-law instances. Certainly statutes are not to be treated as governed by a constative logic of inference that is largely independent of interpretative context.

Certain problems may be solved by appealing (like Hart) to the notion of *performative* utterance as a means of explaining how language takes effect in law. But performative 'explanations' of any kind create problems of their own, as deconstructionists are fond of pointing out. The founding text of speech-act philosophy – J. L. Austin's *How to do Things with Words*[17] – tries its hand at a number of explanatory schemes but discards them one by one. Austin starts out with the idea that language divides into two main classes of utterance, 'constatives' on the one hand and 'performatives' on the other. Then, as the refinements pile up, he abandons this paradigm and talks instead about the various kinds of 'illocutionary force' attaching to *all* forms of utterance. Constatives effectively partake of this condition, since (as Austin notes) any statement of fact can rendered in the form 'I hereby assert' (and so on). And the opposite also holds, since explicit performatives – vows, promises, etc. – achieve their end by purporting to state some *fact* about the utterer's present intention. In his own words, Austin 'plays Old Harry' with any attempt to *theorize* the nature or limits of speech-act parlance. Yet his followers – linguists and philosophers of language – have tended to set aside Austin's scruples and look for a clear-cut *theory* of performatives. Shoshana Felman has gone furthest towards deconstructing these systematic claims by reading them alongside Austin's endlessly elusive and playful text.[18] The upshot is to show that speech-act 'theory' works to undermine any generalized argument couched in categorical or 'constative' terms.

This throws an awkward paradox into Hart's application of Austin's ideas to the philosophy of law. He suggests that attention to the varieties of performative utterance can 'clarify' and 'disentangle' many of the confusions that beset legal philosophy. In particular it helps to clear away the various 'allegorical' notions conjured up by theorists in the grip of a narrowly constative philosophy of language. Hence the creation of abstract entities, the picture (as Hart describes it) of 'Law breathing into the nostrils of a Limited Company a Will Fictitious but, like that of its Creator, Good' (p. 46). Such pictures lack even the consistency of a 'good' allegory, since they break down into nonsense as soon as one tries to apply them. What they work to conceal, according to Hart, is

the fact that the word 'will' shifts its meaning when we use it of a company: the sense in which a company has a will is not that it wants to do legal or illegal actions but that certain expressions used to describe the voluntary actions of individuals may be used of it under conditions prescribed by legal rules. (p. 46)

It is the business of philosophy, therefore, to attend to these shifts of performative status in the legal uses of language. It will then become clear that all those fictions, 'allegories' and abstract entities result from nothing more than a species of mystifying word-magic.

Such, at least, are the claims for speech-act theory as a means of dissolving philosophical perplexities. Yet Hart continues to speak of legal 'rules' as if these remained largely unaffected by the shift to a performative idiom. Such rules, he says, 'may be conceived from one point of view as giving to the language used a certain kind of force or effect which is in a broad sense their meaning' (p. 94). His own language here is notably evasive and hedged around with qualifying phrases. The 'rules' that apply to legal enactments are effectively equated with their 'meaning', though only 'in a broad sense' and 'from one point of view'. Such departures from plain, categorical statement might perhaps be expected in a passage that enunciates the other, 'performative' aspect of language. Yet there is always a claim – implicit in the grammar of Hart's sentence, no matter how heavily qualified – that speech-act theory can indeed produce 'rules' sufficient to establish the operative logic of juridical discourse. To renounce those claims would be to play into Austin's hands as he follows out the furthest, most unsettling implications of his new discovery. It would amount to 'playing Old Harry' with the rule of law. Hart takes the line of those linguists and philosophers who want to preserve the 'constative'/'performative' distinction, at least in some residually workable form. He assumes that there *must* exist 'rules' of some kind, even though their meaning (or range of application) can only be established by the broadest of contextual definitions.

One finds the same ambivalent reasoning at work whenever Hart appeals to speech-act theory. It mostly arises through his wanting to insist that legal entailments are 'like' the obligations created by ordinary-language performatives, but *only up to a point*. Beyond that, legal usage creates special kinds of meaning or 'force' whose sense can only be obscured by the analogy with everyday language. If 'clear cases' are those where 'there is general agreement that they fall within the scope of a rule', then it is tempting to suppose that such rules and agreements exist simply by virtue of the 'shared conventions of language'. But this gives an oversimplified picture, since, according to Hart,

> it does not allow for the special conventions of the legal use of words, which may diverge from their common use, or for the way in which the meanings of words may be clearly controlled by reference to the purpose of a statutory enactment which itself may be either explicitly stated or generally agreed. (p. 106)

This passage perpetually weaves back and forth between constative and performative assumptions. 'Clear cases' in the end come down to nothing more than a widespread *agreement* that the rules in question have this or that conventional force. Yet there also exists a set of 'special' (distinctively legal) conventions, such that the informal rules and obligations of ordinary language are more rigorously held to account. These statutes would presumably leave no room for the common ambiguities of meaning and force which go along with language in its everyday role. Their legal entailments would perhaps be so clear as to place them on the side of constative, rather than performative utterance. Yet this seems at odds with Hart's steady insistence, here and elsewhere, that the operative force of legal enactments can only be construed in performative terms. The problem is compounded when he goes on to distinguish between statutes 'explicitly stated' and those 'generally agreed'. On Hart's own reasoning no law could be so 'explicit' as to require no support from existing conventions. But performatives only exert their force within a given community of shared understanding whose 'rules' are at most a matter of 'general agreement'. So it is difficult to see what grounds could exist for Hart's distinction between everyday language and the specialized or statutory powers of law.

One way to avoid this aporia is to argue, like Fish, that *all* laws are products of interpretation, so that any talk of 'rules' can henceforth be understood as referring to communal conventions. But this – as we have seen – translates into a levelling consensus view which works to impose its own covert norms. An alternative response would be to press the contradictions of Hart's reasoning to the point where they reveal significant facts about the structure of legal discourse in general. An essay by Paul de Man on Rousseau's *Social Contract* offers perhaps the most rigorous example of this second – deconstructionist – approach.[19] De Man finds a tension everywhere at work between the constative and performative functions of language. This tension is raised to a point of maximal complexity and interest in texts like the *Social Contract* which claim a certain legislative force. Here we can see the effects of that uncoupling between logic and rhetoric which becomes the more apparent as the text strives constantly to cover its disruptive potential. Thus it turns out, according to de Man, that the text takes on a machine-like property of self-supporting language (or 'grammar'), while its workings are ceaselessly exposed or undermined by the presence of rhetorical sleights of hand.

Deconstruction insists on *thinking through* the problems thrown up by performative theories of language. It goes far beyond the consensus view represented by a critic like Fish. 'What remains hidden in the everyday use of language, the fundamental incompatibility between grammar and meaning, becomes explicit when the linguistic structures are stated, as is the case here, in political terms' (de Man, p. 269). A legal text like the *Social Contract* is especially suited to showing up this radical divergence between language as a rule-governed system of *production* and language as a discourse of rhetorical intent. On the one hand it is vital that we read such a text as referring to some real-life state of affairs whose political governance it claims to describe in broadly legislative terms. 'Only thus by referring it back to particular praxis can the *justice* of the law be tested, exactly as the *justesse* of any statement can only be tested by referential verifiability, or by deviation from this verification' (de Man, p. 269). But this is precisely what cannot be done where the text turns out, on a close reading, to rely for its effect on a constant exchange between different (and incompatible) functions of language. It then begins to look as if the 'law of the text' is an alien logic which prevents it from meaning what the legislative function would require it to mean.

It is here that deconstruction poses its challenge to philosophies of language that tacitly assume the unproblematical link between sense and reference. 'The indifference of the text with regard to its referential meaning is what allows the legal text to proliferate, exactly as the coded, preordained repetition of a specific gesture or set of gestures allows Helen to weave the story of the war into the epic' (de Man, p. 268). Hence de Man's claim that the tensions within language are pushed to an extreme where the text tries to state the conditions of its own applicability. On the one hand the *Social Contract* can be read as a series of connected propositions arguing the case for a certain working model of political and legal government. From this point of view it would function as a work of social science, its arguments valid in so far as they presented a consistent and intelligible *theory* of the state. But there is also a performative aspect to Rousseau's language, a series of suasive (illocutionary) precepts whose force cannot possibly be accounted for by any such constative theory. Thus it seems that 'as soon as a text knows what it states, it can only act deceptively, like the thieving lawmaker in the *Social Contract*, and if a text does not act, it cannot state what it knows' (de Man, p. 270). The reader is confronted with a strictly *undecidable* choice between two opposed 'logics' of signification whose effects perpetually disrupt the progress of a straightforward expository reading. The 'law of the text' is too complex and devious to allow for any simple correspondence between theory and practice, 'model' and 'example'. As the *Contract* aspires to a condition of law-like regulative force, so it works to undercut such pretensions by constantly reverting to the language of everyday suasive utterance. Thus the 'theory of politics' transforms itself at last into 'the allegory of its inability to achieve the status of a science' (de Man, p. 271).

IV

These tensions are passed over by theorists like Fish who regard the existence of an ongoing 'enterprise' as sufficient to ensure the intelligibility of legal writ. In Hart they are more prominent, not through any willingness to follow in de Man's direction, but because he is more occupied than Fish with particular problems and detailed arguments. They surface most visibly when he comes to consider the difference between statements of legal *fact* and those binding (or 'operative') forms of expression which carry contractual obligations. Thus lawyers commonly distinguish 'the words used in a lease to create a tenancy from the merely descriptive language of the preliminary recital of the facts concerning the parties and their agreement' (Hart, p. 94). But to keep such obligations in force there must exist 'rules', Hart continues, by which – if the due formalities are met – 'the general law or the legal position of individuals is to be taken as changed'.

This creates a number of problems which Hart – here at least – fails to notice. At what precise stage in the legal proceedings does language assume a binding illocutionary force? If this comes about only *after* the decisive 'change' takes effect – as seems to be implied – then the 'rules' and attendant formalities are empty conventions up to that moment. Performative commitments can only ensue from speech acts that are uniquely empowered to confer an 'operative' force on some particular nexus of words, 'rules' and relevant facts. Such powers cannot attach to the mere 'recital' of background conditions and agreements which make up the appropriate *setting* of the utterance in question. But this bears a curious resemblance to that bad allegorical picture of the Law breathing life into abstract conventions and endowing them with some mysterious Will of its own. What cannot be explained in performative terms – unless by a species of 'verbal alchemy' – is how such utterances acquire a legal force that exceeds and transforms all antecedent rules or conventions. Furthermore, since this applies to 'general laws' as well as to 'the legal position of individuals', there would seem to be no limit to the self-transmuting powers of performative utterance.

This may remind us of de Man's deconstructive reading of Rousseau, where the legal text turns out to exhibit a rhetorical force that everywhere subverts its own best attempts at theoretical statement. Any 'rules' that can be offered are immediately subject to a generalized performative stress which exceeds their powers of explanation. Hart comes up against these problems most directly in a chapter on the status of so-called 'self-referring' laws (pp. 170–8). He distinguishes two main varieties, both of which have struck some theorists as giving rise to awkward implications of paradox or infinite logical regress. On the one hand are those 'self-entrenched' clauses designed to protect some particular piece of legislation by ruling against its later repeal by any normal process of law. Of course such provisions would be useless if the special clause could itself be revoked and the obstacle thus cleared away. To prevent this happening, 'a skilful draftsman will entrench also the clause prescribing the special procedure by making the provisions of his clause apply both to the other clauses and to itself' (Hart, pp. 173–4). The second kind of self-referring law is that which, on the contrary, allows for its own subsequent revision by building in a suitable clause to that effect. Thus Article V of the American Constitution explicitly provides for the amendment of any article therein *including itself*. The problem here is to explain how such a law could still be invoked – or its authority persist – once the repeal had been carried through. It could thus be argued that 'any amendment of Article V which is in fact carried out is an alegal act and not the creation of law by way of a procedure that has been instituted'.[20] The process of repeal might indeed take place, but this would amount to nothing more than a 'social-psychological fact', and would have no genuine or binding force in law.

Hart compares the case of an absolute monarch who agrees to implement a new constitution setting strict limits to his own executive powers. It could be argued that no such self-denying ordinance could ever take effect, since the powers that attach to absolute monarchy are constitutionally unable to revoke their own rule. There is a parallel here with theological debates about the nature of God's omnipotence and the question of whether he could choose so to limit his powers as to leave a decent margin for human freedom. William Empson puts the argument at its most extreme when he suggests that Milton entertained the idea of God's finally deciding to 'abdicate', or give up his authority in favour of some better (maybe pan-theist) scheme of things. This notion is distinctly suggested, Empson finds, in the passage of *Paradise Lost* (III. 305 ff.) where God has his 'best moment'. The uplift is felt 'because he is envisaging his own abdication, and the democratic appeal of the prophecy of God is what makes the whole picture of him just tolerable'.[21] But still the idea creates problems, as Empson concedes in a footnote. 'It had occurred to him [Milton] that, after perfection was attained, God would never issue another order; this would be a great relief, but in a philosophical sense God would be in power as never before.'[22] The projected 'abdication' could only take effect through a somehow *con-tinued* exercise of will made possible by God's omnicompetent foreknowledge. The moral situation might scarcely be improved by adding yet another twist of paradox to the divine character.

Hart thinks that these problems about self-referring laws are nowhere near as difficult as they look. The theorists have mostly gone wrong, he suggests, by assuming that legal consequences follow in the same way as valid deductions in strict logic. From this it appears that no law could possibly be framed in such a fashion as to provide for its own later repeal. With 'self-entrenching' clauses the objection would be that they committed the fault of referring *internally* to their own logical status, thus producing the kinds of vicious paradox that Russell has made familiar. But Hart sees no force in these arguments. The process of amending laws in accordance with their own provisions is not, he insists, a matter of deductive inference. Deduction has to do with timeless *a priori* laws of thought, whereas legal enactments always relate to some particular time and place. Thus: 'the statement that a monarch has unlimited powers until he limits them is quite compatible with the statement that after he limits them they are limited' (Hart, p. 177). The problem about the monarch's (or God's) continuing authority is best got over by regarding his absolute power as 'self-embracing' in the sense that it inclusively provides for its own possible dissolution. Likewise with Article V: its effect is simply to prescribe 'the use of a certain procedure until that procedure is replaced by a new procedure introduced by the old procedure' (Hart, p. 176). If courts *do*, in practice, uphold the difference between changes made in accordance with due procedure and those which lack such warrant, how can it be said that their rulings are 'alegal' or merely 'social-psychological facts'?

Thus Hart once again appeals to the standard *conventions* of legal understanding as a means to avoid the contradictions thrown up by examining their logic too closely. In this he might be thought to converge unexpectedly with a theorist like de Man. Both (one could say) give reasons for abandoning the truth-claims of 'theory' when these come up against forms of legislative utterance which cannot be accounted for by any model of explanatory concepts. 'The legal machine', according to de Man, 'never works exactly as it was programmed to do. It always produces a little more or a little less than the original, theoretical input' (p. 271). But, where Hart concludes that such problems are irrelevant to the practical business of legal inter-pretation, de Man insists on thinking them through to the point of recurrent aporia. This is what gives deconstruction its radical edge in any dealing with matters of interpretative politics. It brings out the latent strains and contradictions which find no place in philosophies of meaning founded on the dominant consensus view. In this way it answers to Dworkin's demand for a critical awareness of the deep-laid differences of *principle* at work within the seamless 'institution' imagined by Fish.

Deconstruction is sometimes attacked as a form of unbridled linguistic nihilism whose effects – if somehow put into practice – would include the dissolution of the individual subject and his or her ethical rights before the law. It can hardly be denied that de Man's account of Rousseau (and, even more, his chapters on Nietzsche[23]) reduce the 'subject' to something like a figment of textual operations beyond its knowledge or power to comprehend. In novelistic terms the analogy with Kafka again comes closest to suggesting the alien, self-estranged logic which de Man finds everywhere at work in these 'exemplary' texts. Yet, as Dworkin says, any 'theory' of law or literature will also entail 'a theory of personal identity adequate to mark off the boundaries of a person from his or her circumstances, and from other persons, or at least to deny the reality of any such boundaries'.[24] Liberal theories will typically attach great importance to the autonomy of individual subjects, their status as defined by some unique combination of 'experience, self-consciousness, and the per-ception or formation of values'. Marxist or sociological theories will, of course, place the emphasis elsewhere.

Deconstruction insists on the *written* character of legal in-stitutions, the extent to which language generates a perpetual tension between 'the text of the law' and 'the law of the text'. It measures the distance that separates those ideal constructions of systematic theory from the process of law as a field of competing political interests and ideologies. If this approach is stigmatized as 'merely' textual, it is well to remember the system of punishment envisaged by Kafka in his tale about the penal colony:

'. . . Whatever commandment the condemned man has disobeyed is written on his body by the Harrow. This condemned man, for instance' – the officer indicated the man – 'will have written on his body: HONOUR THY SUPERIORS!'[24]

The enactments of law are none the less real for existing in the form of (literally) textual inscriptions. Nowhere else do words take effect with such drastic and (as deconstruction would have it) such arbitrary force. Hart muses at one point on the different direction his own early writings might have taken had he then 'commanded' the Austinian distinction between constative and performative language (p. 2). Deconstruction gives reason to doubt such powers of assured theoretical command. It raises questions of interpretative method and principle which legal philosophers have yet to confront. And the results of this encounter – as I have argued here – would differ very sharply from current, more accommodating theories of 'law as interpretation'.

8

On not going relativist (where it counts): deconstruction and 'Convention T'

I

Philosophers have a number of knock-down arguments against relativism in its more extreme or unguarded forms. One such response is to point out simply that relativists undermine their own position as soon as they state it as a matter of consistent doctrine. To say that 'all truths are relative' (or other variations on that theme) is inherently to claim that relativism is in some sense *true*, or closer to the truth than competing ideas of how to get there. Then again, the question 'relative to *what*?' is one that has to be sidestepped if the argument is not to contradict its own premisses. The very word implies that our truth-claims, though lacking any ultimate authority, still must be relative to *something* against which we measure the sheer multiplicity of viewpoints, languages, conceptual schemes, and so on. Of course, it is open to the relativist to argue that no such ultimate relation holds, that viewpoints are relative only to each other and not to some imaginary God's-eye perspective which would finally put them in order. But still there is a problem as to where the relativist gets the authority for making any such claim. It is hard to see where his or her statements could issue from, if not from a standpoint somehow above all the shifting perspectives on offer.

The case can be put from a slightly different angle by asking what grounds relativists can show for taking their particular view of things. Any reasons adduced will always be subject to

the inbuilt proviso that they represent just one line of argument among all the others with an equal claim to truth. But this
puts relativists in an awkward position, since they need to
assume at least a limited background of shared understanding
if their reasons are to carry any kind of conviction. That some
arguments are better than others – more cogent, persuasive or
(in some sense) rational – is the minimum requirement for
putting up a case. Relativism presupposes a framework of
common assumptions, first to give a handle for comparing
different viewpoints, and secondly to explain just *how* and *why*
such differences come into play. Relativists have to suspend
their doctrine at least for the purposes of drawing an intelligible set of distinctions between this or that variety of truth-
claim. Otherwise their argument will lack any genuine force
and leave itself open to all those forms of self-refuting paradox
encountered by out-and-out sceptical philosophies.

This incoherence at the heart of relativist thinking can also
give rise to a subtle form of cultural imperialism. The argument
may start out from a healthy sense of the diverse beliefs and
ideas which make up a flourishing world culture. But it also
carries the suggestion that the only way to take this variety on
board is to adopt the kind of tolerant pluralist position which
tends to characterize the more 'advanced' forms of western
cultural consensus. Thus Richard Rorty, for one, equates his
neo-pragmatist outlook with the virtues and values of present-
day North American society.[1] Pragmatism and relativism are
not to be confused, Rorty argues. The pragmatist holds that
'truth' is a matter of what *works best* in any given situation,
while relativism – at least in its full-blown form – comes down
to a wholly untenable philosophy of 'anything goes'. All the
same, Rorty is willing to dispense with any notion of truth
which looks to legitimize its own special claims by appealing to
standards of rational argument outside some existing social
consensus. For Rorty, that consensus now takes the form of a
broad-based liberal pragmatism, an outlook which welcomes
all manner of competing ideas so long as they don't set up as
purveyors of systematic method or truth. To this extent Rorty's
is indeed a relativist argument. Confronted with the question
'relative to what?' he would cheerfully answer: 'relative to the
interests of culture at large, and American "post-modern"

liberal culture in particular'.[2] Further than that it is impossible to go, he argues, unless by embracing some outworn absolute (Marxist, rationalist, logical positivist or whatever) whose truth-claims no longer have much to offer.

Rorty thus provides a rather striking example of the way that relativist arguments tend to privilege their own cultural values even while professing an attitude of open-minded tolerance. Relativism always has the last word, if only by effectively staging the debate so that nothing would *count* as a challenge to its own line of reasoning. Such arguments gain much more than they lose by relinquishing all claims to ultimate truth. They purport to speak for that stage of 'post-philosophical' wisdom where reason has come to accept its own limits and take on a socially useful role. But they also represent a kind of covert self-interest on behalf of those values, beliefs and ideas which make up the present socio-political consensus. There are no truths to be discovered except by sensibly acknowledging that *all* truths are relative to the context of social values and assumptions from which they take rise. And those interests are at present best served, Rorty thinks, by giving up 'philosophy' as traditionally conceived, and making it play the less elevated role of a moderating partner in the ongoing dialogue of western humanistic culture at large.

Hilary Putnam has argued the case against Rorty on precisely the grounds that relativism entails an element of covert ideological bias. Putnam sets the scene by imagining a cultural relativist (one 'R.R.') confronted by a foreigner, Karl, who comes out with the statement 'Schnee ist weiss' ('snow is white'). True to his lights, R.R. will set out to interpret this sentence in keeping with its own implied background of semantic and cultural norms. It will then be the case that Karl ('whether he knows it or not') can only be speaking the truth of the matter in so far as the conventions of his language allow. But, as Putnam points out,

> the sentence 'Snow is white as determined by the norms of German culture' is itself one which R.R. has to *use*, not just mention, to say what Karl says. On his own account, what R.R. means by *this* sentence is: 'Snow is white as determined by the norms of German culture' is true by the norms of R.R.'s culture (which we take to be American culture).[3]

This amounts to a subtle form of cultural imperialism, since it is always by his or her *own* cultural lights that the relativist decides what role might be played by other interpretative norms. 'Other cultures become, so to speak, logical constructions out of the procedures and practices of American culture.' And this holds inescapably for R.R.'s pronouncements on the problems of radical translation, 'no matter how many footnotes, glosses, commentaries on the cultural differences, or whatever, he accompanies them by'.[4]

There is no way out, according to Putnam, by simply applying the doctrine in reverse and imagining how things would look from the other (i.e. Karl's) cultural standpoint. This could only lead to a form of 'methodological solipsism', since there would then be no grounds whatsoever for advancing intelligible truth-claims in either direction. As Putnam writes:

> the transcendental claim of a *symmetrical* situation cannot be *understood* if the relativist doctrine is right. And to say, as relativists often do, that the other culture has 'incommensurable' concepts is no better. That is just the transcendental claim in a special jargon.[5]

So the move to do away with *a priori* grounds of rational critique – and hence to keep the dialogue flexible and open – can often go along with a roundabout form of ideological self-endorsement.

One prominent line of relativist thinking derives from modern linguistics and philosophy of language. This doctrine assumes a similar guise in current post-structuralist theory and in those versions of radical empiricism (like Quine's) which reject the traditional distinction between matters of contingent *fact* and matters of *a priori* logical *truth*. For Quine, the field of knowledge at any given time is best pictured as a fabric of interrelated propositions, some of them (those near the centre) counting as analytic truths, while others (nearer the periphery) are open to empirical checks and corrections.[6] There are no fixed and permanent laws of thought, such as Kant maintained, to distinguish the one kind of truth from the other. Any wholesale change of *a priori* beliefs is likely to effect some corresponding shift of boundary conditions, though resistance to change is naturally great where perception seems to be in touch with empirical reality. Conversely, any radical change on the 'periphery' – like new observations thrown up by scientific experiment – may force us to revise what shall henceforth count as self-evident (analytic) truth. Hence Quine's well-known argument against any form of universalized reason which would claim to transcend the relativity of knowledge and belief by appealing to *a priori* structures of mind. There is always left an opposite appeal open from logic to the 'facts' of empirical experience, including the way in which those 'facts' may be subject to changes unlooked for in the logic of present-day thinking.

This leads Quine to formulate his argument against the assured possibility of 'radical translation' from one language to another. Along with every language goes a set of ontological assumptions which are nowhere spelled out explicitly in terms of unambiguous semantic or structural features. The hypothetical test case for Quine is that of an anthropologist confronted with a tribe whose language and culture are maximally remote from his or her own.[7] Any word they might utter, even with the simplest of didactic intents – say, while actually *pointing* at an object – would still leave its meaning open to doubt. For they could always have intended some significance other than straightforward ostensive definition, or perhaps have been referring to some *aspect* of the thing as apart from its unitary thinghood. The alien observer would have no way of knowing *for sure* that he or she shared with the tribe enough basic conventions even to get a start in learning their language. Such are Quine's reasons for adopting 'ontological relativity' as a doctrine counter to normal ideas about language, truth and logic. Our thinking on these matters is so much bound up with our own particular set of concepts and categories that we 'naturally' assume they must hold good across all varieties of cultural experience.

Quine's arguments find a parallel in the species of linguistic relativism advanced by thinkers like Whorf and Saussure. Again, it is taken as axiomatic that language provides the conceptual scheme by which a given community of speakers will habitually interpret their world. Any difference at the level of linguistic structure will reflect (or create) a corresponding

difference in the framework of organized thought and perception. In semantic terms the point is often made by alluding
to the various ways in which natural phenomena (like the
spectrum of colours) are divided up by different linguistic
cultures.[8] What is in question here is obviously nothing in the
nature of a 'proper', one-to-one relation between word and
referent. Rather it is a case of language creating alternative
structures of sense according to its own internal logic of
differential signifying features. And this applies as much to
syntax as to semantics, in so far as patterns of thought take rise
from the logical resources apparently vested in grammatical
forms.

Whorf approaches this question from the standpoint of
ethnolinguistics, arguing that certain languages (for instance,
Hopi Indian) differ markedly from our own in the way they
construe the *realia* of discrete sensory perception.[9] Hopi grammar has nothing like the clear-cut system of subject, verb and
object which the European languages take as their basis for
describing and explaining reality. It elides such distinctions
and works instead with a relativized notion of *processes* – rather
than objects and attributes – which manifest shifting states of a
fluid space–time continuum. There is no need here to dwell on
the details of Whorf's argument. What is crucial is the claim
that language determines the way we make sense of experience, and that differences of language may indicate widely
divergent – perhaps incommensurable – schemes of understanding.

II

Putnam's objections to cultural relativism would seem to have
equal force when applied to post-structuralist theory. Thus
Foucault must be counted a relativist, Putnam writes, 'because
his insistence on the determination of beliefs by language is so
overwhelming that it is an incoherence on his part not to apply
his doctrine to his *own* language and thought.'[10] It is not
entirely clear that this objection hits the mark in Foucault's
case. What he is precisely *not* claiming is a standpoint above all
the various 'discourses' of knowledge and truth which make

up the archaeology of western tradition. Foucault is at least a consistent relativist to the point of accepting that his own texts are to be read as just one more documentary source among the others that research brings to light. They don't, that is to say, claim any kind of privileged or 'metalinguistic' explanatory power. Foucault's position is in this respect similar to Nietzsche's, at least on that reading of Nietzsche which he and other post-structuralists have lately advanced.[11] Knowledge and power are inseparably bound up together, since what counts as 'truth' for any given culture is a product of forces which work to legitimate certain forms of knowledge and repress or marginalize others. Anyone who sets out to argue such a case will, of course, have to recognize the same laws at work in his or her own field of discourse. Whatever kinds of 'truth-effect' their writings may produce, it won't be a matter of finally displacing or transcending alternative versions. Any change of perspective brought about by Foucault's reading of the cultural 'archive' will result from his strategically contesting all claims to truth which ignore the diversity of possible viewpoints. This assemblage of sources in the form of a Nietzschean 'genealogy' is precisely designed to relativize truth and error beyond any hope of deciding reliably between them.

So it appears that Foucault is not so easily trapped in the kind of self-refuting paradox that Putnam detects within all forms of cultural relativism. The same round of argument might take place over again if it were asked what cognitive status could possibly attach to Foucault's more explicit relativist pronouncements. Would they not fall victim to the standard riposte: that any statement of the general form 'all truths are relative' must *ipso facto* apply to itself and hence undermine its own categorical force? But this is to assume (like Putnam) that Foucault's propositions ask to be judged according to the standards of truth or logical consistency. If one takes them as a species of suasive *rhetoric* – on performative rather than constative terms – then Putnam's line of argument no longer applies. Such is the lesson that Paul de Man reads in Nietzsche's 'exemplary' deconstructions of the philosophic will-to-truth.[12] Philosophy ignores its own rhetorical dimension by staging its argument in the form of 'logical' statements which apparently have no dealing with mere suasive rhetoric. But on a closer (deconstructive) reading those statements turn out to rest on a whole range of metaphors and figural ruses which effectively acknowledge their own rhetorical status. 'Thinking,' says Nietzsche, 'as epistemologists conceive of it, simply does not exist: it is a quite arbitrary element, arrived at by singling out one element from the process and eliminating all the rest, an artificial arrangement for the purpose of intelligibility.'[13] Foucault's texts start out from this position of thoroughgoing Nietzschean scepticism. It is therefore arguable at least that Putnam's objection misses the mark by assuming a commitment to logical (constative) norms of understanding which Foucault implicitly denies.

But this is just to say that relativism can make itself proof against attack by advancing no truth-claims on its own behalf and refusing to be budged by any form of *reductio ad absurdum* argument. What Putnam says of Rorty – that his position comes down to a form of 'methodological solipsism' – can also be applied to Foucault, or indeed to that strain of Nietzschean deconstruction which de Man so strenuously promotes. The outcome of American neo-pragmatism is to view other cultures (in Putnam's phrase) as 'logical constructions' out of the ideas and values of modern American society. In much the same way one could argue that Foucault deploys his relativized notions of truth and knowledge to remove the very grounds of rational debate upon which other discourses ask to be judged. In *Les Mots et les choses* (1966) he traced the structural genealogy of western tradition over the past three centuries through a series of 'epistemological breaks' in the various interrelated fields of knowledge.[14] Underlying this massively ambitious project was the assumption that these diverse disciplines (including both the 'natural' and the 'human' sciences) were grounded in structures of *representation* which shifted arbitrarily from age to age. Their specific claims to truth, 'scientific' or otherwise, were seen as nothing more than a species of enabling fiction. Knowledge, Foucault argued, is a product of discourse, a temporary arrangement of privileged conventions whose 'truth' derives solely from their present command of an otherwise open and heterogeneous field.

According to Foucault, the last great mutation in the order of knowledge was that which focused attention on *language* as the site and source of all understanding. Modernity is seen as issuing directly from this widespread linguistic turn, its emergence signalled by a whole range of movements and ideas that tend to place language – or representation – at the centre of their various concerns. Thus Mallarmé's poetics show language at the point of casting off all taint of a referential function and attempting to grasp its own genesis in the act of reflexive self-interrogation. With Saussure, modern linguistics becomes not only a self-respecting 'science' in its own disciplinary right, but a discourse whose truth-claims extend to fields far beyond that of 'language' as such. Hence Foucault's much-quoted pronouncements of an end to those philosophies of history and reason which elevated 'man', the transcendental subject, to a role of sovereign authority. 'Man' is henceforth dissolved into a figure of language, a transient 'fold' in the fabric of representations which compose the human sciences. Relativism could scarcely go further in denying the existence of ultimate truths or rational grounds for debate. Yet Foucault's entire archaeology of knowledge is narrated from the stand-point of a modern (post-structuralist) philosophy of language with its own very definite grounding assumptions. 'Relative to what?' receives a plain answer in Foucault's case: relative to the ethos of radical scepticism inaugurated on the one hand by Nietzsche's critique of epistemological truth, and on the other by structuralist theories of language and representation.

In short, Foucault is open after all to something like Putnam's formal counter-argument. That is, he relativizes knowledge and truth only only in so far as those notions attach to thought-systems other than his own. This objection has a similar force when applied to other versions of the relativist argument like Whorf's reflections on Hopi Indian grammar. As Donald Davidson shrewdly points out:

> Whorf, wanting to demonstrate that Hopi incorporates a metaphysics so alien to ours that Hopi and English cannot, as he puts it, 'be calibrated', uses English to convey the contents of sample Hopi sentences.[15]

If conceptual schemes are relative to languages, and if trans-lation *between* such schemes can never be more than approximate, then Whorf is doing just what Putnam suggests: imposing his own cultural norms under cover of ethno-comparative credentials. Post-structuralism invites the same charge in so far as it ignores the strong theoretical commitments which characterize its arguments at every point. There seems to be a vicious circularity built into all these versions of the relativist case. They start out with what appears a generous sense of the rich variety of cultures and the need to prevent one's own 'rational' norms from imposing a uniform view. They end up by suggesting just the opposite: that the only possible way to make *sense* of that variety is to lay it out for detailed inspection in the light of one's own deep-laid cultural conventions.

Where the relativist goes off the rails, according to this argument, is in taking it more or less for granted that language determines what will count as 'logic' or 'truth' for any given culture. This makes knowledge entirely a matter of convention, since different languages fix their own rules for distinguishing valid from invalid statements. Post-structuralism has this much in common with Quine's doctrine of 'ontological relativity' and his limit-case arguments against the possibility of translating from one conceptual scheme to another. The two main casualties here are *truth* and *reference*, both of which (as commonsense working notions) get relativized out of the picture. Truth becomes a product of semantic variables (Quine), of signifying structures (Saussure) or of shifting relations between power and knowledge (Foucault). Reference is likewise stripped of any privileged status *vis-à-vis* the 'facts' of experience, and treated as a function strictly relative to the various semantic schemes (or languages) within which it plays a role.

The argument that 'sense precedes reference' (in Frege's dictum) is the starting-point of much analytic philosophy and structuralist theory alike. It comes down to the claim that we can't be *sure* what words refer to unless we have a grasp of the various co-implicated senses which enable them to function as they do. Thus the structuralist would argue that each language constitutes a network of signifying contrasts and relationships which map out its conceptual terrain. Words thus refer not discretely, to this or that object of real-world experience, but always by virtue of the structured economy of sound and sense which makes up a given language. The analytic philosopher reaches much the same conclusion by a somewhat different route. Acts of reference, it is argued, can only come about through a double operation whereby language (1) provides a cluster of semantic attributes held to distinguish the referent in question, and (2) allows the speaker to apply these criteria in picking out the object referred to. Thus reality is structured according to conceptual schemes which in turn derive their operative logic of sense from the language that articulates their meaning.

To Frege this seemed the best, most perspicuous means of coping with the problems thrown up by other (less sophisticated) notions of sense and reference.[16] It looked like preserving the basic distinction between statements of contingent fact and statements whose truth was known *a priori* as a matter of logical analysis. Thus in Frege's well-known example, 'The Morning Star is identical with the Evening Star', the proposition is effectively asserting nothing if it just makes the point that a particular referent (in this case the planet Venus) is identical with itself. The only way to give the statement significant force is to take it as bearing on the *senses* of 'Morning Star' and 'Evening Star', or the fact that people have often (mistakenly) thought of them as two different entities. Asserting their equivalence – as a matter of referential fact – then amounts to both a truth-claim in respect of empirical reality and a logical account of how the senses in question are properly construed. The proposition is no longer redundant or vacuous, since it offers an improved – a more conceptually adequate – grasp of the way that language matches up with the shape of perceived reality. Thus the sense-reference dualism serves to maintain such further crucial distinctions as that between contingent and *a priori* orders of truth.

It remained, however, for sceptics like Quine to push this reasoning one stage further and deny that those distinctions can be known to hold good across all varieties of language and culture.[17] Quine simply follows out the logic of Frege's position to its ultimate sceptical conclusion. If we can make sense of the world only through concepts and categories provided by our own particular language, then we had better not erect them – Quine argues – into universal laws of thought. This

extends, as we have seen, all the way to such basic presuppositions as the difference of logical status between contingent
and analytic truths. From the doctrine that 'sense determines
reference' it is no great step to the relativist argument that
language (or cultural convention) fixes the rules at every stage.
And in that case there would even be a problem in knowing
what to make of Frege's cardinal sentence. It could only be true
(= logically binding) that 'sense determines reference' in a
language and cultural context where the dominant *conventions*
are such as to warrant such a statement. Its appearance of
generalized truth would disguise the fact that this is really a
species of recommendation, a performative utterance enjoin-
ing language to behave as the rules require.

Paul de Man has drawn attention to similar shifts of rhetorical stance in Nietzsche's deconstructions of truth, logic and the
principles of reason in general.[18] It is the mark of philosophy,
Nietzsche suggests, to present its arguments *as if* they be-
longed to the constative (or truth-telling) order of language,
rather than accepting that such arguments are performative at
best, seeking to *persuade* us of their universal truth. Even the
most basic logical axioms – like the law of non-contradiction –
represent not so much the immutable forms of thought as our
present inability or disinclination to think without their aid.
Thus, in Nietzsche's words, 'logic . . . applies only to fictitious
truths that we have created. Logic is the attempt to understand
the actual world by means of a scheme posited by ourselves
. . . to make it easier to formalize and compute.'[19] This deconstruction is pressed through a series of metaleptic reversals in
which Nietzsche seeks to demonstrate how 'concepts' are
formed by a species of *rhetorical* substitution always (necessarily) forgetful of its own linguistic origins.

Yet despite this exemplary sceptical rigour, there is a sense
in which Nietzsche's arguments repeatedly fall foul of his own
best insights. The very grammar of language requires him to
assert the unreliability of language and logic in a mode of
generalized constative utterance. 'The text deconstructs the
authority of the principle of contradiction by showing that this
principle is an act, but when it acts out this act, it fails to
perform the deed to which the text owed its status as act.'[20] The
same goes in turn for de Man's reading of Nietzsche, compel-

led to argue its case in terms which necessarily adopt a constative grammar, and thus controvert their own most vigilant deconstructive principles. Such complications, according to de Man, are characteristic of all rigorous reflection on language: 'the deconstruction states the fallacy of reference in a necessarily referential mode'.[21]

Returning to Frege, one can see how this might apply to categorical statements (like 'sense determines reference') where the grammar implies a universal validity undermined by its relativist consequences. One could make the point more simply by remarking how the sentence would take on a very different significance if it figured in the course of a Quinian argument on the theme of ontological relativity. In Frege the context works to debar such a reading: here it is the *logic* of truthful propositions which supposedly sets the terms for analysis of 'sense' and 'reference' alike. Familiarity with Frege's grounding assumptions is sufficient to prevent us from glossing the sentence as a full-blown relativist claim. But then one might ask – from a Quinian standpoint – just *why* such statements should be treated as absolute truths exempt from the general relativity of language and belief. The very logic of Frege's dictum then seems to require that we follow through to some kind of relativist conclusion. If 'sense determines reference', then this must be the case (Quine might argue) for *each particular language* and the framework of beliefs, truth-claims, etc., that goes along with it. The statement is not to be lifted clean out of its linguistic context and treated as a matter of absolute, *a priori* truth.

This essay started out by noting some of the obvious, first-order objections to relativist arguments. These took the form of what is sometimes called the 'transcendental *tu quoque*': the question, that is, why we should attend seriously to the relativist's arguments, given his or her professed disbelief in any binding protocols of truth and reason. This line of attack assumes a more sophisticated analytic form in Putnam's demonstration of the problems attendant upon any form of thoroughgoing relativist (or pragmatist) outlook. Finally, the instance of de Man on Nietzsche shows how radically unsettling are the consequences for philosophy of language if the sceptical-relativist position is pushed to its rigorous (non-)conclusion. In Nietzsche, according to de Man, 'the burden of proof shifts incessantly back and forth between incompatible propositions such as A = A, A better be equal to A or else, or A cannot be equal to A, etc.'[22] This holds as much for Nietzsche's own texts as for the discourse of traditional reason upon which those texts exert their deconstructive power. It is a resolutely no-win species of sceptical argument which equates 'true' rigour with the final dissolution of all claims to truth, including its own less canny formulations.

I have argued that this is the inevitable upshot of those relativist doctrines, whatever their 'logical' form, which start out by assuming that language in some sense *precedes and determines* the structure of thought. This assumption cuts across a wide range of otherwise disparate philosophies, from Quine's radical empiricism to Foucault's post-structuralist genealogies of power and knowledge. Furthermore, it works to complicate such arguments as Frege's, making them appear a form of halfway compromise position between the relativist standpoint and the claims of an *a priori* logical analysis of reference and sense. Deconstruction puts all these theories to the test by taking their central premiss strictly *at its word* and discovering how far their arguments stand up in the light of a rigorous sceptical critique. To use the term 'rigorous' in such a context might seem to beg all those same questions about the self-refuting nature of relativist claims. It is warranted only in the sense that Nietzsche, according to de Man, has 'earned a right to this inconsistency by the considerable labor of deconstruction that makes up the bulk of his more analytical writings'.[23] The suggestion is that other philosophies of language have no such hard-earned right, their proponents having scarcely begun the critical 'labour' that de Man carries over from Nietzsche's texts. Deconstruction thus confronts the inbuilt paradoxes of relativist doctrine by pressing them to the limit and admitting no kind of saving compromise 'solution'.

III

It remains to ask whether modern philosophy holds out any comparably rigorous argument which might provide a full-scale alternative to the picture presented so far. One promising candidate is the version of truth-conditional semantics developed by Donald Davidson. I have already quoted Davidson's objection to relativism in its Whorfian or ethnolinguistic form. It is an argument he extends to Quine also, in particular Quine's idea that the 'inscrutability of reference' necessarily leads to an acceptance of 'ontological relativity'. That this is not the case should be evident, Davidson suggests, from the fact that Quine (like Whorf) can 'give us a feel' for thought-systems other than our own – in this case the 'pre-individuative phase in the evolution of our conceptual scheme'.[24] As it stands, of course, this amounts to little more than a slight variation on the stock counter-relativist argument. Where Davidson moves the debate on to new ground is in proposing that *truth*, not meaning, be taken as the starting-point for any workable theory of language. This is to reject the idea common to Quine, Whorf and Foucault (among others): that truth (or all we can know of it) is always relative to the system of meaningful conventions that underlies a given language. For Davidson, the attitude of *holding-true* is the basic assumption that explains how we can, in fact, translate from one 'conceptual scheme' into another with some regular degree of success. To assume the opposite – that meaning effectively determines truth – is to fall into all kinds of paradox and dead-end sceptical argument.

This indicates the outline of Davidson's answer to the Quinian problem of 'radical translation'. We are forced to a sceptical conclusion, he argues, only if we hold to the relativist precept that truth is entirely a product of linguistic convention. Reverse this order of priorities – make *holding-true* the basis of all understanding – and the sceptic's case begins to look less impressive. Put simply, 'the methodological problem of interpretation is to see how, given the sentences a man accepts as true under given conditions, to work out what his beliefs are and what his words mean' (Davidson, p. 162). This shows the extent of Davidson's disagreement with those thinkers (like Whorf and Foucault) who relativize truth to the point of treating it entirely as a matter of linguistic and sociocultural convention. According to Davidson, this is a mistaken order of priorities which creates all manner of unnecessary puzzles. 'Philosophers who make convention a necessary element in language have the matter backwards. The truth is rather that language is a condition for having conventions' (p. 280). Language, thus delivered from the forcing-house of relativist doctrine, becomes an altogether less mysterious object: 'All that we can say gets fixed by the relativization is the way we answer questions about reference, not reference itself' (p. 239). The sceptic's problems have more to do with a particular (mistaken) philosophical doctrine than with a genuine difficulty in the nature of language. Thus the best way to answer those problems is to reverse the sceptic's system of priorities and start out from the idea that questions of meaning are supervenient upon questions of truth.

It is well to be clear what Davidson is *not* arguing in this case for a version of truth-conditional semantics. He is not, like the logical positivists, suggesting that the only meaningful statements are those which involve either empirical facts-of-observation or strictly analytic (*a priori*) truths. This would make the theory logically watertight but leave it without any useful application in the field of natural language. Davidson's claim is less exclusive and a great deal more useful. What counts in his theory is not that every language should be thought of as conforming to some abstract ideal, but that *certain sentences* within every language should point towards their governing truth-conditions. As Davidson puts it:

> knowledge of the circumstances under which someone holds sentences true is central to interpretation. . . . Although most thoughts are not beliefs, it is the pattern of belief that allows us to identify any thought; analogously, in the case of language, although most utterances are not concerned with truth, it is the pattern of sentences held true that gives sentences their meaning. (p. 162)

Again, Davidson is *not* pitching his argument at such an abstract level that all considerations of time, place and circumstance drop out of the picture. That is to say, he is not dealing with the tightly restricted class of propositions (like 'Socrates was mortal') which often serve the logician's purpose in sorting out orders of logical entailment. For Davidson, any theory of truth which rates itself applicable to natural language must admit that its claims are relative at least to the circumstantial context at hand. This requirement can be managed, he writes, 'either by declaring that it is particular utterances or speech-acts, and not sentences, that have truth-values, or by making truth a relation that holds between a sentence, a speaker, and a time' (p. 58). But truth can be relativized in this way without letting go of the basic assumption that language makes sense only against a background of knowing what *counts* as a truthful sentence. And this provides Davidson with his main grounds for arguing that the vaunted 'problem' of radical translation is largely a product of false ideas about the cognitive structure of language.

Still there are passages in Davidson's essays where the case appears weakened to such a degree that the relativist would scarcely want to challenge it. Thus he writes at one point that a 'reasonable way' of conducting the argument might be to claim simply that 'sentences are true, and words refer, relative to a language' (p. 240). Transposing this sentence into a Quinian context would yield something almost indistinguishable from the full-blown relativist case against radical translation. Again, Davidson is not trying to save the notion of reference in anything like a dogmatic or hard-line realist form. He goes along with the relativist argument at least to the extent of declaring that his theory gives no 'empirical content' to the relation between names and objects. Such content can only be assigned *indirectly*, he argues, by looking to the larger background of truth-conditional rules and assumptions which make up our grasp of a language. Indeed, Davidson seems on the point of agreeing with Quine when he remarks that 'the theory gives up reference . . . as part of the cost of going empirical' (p. 223). Concessions like these could well be construed as meeting the relativist more than halfway, and on ground moreover of the relativist's own canny choosing.

But this is where Davidson again turns the argument round by insisting that language can be relativized in this limited way *without* giving up the essentials of a properly constructive theory of meaning: 'Doing without reference is not at all to embrace a policy of doing without semantics or ontology' (p. 223). This is because language *presupposes* a generalized grasp of what it is for a word to refer or for a sentence to articulate some truthful proposition. The sceptic is too easily impressed by local relativities and fails to take account of the complex logical relations that exist in and between all varieties of language use. It is more rational to assume, says Davidson, that 'we compensate for the paucity of evidence concerning the meaning of individual sentences not by trying to produce evidence for the meanings of words but by considering the evidence for a theory of the language to which the sentence belongs' (p. 225). This theory need not rest on any questionable doctrine of linguistic universals or 'deep' transcultural structures of mind. All that is needed is the basic recognition that even *disagreements* about meaning must always involve some common appeal to imputed norms of adequate explanation. Thus the theory, far from claiming to eliminate such differences, seeks to make them more intelligible by explaining how and why they might develop. Without at least a modicum of shared truth-conditional assumptions it is hard to see how such specific disagreements could get off the ground.

This argument connects with what Davidson calls the 'principle of charity', the belief (roughly speaking) that the best interpretation in any given case is the one which enables us to best *make sense* of the utterance concerned. This principle is not an option, Davidson asserts, but a precondition of trying to provide any genuinely workable theory. Since this is the case, 'it is meaningless to suggest that we might fall into massive error by endorsing it' (p. 197). Sceptics have it both ways here, denying that we can know what it means to make sense of languages other than our own, but still going ahead (like Whorf) to give us a 'feel' for such supposedly alien systems. Post-structuralism is open to a similar line of counter-argument. It claims to deconstruct the very notions of knowledge and truth by showing them up as mere emanations of the will-to-power vested in language. But this relativism turns out to have sharp limits (as we have seen) when the question arises how it can achieve this demystified standpoint above all the rival systems on view. According to Davidson, such paradoxes only come about through the sceptics' refusal to acknowledge what their arguments always tacitly assume, i.e. the large measure of conceptual agreement that underlies even the most 'radical' differences of imputed meaning. Thus Davidson's theory can readily accept that misinterpretation not only occurs – as a matter of fact – but must be in some sense *built into* the structure of linguistic understanding. Its purpose, he writes, 'is to make meaningful disagreement possible, and this depends entirely on a foundation – *some* foundation – in agreement' (p. 197).

It might seem that Davidson is heading from a different direction towards the same kind of cultural-imperialist stance that Putnam objects to in Rorty. Certainly the terms of 'agreement' in question can only be inferred, or their logic reconstructed, from a standpoint possessing its own claims to truth and willing to extend them to other systems. In Davidson's words,

> the agreement may take the form of widespread sharing of sentences held true by speakers of 'the same language', or agreement in the large mediated by a theory of truth contrived by an interpreter for speakers of another language. (p. 197)

In short, the theory holds that interpreters are justified in taking a set of shared rational norms, as embedded in their *own* linguistic culture, and using these to make sense of whatever meaningful utterances come their way. So this – it might be argued – is just another, more blatant form of the tendency to exclude one's own discourse from the general relativity of knowledge. But Davidson effectively avoids this charge in so far as he makes it a basic requirement of the theory that it work to maximize the logical sense (or the range of truth-related sentences and meanings) assumed to exist in the language under scrutiny. Relativists recognize no such constraints and are therefore free to impose whatever *covert* system of assumptions happens to characterize their own discourse. Davidson's theory, on the contrary, takes it as axiomatic that languages tend to make rational sense if only one approaches them with a mind unwarped by fashionable relativist doctrine.

It is an essential part of this argument that 'a theory is better the more of its own resources it reads into the language for which it is a theory' (p. 229). The relativist mounts a sophisticated case for the incommensurability of truth-claims, the fallacy of radical translation, etc., and then proceeds to generalize about 'other languages' in terms which allow them no comparable powers of thought. On Davidson's theory, this violates the basic principle of charity, according to which, 'whether we like it or not, if we want to understand others, we must count them right on most matters' (p. 197). Otherwise there is simply no reason to assume that their language makes sense by rational standards that we (or they) could hope to grasp. And to take this line, Davidson argues, is to end up confronting all the puzzles and paradoxes of a radical scepticism. The alternative is simply to assume that speakers of different languages tend to operate with much the same kinds of logical or truth-seeking expectation. Hence the Davidsonian requirement that 'theory', if it is going to work properly, should expect to find its own conceptual resources implicitly prefigured in language at large.

> If we can produce a theory that reconciles charity and the formal conditions for a theory, we have done all that could be done to ensure communication. Nothing more is possible, and nothing more is needed. (p. 197)

'Charity' is therefore not an option but a part of the basic understanding we bring to all communicative contexts, no matter how remote or familiar the language. Such might be termed the 'weak' or most generalized requirement of Davidson's theory. Its 'strong' counterpart is the claim that we can only exercise this principle of charity by assuming that *truth* – and not meaning – is the 'central primitive concept' upon which any such theory must be based.

To the question 'What is truth?' Davidson responds by introducing a form of canonical notation supplied by the logician Alfred Tarski. At first sight this device – the so-called 'Convention T' – appears quite redundant and wholly uninformative. It consists of taking a declarative sentence (say, 'Snow is white') and expanding it so as to form a tautological proposition, i.e. one that satisfies its own truth-conditions merely by virtue of its logical structure. Thus:

> '"Snow is white" is true if and only if snow is white.'

Since we recognize this to be 'trivially true' (as a purely analytic statement), it can serve as the basis for a generalized theory of truth, albeit a theory without the least empirical content.

Where its usefulness lies, according to Davidson, is in setting out the formal precondition of other, more specific truth requirements. That is, one can take Convention T as a means of explaining how the 'primitive concept' of truth might apply both *within* and *across* all varieties of natural language. It thus becomes a kind of working assurance that the problems thrown up by radical translation are not, after all, so great as to defeat any hope of rational solution.

To see how this argument works it may be useful to present Tarski's theorem in its most abstract ('trivial') form, and then follow out its larger implications. According to Convention T, in Davidson's summary,

> a satisfactory theory of truth for a language L must entail, for every sentence *s* of L, a theorem of the form '*s* is true if and only if *p*' where '*s*' is replaced by a description of *s* and '*p*' by *s* itself if L is English, and by a translation of *s* into English if L is not English. (p. 194)

This is not, Davidson stresses, a 'definition' of truth, or a theory that could simply be applied to determine which sentences were true in any given language. What it does is suggest one feature common to all the more specific (and useful-in-practice) notions of truth. This comes down to the 'simple idea' – as Davidson describes it – that 'something is an acceptable conceptual scheme or theory if it is true' (p. 194). Of course this doesn't mean that such ascriptions of truth must always turn out to be *right* or warranted once enquiry reaches an end. Ultimate truth of that kind is not in question for Davidson's theory. It argues only – on formal grounds – that the attitude of 'holding-true' is a primitive concept which logically precedes any genuine attempt to make sense of language. If Convention T (as Davidson claims) 'embodies our best intuition as to how the concept of truth is used', then it also clears away a great deal of relativist mystification. It suggests (as in Davidson's summary above) how the same general conditions hold both for understanding sentences of one's own language and for knowing what would count as adequate translation from another.

Thus *truth* and *translatability* figure as closely connected ideas in Davidson's theory of language. This follows from his argument for treating truth (or the attitude of holding-true) as logically prior to questions of semantic interpretation. It would then be strictly pointless to ask, like the sceptic or radical relativist, what *sense* attached to 'true' for the language in question. As Davidson sees it,

> there does not seem to be much hope for a test that a conceptual scheme is radically different from ours if that test depends on the assumption that we can divorce the notion of truth from that of translation. (p. 195)

Problems of translation are in this sense much on a par with problems of conceptual adjustment within a single language. Philosophers, Davidson remarks, tend to be 'peculiarly tolerant of systematic malapropism, and practised at interpreting the result' (p. 196). This they can do because local confusions or anomalies of meaning are soon referred back to some regulative notion of what makes best, most adequate sense. 'Off-the-cuff' compensations of this kind are a vital part of our standard linguistic competence. They involve reinterpreting words in context so as to preserve a reasonable working system of assumptions. And the governing process, as Davidson argues, is 'that of constructing a viable theory of belief and meaning from sentences held true' (p. 196). Otherwise we could scarcely make a start in understanding sentences of our own, let alone of other languages.

IV

Davidson's arguments are couched in the idiom of modern analytic (or, in some respects, 'post'-analytic) philosophy. But they also have an important bearing on those issues that preoccupy literary critics in the structuralist line of descent. Most important here is Davidson's challenge to the deep-seated structuralist principle that linguistic *conventions* are the bedrock of meaning beyond which thought cannot go in its quest to make sense of language. On the contrary, he argues: this position is strictly incoherent in so far as it provides no grounds for deciding what shall *count* as a meaningful convention. Knowledge of the conventions that operate in any given language is, Davidson writes; 'a practical crutch to interpret-ation', a support that we often need in practice but one that we could – 'under optimum conditions' – afford to throw away. In theory at least we could make do without it from the start, since conventions belong to the second-order (socialized) level of linguistic competence where primary questions of truth and belief have already been settled as far as we require for basic understanding. If language was conventional through and through, then we would need, in effect, a new theory of interpretation not only for every new language but for every new speaker. What saves us from this impossible situation is the fact that 'from the moment someone unknown to us opens his mouth, we know an enormous amount about the sort of theory that will work for him – or we know we know no such theory' (p. 278). And even in the latter case our knowledge goes far enough to start up rational conjectures and take us beyond the mere puzzlement at alien conventions.

This argument puts Davidson squarely at odds with the relativist conclusion that post-structuralists draw from Saussure's doctrine of the 'arbitrary' nature of the sign. What is wrong with such reasoning, he suggests, is the fact that it concentrates on issues of *semantics* (i.e. the relation between individual words and meanings), and tends to ignore the syntactic component of language. Relativism may have a certain *prima facie* plausibility when applied at the wholly artificial level of discrete signifying units. It can then be erected into a generalized theory by arguing, like Saussure, from the isolated 'sign' to the full-scale system of relationships and differences which supposedly make up language at large. But the picture changes if one shifts attention to the complex regularities of logic and entailment to be found at the level of syntax. Thus: 'what forms the skeleton of what we call a language is the pattern of inference and structure created by the logical constants: the sentential connectives, quantifiers, and devices for cross-reference' (p. 279). It is for this reason, Davidson says, that 'syntax is so much more social than semantics'.

But this is not to privilege the 'social' in the same way that relativist doctrine would have it. In Davidson's view it is the 'logical constants' in language – those aspects pertaining most directly to questions of truth and belief – that determine its social and communicative character. To make 'convention' the ultimate ground of appeal is to relativize language without leaving anything to which it could intelligibly be said to relate. Thus a thoroughgoing conventionalism explains precisely nothing, in so far as it removes the very grounds of rational explanation. Hence Davidson's argument that 'linguistic communication does not require, though it very often makes use of, rule-governed repetition'. And in that case, he concludes, 'convention does not help explain what is basic to linguistic communication, though it may describe a usual, though contingent, feature' (pp. 279–80).

Of course this doesn't amount to a straightforward *refutation* either of relativism in the broad general sense or of post-structuralist theory in particular. At most it provides strong grounds for supposing that a different set of logical priorities will make better sense of language and avoid some of the worst (most counter-intuitive) features of the relativist position. Tarski's 'disquotational' theory of truth serves the purpose only in so far as it offers a powerful but *abstract* (because wholly *a priori*) statement of the basic position. The rest is a matter of applying such principles so as to maximize the degree of practical 'fit' between language, logic and belief. 'When all the evidence is in', Davidson writes, 'there will remain . . . trade-offs between the beliefs we attribute to a speaker and the interpretations we give his words' (p. 139). No theory of truth can eliminate these areas of intuitive adjustment, since truth must always 'go relative' to some extent when applied to natural (as distinct from formal or artificial) languages. All the same, Davidson writes, 'the resulting indeterminacy cannot be so great but that any theory that passes the tests will serve to yield interpretations' (p. 139). The point of appealing to Convention T is to back up the loose but (in practice) indispensable conviction that we know far more than relativist doctrine *allows* us to know.

It seems to me that some such truth-related theory of meaning is the only alternative to the sceptical rigours of deconstruction. Linguistic philosophers mostly feel safe in ignoring deconstructionists like Derrida and de Man because they (the deconstructionists) appear to ignore all the protocols of logic and truth. Such reactions are perhaps understandable, given the extreme and unsettling nature of what these critics have to say. Taking 'literature' as a field coextensive with 'rhetoric', the upshot (in de Man's summary statement) is that 'philosophy turns out to be an endless reflection on its own destruction at the hands of literature'.[25] But this position is reached by a rigorous following-through of premisses which – as we have seen – also characterize a good deal of modern analytic philosophy. Deconstruction is simply the most hard-pressed and consequent of relativist doctrines applied to questions of meaning, logic and truth. From the assumption that all truths are 'relative to language' it is strictly impossible *not* to arrive at some form of wholesale epistemological scepticism. Only a theory that reverses that assumption – and offers good grounds for so doing – can hope to turn back the more unwelcome effects of this widespread relativist drift.

9

Conclusion

I

After so much complex argumentation I should perhaps offer my reader the courtesy of a generalized summing-up. To do so might seem to fly in the face of at least one major deconstructionist principle: that conclusions are simply not to be had, or only in so far as one ignores the problems thrown up by textual close reading. In Chapter 4 – on Descartes and Husserl – I explored the implications of this argument by pursuing a rhetorical (or 'literary') reading of texts that set out to ground or refurbish the very conditions of rational thought. Such is the idea of 'deconstruction' most widely entertained by its Anglo-American proponents and detractors alike. On this account, the upshot of a deconstructive reading is to show how concepts reduce to metaphors, or how philosophic arguments come down in the end to a variety of *narrative* pretexts and alibis. By some, this move has been taken to portend a turning of the tables on philosophy itself, a demonstration that its texts are just one kind of writing among many, with no special claim to authority and truth. The undoing of philosophic reason would then go along with a marked elevation of literary criticism as a discourse of henceforth unlimited scope and interpretative power.

I have argued, on the contrary, that deconstruction is (or should be) a rigorous thinking-through of precisely those issues that are pushed out of sight by other, more accommodating versions of cultural critique. To treat it as a form of sophistical word-play or a free-for-all interpretative romp is grossly to misread the texts of Derrida and de Man. It fastens on their seemingly 'irrational' conclusions and ignores those other qualities – of logical tautness and dialectical rigour – that characterize their writing. Of course, such terms are open to challenge on well-rehearsed deconstructionist grounds. That Derrida *argues*, and moreover argues 'rigorously', is a claim that some might reject altogether. And is it not the case that these texts are aimed at dismantling the very conceptual foundations of what normally counts as 'dialectical' thought? These objections must be granted a certain force. Yet where does that force derive from, in the end, if not from the detailed and scrupulous working-through that these arguments receive in Derrida's texts?

This is perhaps a variant of that rationalist riposte which Jürgen Habermas has termed the 'transcendental *tu quoque*'. It is also an argumentative tactic that Derrida's opponents have used against him on more than one occasion. If meaning is indeed indeterminate, or logic suspended by the play of rhetorical signification, then what is to prevent us from reading Derrida specifically *against* his (supposed or imputed) argumentative drift? Deconstruction would appear wide open to any such line of counter-attack. What could it mean to 'misread' Derrida, given that (first) any notion of 'true' interpretation is a vestige of the old metaphysical desire for logocentric closure, and (second) any argument against such misreading can only be enmeshed in the same metaphysical toils? There is a real problem here, which the celebrants of deconstruction have not been sufficiently willing to address. They have mostly fastened upon texts (like the much-quoted 'Structure, Sign and Play'[1]) which appear to come out in favour of a limitless hermeneutic freedom, an ultimate break with the grim paternal law of interpretative logic and truth. Certainly this is one side of Derrida's strategy, and the side he has shown most often of late in writing (via translation) for a largely American readership. What it always *presupposes* – by way of enabling background – is the rigorous work of deconstruction as practised in other, more scrupulous texts like *Of Grammatology*.

Again it may be argued that any such distinction is beside the point in deconstructionist terms, since no one kind of writing can exert any ultimate or privileged claim to knowledge. Surely it is a cardinal error – and one that Derrida ceaselessly denounces – to equate 'philosophy' with a special form of *rigour* unavailable (say) to literary texts? Such hierarchies of discourse are the first thing to go when deconstruction insinuates its doubt as to the sovereignty of logic over rhetoric. Literary critics are particularly keen to have done with such truth-claims, the more so where they tend to elevate philosophy above the mere practice of literary interpretation. No doubt this goes a long way towards explaining why Derrida's influence has been exerted far more upon literary critics (who have much to gain) than on mainstream academic philosophers (who, by their own current lights, have a great deal to lose). But there remains the question of what gets lost in this assimilation of Derrida's texts to a 'literary' ethos of joyously post-New-Critical interpretative licence. One result is a marked disinclination to engage with the complex details of Derrida's argument, and a corresponding tendency to seize on such passages of his writing as promise a final, spectacular release from the protocols of logic and truth.

Thus the first of his texts to make a sizeable impact in translation was 'Structure, Sign and Play', delivered on the occasion of a 1966 Johns Hopkins University conference. The conference was planned as a meeting-ground of French and American scholarship, designed to put 'structuralism' firmly on the map and to emphasize its manifold interdisciplinary interests. In the event, it was Derrida's *critique* of structuralism – more specifically, of latent problems and contradictions in the structural anthropology of Lévi-Strauss – which left the deepest mark on subsequent American thought. The structuralist 'movement' was no sooner granted an import licence than it was pushed aside in the scramble for other, more exotic goods. And the closing paragraphs of 'Structure, Sign and Play' were perfectly adapted to catch the current mood of critics chafing under the rigid dispensation of 'old' New Critical precept. Derrida's writing took on its most apocalyptic tone as he proclaimed the imminent demise of a structuralism turned back nostalgically towards metaphors of origin, truth and authority. In their place he envisaged a new kind of discourse, a language of Nietzschean affirmation which would finally have freed itself from those old, consolatory props and devices. Structuralism is seen as the last problematical episode in a long history of similar attempts to master the disseminating play of language. To think through and beyond the structuralist 'moment' is to come out on the side of a new-found and limitless interpretative freedom.

This helps to explain the selective appropriation of Derrida's texts by critics in search of a more adventurous hermeneutic model. It also accounts for the widespread tendency to pass over the detail of his 'philosophic' arguments and latch on to their radical conclusions without fully grasping the structured genealogy of concepts which holds them in place. There is a parallel here with the intellectual afterlife of Kant's philosophy, subject as it was to a series of critiques (by Hegel and Nietzsche, among others) which sought to undermine its conceptual claims. Hegel objected to the Kantian presumption that philosophy could arrive at timeless truths about the scope and limits of human reason. Only by reflecting on its own prehistory could thought come to recognize the various stages or degrees of self-knowledge through which it had to pass on the way to enlightened understanding. Kant's *a priori* system of argument ignored this whole historical (or narrative) dimension, and thus produced nothing but a set of purely formal concepts and categories, devoid of any genuine experiential grasp. Nietzsche pressed his case against both Kant *and* Hegel by arguing for a yet more radical scepticism, one that treated all the truth-claims of philosophy as mere emanations of an arbitrary will-to-power. This he identified in turn with the figurative drive within language that everywhere concealed its operations by passing off metaphors as concepts, rhetorical tricks as immutable truths. Only recently has Nietzsche found readers (like Derrida and de Man) prepared to pursue such arguments to their limit in the deconstructive reading of philosophic texts. It can therefore be seen how the movement 'beyond' structuralism has tended to recapitulate that same post-Kantian chapter of intellectual history. Yet structuralism is no more a *closed* chapter than the Kantian revolution in philosophy, which continues to set the main terms for debate, even where its claims are most vigorously contested.

Paul Ricœur once characterized the structuralist project as

'Kantianism without the transcendental subject', a description that is often repeated as if thereby to discredit the whole enterprise. There is certainly no room for the transcendental subject, where subjectivity is conceived – in post-structuralist terms – as a ceaseless undoing of the unitary self through effects of unconscious desire, themselves made manifest in the play of linguistic figuration. Hence the antagonism between structuralist theory and those varieties of 'textualist' critique which deny its methodological claims. If the unconscious is indeed 'structured like a language', as Lacan says, then its workings must elude any rational attempt to explain either the unconscious *or* language in terms of some generalized theory. Such attempts will always founder on the surplus of unconscious figuration which cannot be mastered or effectively encompassed by any logic of explanatory concepts. Structuralism renounces the Kantian 'transcendental subject', only to replace it with a kind of linguistic *a priori*, a regulative concept of 'structure' which seeks to place firm juridical limits on the play of signification. Such, at least, is the critique brought to bear upon structuralist thinking by those – like Lacan and Derrida – who read in it the last, lingering signs of a rationalist tradition forced up against its own (unconscious) limits.

But, if structuralism has indeed been rendered problematic by these later developments, it has not been superseded or its enterprise quietly laid to rest. According to Derrida, a certain 'spontaneous structuralism' has always been philosophy's most characteristic mark and gesture.[2] That is to say, philosophy has rested its claims upon the appeal to such regulative notions as reason, method and 'structure' itself – concepts whose purely *metaphorical* nature it has not been able to recognize, since this would entail the dissolution of philosophy, the unthinkable step 'beyond' logocentric tradition. 'Structure is perceived through the incidence of menace, at the moment when imminent danger concentrates our vision on the keystone of an institution, the stone which encapsulates both the possibility and the fragility of its existence.'[3] Yet Derrida is equally insistent that deconstruction must work from *within* this edifice of concepts, seeking to shake (or 'solicit') its structure, rather than thinking to bring it down at a single, apocalyptic stroke. There is no passing 'beyond' structuralism except by a constant and vigilant awareness that the structuralist enterprise is deeply complicit with the whole prehistory of philosophic reason. And – as Derrida shows in his essay on Foucault, 'Cogito and the History of Madness'[4] – there is no way of breaking with philosophic reason that doesn't at the last use strategies borrowed from that same ubiquitous tradition.

II

There is, I have suggested, a more than incidental relation between the irrationalist leanings of 'American deconstruction' and the fact that it sidestepped any serious involvement with the structuralist enterprise. The result has been a kind of radical euphoria, much like the consequence of reading Nietzsche before one got round to reading either Kant or Hegel. It has produced a one-sided account of Derrida's texts whose partiality can best be shown up by returning to those texts and reading them afresh with a view to what is often passed over on the standard 'deconstructionist' view. Then – as I have argued – there emerges the outline of a counter-interpretation, more rigorous in its 'philosophic' bearing and far less amenable to the purposes of straightforward literary-critical use.

Derrida's essay 'White Mythology' is perhaps the most crucial example here.[5] Its theme is metaphor in the discourse of philosophy, a theme which Derrida broaches only to insist that the resultant problems cannot be grasped in any language available to analytic thought. On the one hand, all *definitions* of metaphor proceed from philosophic premises deeply complicit with the whole genealogy of western intellectual tradition. 'Each time that a rhetoric defines metaphor, not only is *a* philosophy implied, but also a conceptual network in which philosophy *itself* has been constituted' (p. 230). From Aristotle to the present, metaphor has been theorized in accordance with the need for philosophy to subdue figural language to its own operative terms and concepts. On the other hand, those concepts are themselves metaphorical through and through, the product (as Nietzsche first perceived) of a figural will-to-power masquerading as absolute knowledge. 'Metaphor has

been issued from a network of philosophemes which themselves correspond to tropes or figures, and these philosophemes are in systematic solidarity with those tropes or
figures' (p. 219). It is therefore impossible, strictly speaking, to
think through the relationship between metaphor and philosophy, since the two are bound up in a shuttling exchange of
reciprocal definition which nowhere permits of any rigorous
distinction between them. Philosophy is unable to subjugate
figural language, on account of the manifold residual
metaphors (and other figures of thought) that inhabit its own
language. But neither is it possible simply to reverse this
prejudice and conceive of philosophy as wholly governed and
structured by metaphor. There remains the insuperable problem that metaphor has always been defined and conceived on
terms laid down by philosophy itself.

This leads, in Derrida's words, to a 'double and contradictory' situation:

> On the one hand it is impossible to dominate philosophical
> metaphorics as such, *from the exterior*, by using a concept of
> metaphor which remains a philosophical product. Only
> philosophy would seem to wield any authority over its own
> metaphorical productions. But, on the other hand, for the
> same reason philosophy is deprived of what it provides
> itself. Its instruments belonging to its field, philosophy
> is incapable of dominating its general tropology and
> metaphorics. (p. 228)

It is instructive to compare this scrupulously hard-won position with the account often given (by literary critics) of Derrida's thinking on the topic of metaphor. One might gather
that Derrida had done no more than assert the omnipresence
of metaphor in language and the problems that confront any
attempt to distinguish 'literal' from 'figurative' sense. From
here it is a short enough step to the ecstasies of liberated
signifying practice which critics have been quick to seize upon
as the upshot of Derrida's arguments. Hence what might be
called the 'vulgar-deconstructionist' view: that logic and rigour
are beside the point, since all concepts come down to
metaphors at root, and 'philosophy' is merely the chronic
delusion that results from not acknowledging that fact. But

'White Mythology', properly read, gives little encouragement to such notions. It is a text of extreme analytical precision, scrupulously argued and utterly consequent in its various (albeit paradoxical) conclusions. If concepts are metaphors, then equally it is the case that metaphor – the *concept* of metaphor – is an idea so thoroughly worked over in western tradition as to need thinking through with the utmost 'philosophical' precision.

'The Supplement of Copula' is another text which presses well beyond the commonplace account of deconstructionist strategy.[6] Its subject is the issue of priority between language and philosophic thought, the question whether concepts are ultimately structured by linguistic forms and categories. The point of departure for Derrida's text is an essay by the linguist Emile Benveniste, which argues for a straightforward one-way dependence of thought upon language. Benveniste's chief example is Aristotle and his attempt to erect a wholesale logic and epistemology on the basis of certain (culture-specific) grammatical norms. It is evident, Benveniste writes, 'that these distinctions are primarily categories of language and that, in fact, Aristotle, reasoning in the absolute, is simply identifying certain fundamental categories of the language in which he thought' (p. 180). One might expect Derrida to embrace what amounts to a grounding supposition of current post-structuralist theory. That thought is always already enmeshed in the signifying codes of language is a notion so widely accepted that it is almost an article of faith. Yet it is here precisely that Derrida exerts the critical leverage of a deconstructive counter-reading. Just as metaphor (or rhetoric) failed to command the field of philosophy – the very *concept* of metaphor having always been defined in philosophical terms – so linguistics cannot provide the means for a thoroughgoing deconstruction of Greek (or western post-Hellenic) thought. There is no way of marking out the 'proper' domain of linguistics that does not at some point rejoin that tradition, appealing to philosophic reason (expressly or implicitly) by way of distinguishing 'thought' and 'language'. Thus, as Derrida remarks: 'none of the concepts utilized by Benveniste could have seen day, including that of linguistics as a science and the very notion of language, without a certain small "document" on the categories' – the 'document' in question being Aristotle's text (p. 188).

There is analytic rigour here, though philosophers in the 'other' tradition may disdain to perceive it. What generates this misunderstanding is Derrida's insistence that *texts*, not concepts or 'propositions', are the element within which philosophy must always work. It is clear that an essay like '*Ousia* and *grammē*' (on Aristotle's concept of time) raises questions in the 'textualist' mode which are none the less crucial for analytic thought.[7] Derrida shows – in exemplary close-reading style – how Aristotle's entire metaphysics rests on a notion of self-present momentary consciousness which his text simultaneously works to undo. On the one hand it develops a thematics of being and presence (*ousia*) which seeks to ground all knowledge in a plenitude of lived experience. Time could then be understood from the standpoint of a 'now' which coincided promptly with the self-possessed grasp of a transcendental subject. But there also emerges, interwoven with this argument, another train of reasoning which works to suggest an irremovable paradox at the heart of Aristotle's metaphysics. 'The now is given simultaneously as that which is *no longer* and as that which is *not yet*' (p. 39). Time cannot be conceptualized except at the cost of admitting other terms and critical motifs which destabilize the overt structure of argument. These have to do with spacing, alterity and difference, the complex of problematic themes that reason seeks to repress in its quest for a grounding philosophy of being and presence. In Aristotle's text their operations are focused upon the key-term *grammē*, which in turn sets up a train of associated meanings (writing, trace, differential spacing) whose repercussive symptoms Derrida reads.

Grammatology is thus installed at the origin of a tradition which henceforth has to deny or repress its effects. A primordial *différance* opens up within the concepts by which philosophy thinks to secure its transcendental claims. This differing/deferring can be carefully descried in the slippage of logical argumentation – more precisely, the non-coincidence of logic and language – as Aristotle presses his conclusions home. 'What Aristotle has set down, then, is both traditional metaphysical security, and, in its inaugural ambiguity, the critique of this security' (p. 49). At no point in this powerful reading does Derrida abandon the protocols of reasoned argument. Indeed, it is one of his contentions that later thinkers (among them Hegel, Bergson and Heidegger) failed to grasp the full complexity of Aristotle's text, and were thus content with various forms of premature ('metaphysical' or 'dialectical') resolution. To *think through* the central problems of philosophy is to think them in the rigour of a textual formulation that resists – as far as possible – the drift toward abstract concepts. Thus Hegel's treatment of the issue becomes, in Derrida's words, 'the repetition, the paraphrastic reedition of an exoteric aporia, the brilliant formulation of a vulgar paradox' (p. 43).

Analytic philosophers have a different idea of what it is to be rigorous and consequent in reasoning. For them – even when expressly devoted to the forms and usages of 'ordinary language' – the necessary drive is more quickly and directly from word to regulating concept. Hence the extreme reluctance of philosophers to engage with Derrida's *texts*, as distinct from his generalized arguments as gleaned from a cursory reading of those texts. I have argued, on the contrary, that deconstruction both warrants and requires the kind of scrupulous close reading that Derrida brings to bear. It will then be seen that there is not, after all, such a sharp disjunction or conflict of aims between the 'textualist' and the 'analytic' modes of philosophic writing. Deconstruction is preoccupied with the central questions of meaning, reference and truth, as addressed by analytical philosophers from Frege to Putnam and Davidson. It is a flat misreading of deconstruction that sees it as merely suspending these issues in favour of an infinitized 'free play' of language devoid of logical rigour or referential grasp.

One could apply to de Man what he writes about Rousseau in a crucial paragraph from *Allegories of Reading*. It must be kept in mind, de Man insists, that

> his [Rousseau's] radical critique of referential meaning never implied that the referential function of language could in any way be avoided, bracketed, or reduced to being just one contingent property among others. . . . Rousseau never

allows for a 'purely' aesthetic reading in which the referential determination would remain suspended or be
nonexistent.[8]

I have argued (in Chapter 2) that de Man's account of these
deep-laid epistemological problems has decisive implications
for linguistic philosophy in the current (post-Fregean) analytic
tradition. It also resists that fashionable line of neo-pragmatist
thinking which would treat deconstruction as a stage on the
path to a 'post-philosophical' consensus view of knowledge
and human interests. Chapter 8 argues that some kind of
truth-conditional semantics is implicit in the nature of linguistic understanding, as well as in those forms of *Ideologiekritik*
where thought takes rational account of its own (or rival)
consensus values. To keep such lines of enquiry open is the
most important function of critical theory. And it is here that
the present-day 'contest of faculties' has an urgent claim upon
the interest of philosophers and literary critics alike.

Notes

Introduction

1 See especially Hans-Georg Gadamer, *Truth and Method*, trans. and ed. Garrett Barden and John Cumming (London: Sheed & Ward, 1975).

2 See Jürgen Habermas, *Theory and Practice*, trans. John Viertel (London: Heinemann, 1974).

3 See Jürgen Habermas, *Communication and the Evolution of Society*, trans. Thomas McCarthy (London: Heinemann, 1979).

4 See the essays collected in Richard Rorty, *Consequences of Pragmatism* (Minneapolis: University of Minnesota Press, 1982).

5 Ibid., p. 156.

6 Ibid., p. 155.

7 Ibid., p. xx.

8 Ibid., p. 153.

9 Ibid., p. 156.

10 Terry Eagleton, *Literary Theory: An Introduction* (Oxford: Blackwell, 1983), p. vii.

11 Rorty, op. cit., p. 165.

12 Ibid., p. 99.

13 Paul de Man, 'The resistance to theory', in Barbara Johnson (ed.), *The Pedagogical Imperative*, *Yale French Studies*, No. 63 (1982), pp. 3–20.

14 Rorty, op. cit., p. 95.

15 Paul de Man, op. cit., p. 11.

16 Ibid., p. 11.

17 Ibid., p. 8.

18 See Paul de Man, 'Phenomenality and materiality in Kant', in Gary Shapiro and Alan Sica (eds), *Hermeneutics: Questions and Prospects* (Amherst, Mass.: University of Massachusetts Press, 1984), pp. 121–44.

19 De Man, 'The resistance to theory', p. 11.

20 Roger Scruton, *The Aesthetic Understanding* (London: Methuen, 1983), p. 8.

21 T. S. Eliot, 'The metaphysical poets', in *Selected Essays* (London: Faber, 1964), pp. 241–50; p. 247.
22 See T. S. Eliot, *The Use of Poetry and the Use of Criticism* (London: Faber, 1964), p. 156.
23 See T. S. Eliot, 'The perfect critic', in *The Sacred Wood* (London: Faber, 1928), pp. 1–16.
24 T. S. Eliot, 'Tradition and the individual talent', in *Selected Essays*, pp. 3–11; p. 11.
25 De Man, 'Phenomenality and materiality in Kant', p. 124.
26 Ibid., p. 140.
27 Jean-François Lyotard, *The Post-Modern Condition: A Report on Knowledge*, trans. Geoff Bennington and Brian Massumi (Minneapolis: University of Minnesota Press, 1983).
28 Ibid., p. 64.
29 Ibid., p. 65.

1 Narrative theory or theory-as-narrative

1 See especially Hayden White, *Tropics of Discourse* (Baltimore: Johns Hopkins University Press, 1978).
2 Richard Rorty, *Philosophy and the Mirror of Nature* (Princeton, NJ: Princeton University Press, 1980).
3 Richard Rorty, *Consequences of Pragmatism* (Minneapolis: University of Minnesota Press, 1982), p. xx.
4 See especially Michel Foucault, *Language, Counter-Memory, Practice*, trans. Donald F. Bouchard and S. Simon (Oxford: Blackwell, 1977).
5 Michel Foucault, *I, Pierre Rivière, having slaughtered my mother, my sister and my brother . . .* , trans. Frank Jellinek (Harmondsworth: Peregrine, 1978).
6 Jean-François Lyotard, *The Postmodern Condition: A Report on Knowledge*, trans. Geoff Bennington and Brian Massumi (Minneapolis: University of Minnesota Press, 1984).
7 See particularly Jürgen Habermas, 'A review of Gadamer's *Truth and Method*', in Fred R. Dallmayr and Thomas A. McCarthy (eds), *Understanding Social Inquiry* (Notre Dame, Ind.: Indiana University Press, 1977).
8 Hans-Georg Gadamer, *Philosophical Hermeneutics*, trans. David E. Linge (Berkeley: University of California Press, 1977). See also Gadamer, 'On the scope and function of hermeneutical reflection', trans, G. B. Hess and R. E. Palmer, *Continuum*, 8, 1 and 2 (1970), pp. 77–95.
9 Jürgen Habermas, *Knowledge and Human Interests*, trans. Jeremy J. Shapiro (London: Heinemann, 1972).

10 Jürgen Habermas, *Communication and the Evolution of Society*, trans. Thomas McCarthy (London: Heinemann, 1979).

11 Jürgen Habermas, 'Summation and response', quoted in David Held, *Introduction to Critical Theory: Horkheimer to Habermas* (London: Hutchinson, 1980), p. 314.

12 Ibid., p. 315.

13 Pierre Macherey, *A Theory of Literary Production*, trans. Geoffrey Wall (London: Routledge & Kegan Paul, 1978), p. 21.

14 Terry Eagleton, *Criticism and Ideology* (London: New Left Books, 1976), p. 43.

15 Roland Barthes, *S/Z*, trans. Richard Miller (London: Cape, 1975).

16 See Barbara Johnson, *The Critical Difference: Essays in the Contemporary Rhetoric of Reading* (Baltimore: Johns Hopkins University Press, 1981).

17 Shoshana Felman, 'Turning the screw of interpretation', *Yale French Studies*, Nos 55–6 (1977), pp. 94–207; pp. 114–15.

18 Ibid., p. 116.

19 See Jacques Lacan, *Ecrits: A Selection*, trans. Alan Sheridan-Smith (London: Tavistock, 1977).

20 Rainer Nägele, 'The provocation of Jacques Lacan', *New German Critique*, 16 (1979), pp. 5–29.

21 Dominick LaCapra, 'Habermas and the grounding of critical theory', *History and Theory*, 16 (1977), p. 263.

22 See Habermas, *Knowledge and Human Interests*, pp. 274–300.

23 Rainer Nägele, 'Freud, Habermas and the dialectic of enlightenment: on real and ideal discourses', *New German Critique*, 22 (1981), pp. 41–62.

24 Habermas, *Knowledge and Human Interests*, pp. 214–18.

25 Michael Ryan, *Marxism and Deconstruction: A Critical Articulation* (Baltimore: Johns Hopkins University Press, 1982), p. 8.

26 Ibid., p. 202.

27 Ibid., p. 174.

28 Ibid., p. 160.

29 Hilary Putnam, *Reason, Truth and History* (Cambridge: Cambridge University Press, 1981), p. 158.

30 Ibid., p. 138.

31 Fredric Jameson, *The Political Unconscious: Narrative as a Socially Symbolic Act* (London: Methuen, 1981).

32 Ibid., p. 53.

33 Ibid., p. 49.

34 Ibid., p. 50.

35 Paul de Man, *Allegories of Reading: Figural Language in Rousseau, Nietzsche, Rilke and Proust* (New Haven, Conn.: Yale University Press, 1979).

36 Ibid., p. 242.
37 See, for instance, Terry Eagleton, *Walter Benjamin, or Towards a Revolutionary Criticism* (London: New Left Books, 1981).
38 De Man, op. cit., p. 258.
39 Ibid., p. 271.
40 Ibid., p. 277.
41 Ibid., p. 157.
42 Ibid., pp. 156–7.
43 Jameson, op. cit., p. 53.
44 De Man, op. cit., p. 259.

2   Sense, reference and logic

1 See, for instance, Terry Eagleton, *Walter Benjamin, or Towards a Revolutionary Criticism* (London: New Left Books, 1981).
2 See Gerald Graff, *Literature against Itself: Literary Ideas in Modern Society* (Chicago and London: University of Chicago Press, 1979).
3 Alex Callinicos, *Marxism and Philosophy* (London: Oxford University Press, 1983), offers a materialist critique of post-structuralism along with some useful elucidating comment on Frege and analytical philosophy. See especially pp. 18–25, 114–26 and 136–53. See also Stephen Gaukroger, 'Logic, language and literature: the relevance of Frege', *Oxford Literary Review*, 6, 1 (1983), pp. 68–96. Ian Hacking's *Why Does Language Matter to Philosophy?* (Cambridge: Cambridge University Press, 1975) concentrates on issues in the 'analytic' mainstream, but shows a lively awareness of post-structuralist debate. On Frege more specifically, see Ian Hacking, 'On the reality of existence and identity', *Canadian Journal of Philosophy*, 8 (1978), pp. 613–32.
4 Michael Dummett, *Frege: Philosophy of Language* (London: Duckworth, 1973). All further references given by page number in the text. See also the supplementary essays and response to various critics in Dummett, *The Interpretation of Frege's Philosophy* (London: Duckworth, 1981). It should be noted that Dummett has not gone unchallenged in his argument that Frege was primarily (or most interestingly) a philosopher of *language* in the sense established by modern analytical tradition (see note 5).
5 For the view that Fregean logic is not so easily assimilated to a theory of meaning, see Gregory Currie, *Frege: An Introduction to his Philosophy* (Brighton: Harvester, 1982).
6 Ferdinand de Saussure, *Course in General Linguistics*, trans. Wade Baskin (London: Fontana, 1974).
7 See Immanuel Kant, *Critique of Pure Reason*, trans. Norman Kemp Smith (London: Macmillan, 1953), pp. 454 ff.

8 Gottlob Frege, 'On sense and reference', in *Translations from the Philosophical Writings of Gottlob Frege*, ed. Max Black and P. T. Geach (Oxford: Blackwell, 1952), pp. 56–78; p. 59.

9 Ibid., p. 59.

10 Ibid., p. 60.

11 Ibid., p. 60.

12 Ibid., p. 58.

13 Saul Kripke, *Naming and Necessity* (Oxford: Blackwell, 1980).

14 Frege, op. cit., p. 63.

15 Ibid., pp. 61–2.

16 Ibid., p. 62.

17 Ibid., p. 57.

18 B. V. Birjukov, *Two Soviet Studies on Frege*, trans. and ed. Ignacio Angelelli (Dordrecht: D. Reidel, 1964).

19 Ibid., p. 44.

20 Ibid., p. 29.

21 Ibid., p. 29.

22 Saussure, op. cit., pp. 108–9.

23 Ibid., p. 109.

24 Ibid., p. 109.

25 Ibid., p. 109.

26 W. V. O. Quine, 'Two dogmas of empiricism', in *From a Logical Point of View* (Cambridge, Mass.: Harvard University Press, 1953), pp. 20–46.

27 W. V. O. Quine, 'On the reasons for indeterminacy of translation', *Journal of Philosophy*, 67 (1970), pp. 178–83.

28 See, for instance, Michel Foucault, *Language, Counter-Memory, Practice*, ed. D. F. Bouchard and S. Simon (Oxford: Blackwell, 1977); *Power/Knowledge*, ed. Colin Gordon (Brighton: Harvester, 1980); *Power, Truth, Strategy*, ed. Meaghan Morris and Paul Patton (Melbourne, Australia: Feral Books, 1979). On the connections between Quine and Foucault (and their common liabilities 'from a logical point of view'), see Christopher Norris, *The Deconstructive Turn: Essays in the Rhetoric of Philosophy* (London: Methuen, 1983), pp. 7–9, 156–7.

29 Sollace Mitchell, 'Post-structuralism, empiricism and interpretation', in Sollace Mitchell and Michael Rosen (eds), *The Need for Interpretation* (London: Athlone Press, 1983), pp. 54–89; p. 76.

30 Ibid., p. 76.

3 Some versions of rhetoric

1 See especially Geoffrey Hartman, *Saving the Text: Literature/ Derrida/Philosophy* (Baltimore: John Hopkins University Press, 1981).

2 See Geoffrey Hartman, *Criticism in the Wilderness: The Study of Literature Today* (New Haven, Conn.: Yale University Press, 1980).

3 W. K. Wimsatt, 'Battering the object: the ontological approach', in Malcolm Bradbury and David Palmer (eds), *Contemporary Criticism* (London: Edward Arnold, 1970).

4 See Jacques Derrida, 'Signature Event Context', in *Margins of Philosophy*, trans. Alan Bass (Chicago: University of Chicago Press, 1982), pp. 207–30.

5 J. Hillis Miller, 'The critic as host', in *Deconstruction and Criticism* (New York: Seabury Press, 1979), pp. 217–53.

6 Paul de Man, 'The resistance to theory', *Yale French Studies*, No. 63 (1982), pp. 3–20.

7 Paul de Man, *Allegories of Reading: Figural Language in Rousseau, Nietzsche, Rilke and Proust* (New Haven, Conn.: Yale University Press, 1979), p. 9.

8 Ibid., p. 12.

9 Barbara Johnson, *The Critical Difference: Essays in the Contemporary Rhetoric of Reading* (Baltimore: Johns Hopkins University Press), p. xii.

10 De Man, *Allegories of Reading*, p. 17.

11 Ibid., p. 270.

12 Ibid., p. 115.

13 Philip Wheelwright, 'On the semantics of poetry', *Kenyon Review*, 2 (1940), pp. 264–83.

14 See, for instance, Cleanth Brooks, 'Empson's criticism', *Accent* (Summer 1944), pp. 208–16.

15 John Crowe Ransom, 'Mr Empson's muddles', *The Southern Review*, 4 (1938), p. 334.

16 John Crowe Ransom, quoted in William Rueckert (ed.), *Critical Responses to Kenneth Burke* (Minneapolis: University of Minnesota Press, 1969), p. 156.

17 Cleanth Brooks, 'My credo' (contribution to 'The formalist critics: a symposium'), *Kenyon Review*, 18 (1951), pp. 72–81.

18 William Empson, *Seven Types of Ambiguity* (Harmondsworth: Penguin, 1961), p. 192. All further references to *Seven Types* given by page number in the text.

19 Paul de Man, *Blindness and Insight: Essays in the Rhetoric of Contemporary Criticism*, 2nd edn, revised and enlarged, ed. Wlad Godzich (London: Methuen, 1983). 'The rhetoric of temporality' appears

among the supplementary essays, pp. 187–228. Quotation from Coleridge, p. 192. All further references given by page number in the text.
20 See Jacques Derrida, 'Differance', in *Margins of Philosophy*, trans. Alan Bass (Chicago: University of Chicago Press, 1982), pp. 3–27.
21 Cleanth Brooks, *The Well Wrought Urn* (New York: Dobson, 1949), p. 138.
22 Paul de Man, 'The dead-end of formalist criticism', in *Blindness and Insight*, pp. 229–45. All further references given in the text.
23 Brooks, op. cit., p. 237.
24 I. A. Richards, *Principles of Literary Criticism* (London: Kegan Paul, Trench, Trubner, 1926), p. 32.
25 Paul de Man, 'Heidegger's exegeses of Hölderlin', in *Blindness and Insight*, pp. 246–66.
26 William Empson, 'Marvell's Garden', in *Some Versions of Pastoral* (Harmondsworth: Penguin, 1966), pp. 97–119. All subsequent references given by page number in the text.

4   Transcendent fictions

1 Plato, *The Republic*, trans. H. D. P. Lee (Harmondsworth: Penguin, 1955), pp. 370–86.
2 See I. A. Richards, *Principles of Literary Criticism* (London: Kegan Paul, Trench, Trubner, 1926).
3 Sir Philip Sidney, 'An Apologie for Poetry', in D. J. Enright and Ernst de Chickera (eds), *English Critical Texts* (London: Oxford University Press, 1961), pp. 3–49.
4 See Edmund Husserl, *Cartesian Meditations*, trans. Dorian Cairns (The Hague: Martinus Nijhoff, 1960).
5 René Descartes, *Discourse on Method, and Other Writings*, trans. F. E. Sutcliffe (Harmondsworth: Penguin, 1967), p. 31.
6 Ibid., p. 29.
7 Ibid., p. 35.
8 Jaakko Hintikka, '*Cogito, ergo sum*: inference or performance?', in Willis Doney (ed.), *Descartes: A Collection of Critical Essays* (London: Macmillan, 1968).
9 Ibid., p. 113.
10 Ibid., p. 122.
11 See J. L. Austin, *How to do Things with Words* (London: Oxford University Press, 1963).
12 On the topic of this general shift of ideas, see Ian Hacking, *Why Does Language Matter to Philosophy?* (Cambridge: Cambridge University Press, 1975).
13 Descartes, *Discourse*, p. 41.

14 See, for instance, P. F. Strawson, *Individuals* (London: Methuen, 1963).

15 Descartes, op. cit., p. 32.

16 Hintikka, op. cit., p. 114.

17 Ibid., p. 139.

18 Ibid., p. 114.

19 John Pilling, *Samuel Beckett* (London: Routledge & Kegan Paul, 1975), p. 113.

20 Ibid., p. 117.

21 For a useful introduction, see J. Hillis Miller, 'The Geneva School', *Critical Quarterly*, 8 (1966), pp. 305–21.

22 Georges Poulet, *Studies in Human Time*, trans. Elliott Coleman (Baltimore: Johns Hopkins University Press, 1956).

23 See, for instance, Wolfgang Iser, *The Act of Reading* (London: Routledge & Kegan Paul, 1978).

24 Husserl, op. cit., pp. 31–2.

25 See Roman Ingarden, *The Literary Work of Art* and *The Cognition of the Literary Work of Art* (Evanston, Ill.: Northwestern University Press, 1973).

26 Edmund Husserl, *Experience and Judgement*, trans. James S. Churchill and Karl Ameriks (Evanston, Ill.: Northwestern University Press, 1973), p. 298.

27 Ibid., p. 298.

28 Ibid., pp. 298–9.

29 Ibid., pp. 167–8.

30 Ibid., p. 168.

31 Ibid., p. 171.

32 Ibid., pp. 171–2.

33 Edmund Husserl, *The Phenomenology of Internal Time-Consciousness*, trans. James S. Churchill (Bloomington, Ind.: Indiana University Press, 1964).

34 Husserl, *Experience and Judgement*, p. 173.

35 Jacques Derrida, *Speech and Phenomena, and Other Essays on Husserl's Theory of Signs*, trans. David B. Allison (Evanston, Ill.: Northwestern University Press, 1973).

36 Poulet, op. cit., p. 51.

37 Ibid., p. 57.

38 Ibid., p. 57.

39 Ibid., p. 65.

40 Ibid., p. 72.

5   Aesthetics and politics

1 I. A. Richards, *Principles of Literary Criticism* (London: Kegan Paul, Trench Trubner, 1926).

2 For a recent collective statement along these lines, see Peter Lamarque (ed.), *Philosophy and Fiction: Essays in Literary Aesthetics* (Aberdeen: Aberdeen University Press, 1983).

3 See, for instance, Stein Haugom Olsen, *The Structure of Literary Understanding* (Cambridge: Cambridge University Press, 1978).

4 Roger Scruton, *The Aesthetic Understanding: Essays in the Philosophy of Art and Culture* (London: Methuen, 1983). All further references to this book are given by page number in the text.

5 See Raymond Williams, *Marxism and Literature* (London: Oxford University Press, 1977), for a discussion of this and related issues in Marxist critical theory.

6 Perhaps the most influential statement of this position is Peter Winch's book *The Idea of a Social Science and its relation to philosophy* (London: Routledge & Kegan Paul, 1958).

7 Paul de Man, 'Hegel on the sublime', in Mark Krupnick (ed.), *Displacement: Derrida and After* (Bloomington, Ind.: Indiana University Press, 1983), pp. 139–53; p. 140.

8 Paul Hamilton offers a most persuasive reading in his recent book *Coleridge's Poetics* (Oxford: Blackwell, 1983).

9 John Casey, *The Language of Criticism* (London: Methuen, 1966). See also his essay 'The autonomy of art', in G. Vesey (ed.), *Philosophy Looks at the Arts* (London: Macmillan, 1973).

10 F. R. Leavis, 'Literary criticism and philosophy', *Scrutiny*, 6 (1937), pp. 59–70.

11 Walter Benjamin, 'The work of art in the age of mechanical reproduction', in *Illuminations*, trans. Hannah Arendt (London: Fontana, 1973), pp. 219–53.

12 See Walter Benjamin, 'The author as producer', in *Understanding Brecht*, trans. Anna Bostock (London: New Left Books, 1973), pp. 85–103.

6   Philosophy as a kind of narrative

1 See, for instance, John R. Searle, 'Reiterating the differences', *Glyph*, 1 (1977), pp. 198–208.

2 Richard Rorty (ed.), *The Linguistic Turn: Recent Essays in Philosophical Method* (Chicago: University of Chicago Press, 1967).

3 See Richard Rorty, 'Overcoming the tradition: Heidegger and Dewey', in *Consequences of Pragmatism* (Minneapolis: University of Minnesota Press, 1982), pp. 37–59.

4 Richard Rorty, *Philosophy and the Mirror of Nature* (Princeton, NJ: Princeton University Press, 1980), p. 12.
5 M. H. Abrams, *The Mirror and the Lamp: Romantic Theory and the Critical Tradition* (New York: Oxford University Press, 1953).
6 W. V. O. Quine, 'Two dogmas of empiricism', in *From a Logical Point of View* (Cambridge, Mass.: Harvard University Press, 1953), pp. 20–46.
7 Rorty, *Philosophy and the Mirror of Nature*, p. 136.
8 Ibid., p. 136.
9 Rorty cites the example of Hans Reichenbach, *The Rise of Scientific Philosophy* (Berkeley: University of California Press, 1951).
10 Rorty, *Consequences of Pragmatism*, p. xxxix.
11 Ibid., p. xviii.
12 Richard Rorty, 'Philosophy as a kind of writing', in ibid., pp. 89–109; p. 106.
13 Rorty, *Consequences of Pragmatism*, p. xviii.
14 Ibid., p. xx.
15 Jean-François Lyotard, *La Condition postmoderne* (Paris: Minuit, 1979).
16 See, for instance, Jürgen Habermas, *Knowledge and Human Interests*, trans. Jeremy J. Shapiro (London: Heinemann, 1972).
17 Lyotard, op. cit., p. 1. The passage is quoted and translated by Richard Rorty in 'Habermas and Lyotard on postmodernity', an unpublished paper circulated at the School for Criticism and Theory, Northwestern University, 1983. I am grateful to Professor Rorty for permission to refer to it here.
18 Lyotard, op. cit., p. 36 (Rorty's translation).
19 Richard Rorty, 'Postmodern bourgeois liberalism', paper presented at Northwestern University, 1983. Again, my thanks to Professor Rorty.
20 Lyotard, op. cit., p. 12 (Rorty's translation).
21 Rorty, *Consequences of Pragmatism*, p. xxiii.
22 In Rorty, 'Postmodern bourgeois liberalism'.
23 See Richard Rorty, 'Pragmatism, relativism, irrationalism', in *Consequences of Pragmatism*, pp. 160–75.
24 Peter Winch, *The Idea of a Social Science and its relation to philosophy* (London: Routledge & Kegan Paul, 1958).
25 Richard Rorty, 'Idealism and textualism', in *Consequences of Pragmatism*, pp. 139–59.
26 Ibid., p. 152.
27 Ibid., p. 156.
28 Ibid., p. 153.
29 See, for instance, David Lodge, *The Modes of Modern Writing* (London: Edward Arnold, 1977).

30 Hayden White, *Tropics of Discourse: Essays in Cultural Criticism* (Baltimore: Johns Hopkins University Press, 1978).
31 Ibid., pp. 42–3.
32 See Richard Rorty, 'Overcoming the tradition: Heidegger and Dewey', in *Consequences of Pragmatism*, pp. 37–59.
33 See, for instance, Geoffrey Hartman, *Criticism in the Wilderness: The Study of Literature Today* (New Haven, Conn.: Yale University Press, 1980).
34 Alasdair MacIntyre, 'Rationalism and the explanation of action', in *Against the Self-Images of the Age* (London: Duckworth, 1971), pp. 244–59; p. 247.
35 Alasdair MacIntyre, 'The idea of a social science', in ibid., pp. 211–29; p. 217.
36 MacIntyre, 'The End of Ideology and the End of the End of Ideology', in ibid., pp. 3–11; p. 7.

7 Suspended sentences

1 Roland Barthes, 'Dominici: or the triumph of literature', in *Mythologies*, trans. Annette Lavers and Colin Smith (London: Fontana, 1972), pp. 43–7.
2 H. L. A. Hart, *Essays in Jurisprudence and Philosophy* (Oxford: Clarendon Press, 1983), p. 99. All further references to this work are given by page number in the text.
3 On the question of textual boundaries, see Jacques Derrida, 'Living on: border lines', in Harold Bloom *et al.*, *Deconstruction and Criticism* (New York: Seabury Press, 1979), pp. 75–175. See also Jacques Derrida, 'The law of genre', *Glyph*, 7 (1980), pp. 202–29.
4 See Charles Altieri, *Act and Quality: A Theory of Literary Meaning and Humanistic Understanding* (Amherst, Mass.: University of Massachusetts Press, 1981). Also Gerald Graff, *Literature against Itself: Literary Ideas in Modern Society* (Chicago: University of Chicago Press, 1979).
5 Stanley Fish, *Is There a Text in this Class?* (Cambridge, Mass.: Harvard University Press, 1980).
6 Stanley Fish, 'Working on the chain gang: interpretation in the law and in literary criticism', *Critical Inquiry*, 9 (1982–3), pp. 201–16.
7 Fish, 'Working on the chain gang', p. 201.
8 Ibid., p. 206.
9 Ibid., p. 212.
10 See Fish, *Is There a Text in this Class?*
11 Fish, 'Working on the chain gang', p. 212.
12 Ronald Dworkin, 'Law as interpretation', *Critical Inquiry*, 9 (1982–3), pp. 179–200. The essays by Dworkin and Fish, along

with a further response from Dworkin, are reprinted in the *Texas Law Review*, 60 (1982).

13 Fish, 'Working on the chain gang', p. 207.

14 Ibid., p. 208.

15 Dworkin, 'Law as interpretation', p. 199.

16 Ibid., p. 200.

17 J. L. Austin, *How to do Things with Words* (London: Oxford University Press, 1963). For a typical attempt to 'apply' Austin's ideas to literary theory, see Richard Ohmann, 'Speech acts and the definition of literature', *Philosophy and Rhetoric*, 4 (1971, pp. 1–19.

18 Shoshana Felman, *Le Scandale du corps parlante: Don Juan avec Austin ou la séduction en deux langues* (Paris: Seuil, 1980).

19 Paul de Man, 'Promises (*Social Contract*)', in *Allegories of Reading: Figural Language in Rousseau, Nietzsche, Rilke and Proust* (New Haven, Conn.: Yale University Press, 1979), pp. 246–77. All further references to this work given by page number in the text.

20 A. Ross, *On Law and Justice* (London: Stevens, 1958), p. 81; cited in Hart, op. cit., p. 175.

21 William Empson, *Milton's God*, rev. edn. (London: Chatto & Windus, 1965), p. 137.

22 Ibid., p. 280.

23 See de Man, op. cit., pp. 79–131.

24 Dworkin, 'Law as interpretation', p. 200.

25 Franz Kafka, 'In the penal settlement', in *'Metamorphosis' and Other Stories*, trans. Willa and Edwin Muir (Harmondsworth: Penguin, 1961), pp. 169–99; p. 174.

8   On not going relativist

1 See the essays collected in Richard Rorty, *Consequences of Pragmatism* (Minneapolis: University of Minnesota Press, 1982).

2 See especially Richard Rorty, 'Overcoming the tradition: Heidegger and Dewey', in ibid., pp. 37–59.

3 Hilary Putnam, *Realism and Reason* (Cambridge: Cambridge University Press, 1983), p. 237.

4 Ibid., p. 237.

5 Ibid., p. 238.

6 See W. V. O. Quine, *Word and Object* (Cambridge, Mass.: Harvard University Press, 1960).

7 See W. V. O. Quine, 'Two dogmas of empiricism', in *From a Logical Point of View* (Cambridge, Mass.: Harvard University Press, 1953), pp. 20–46.

8 See Louis Hjelmslev, *Prolegomena to a Theory of Language*, trans. Francis J. Whitfield (Madison, Wisc.: University of Wisconsin Press, 1969), pp. 53 ff.

9 Benjamin Lee Whorf, *Language, Thought and Reality (Selected Writings)*, ed. J. B. Carroll (Cambridge, Mass.: MIT Press, 1956).

10 Putnam, op. cit., p. 235.

11 See especially Michel Foucault, *Language, Counter-Memory, Practice*, ed. D. F. Bouchard and S. Simon (Oxford: Blackwell, 1977).

12 Paul de Man, *Allegories of Reading: Figural Language in Rousseau, Nietzsche, Rilke and Proust* (New Haven, Conn.: Yale University Press, 1979), pp. 79–131.

13 Friedrich Nietzsche, *The Will to Power*, trans. Walter Kaufmann and R. J. Hollingdale (New York: Random House, 1967), p. 264. The passage is quoted by de Man, op. cit., p. 129.

14 Michel Foucault, *Les Mots et les choses*; translated as *The Order of Things*, trans. Alan Sheridan (New York: Pantheon, 1970).

15 Donald Davidson, *Inquiries into Truth and Interpretation* (Oxford: Clarendon Press, 1984), p. 184. A number of related issues are raised in Davidson's *Essays on Actions and Events* (Oxford: Clarendon Press, 1980).

16 See Gottlob Frege, 'On sense and reference', in P. Geach and M. Black, *Translations from the Philosophical Writings of Gottlob Frege* (Oxford: Blackwell, 1952), pp. 56–78.

17 Quine, 'Two dogmas of empiricism', op. cit.

18 De Man, op. cit., pp. 119–31.

19 Nietzsche, op. cit., p. 280; quoted by de Man, op. cit., p. 121.

20 De Man, op. cit., p. 125.

21 Ibid., p. 125.

22 Ibid., p. 125.

23 Ibid., p. 131.

24 Davidson, *Inquiries into Truth and Interpretation*. All further references to this work given by page number in the text.

25 De Man, op. cit., p. 115.

9 Conclusion

1 Jacques Derrida, 'Structure, sign and play in the discourse of the human sciences', in *Writing and Difference*, trans. Alan Bass (London: Routledge & Kegan Paul, 1978), pp. 278–300.

2 Derrida, op. cit., p. 160.

3 Ibid., p. 6.

4 Ibid., pp. 31–63.

5 Jacques Derrida, 'White mythology: Metaphor in the text of Philosophy', in *Margins of Philosophy*, trans. Alan Bass (Chicago,

Ill.: University of Chicago Press, 1982), pp. 207–71. All further references given by page number in the text.

6 Jacques Derrida, 'The supplement of copula', in *Margins of Philosophy*, pp. 175–205. All further references given by page number in the text.

7 Derrida, '*Ousia* and *grammē*', in *Margins of Philosophy*, pp. 29–67. All further references given by page number in the text.

8 Paul de Man, *Allegories of Reading: Figural Language in Rousseau, Nietzsche, Rilke and Proust* (New Haven, Conn.: Yale University Press, 1979), p. 207.

Index